THE POSTMODERN PREDICAMENT

THE POSTMODERN PREDICAMENT

Existential Challenges of the Twenty-First Century

Bruce Ackerman

Yale
UNIVERSITY PRESS
NEW HAVEN & LONDON

Published with assistance from the foundation established in memory of
Philip Hamilton McMillan of the Class of 1894, Yale College.

Yale University Press books may be purchased in quantity
for educational, business, or promotional use. For information, please e-mail
sales.press@yale.edu (U.S. office) or sales@yaleup.co.uk (U.K. office).

Set in Yale and Alternative Gothic type by Newgen North America.
Printed in the United States of America.

Library of Congress Control Number: 2023942827
ISBN 978-0-300-27350-2 (hardcover: alk. paper)
A catalogue record for this book is available from the British Library.
This paper meets the requirements of ANSI/NISO Z39.48-1992
(Permanence of Paper).
10 9 8 7 6 5 4 3 2 1

CONTENTS

PART TWO: MY BODY, MYSELF

PART THREE: FACING THE FUTURE

ACKNOWLEDGMENTS

I could not have written this essay without the insights contributed by countless conversation partners over the years – and so it is only possible to mark out the people who have made the biggest difference.

Beginning with my wife, Susan: for more than fifty years, she has profoundly shaped my life, my work, my thoughts, in ways that have made me the person that I have become. No words can express my debt, my love.

Then there are my colleagues. Most obviously, on-going collaborations with Anne Alstott and Jim Fishkin enabled me to advance the concrete reforms proposed in the final chapter of this book. But I have been lucky enough to have engaged in similar decades-long engagements with Ian Ayres, Jack Balkin, Guido Calabresi, Mirjan Damaska, Stephen Darwall, Owen Fiss, Erving Goffman, Dieter Grimm, Oona Hathaway, Karsten Harries, Alvin Klevorick, Tony Kronman, Juan Linz, Jerry Mashaw, David Mayhew, Jed Rubenfeld, Ian Shapiro, Scott Shapiro, and Stephen Skowronek. They have made New Haven the vibrant center of my scholarly existence – as have generations of extraordinary students who have worked with me to confront the radical transformations of the late twentieth, and early twenty-first, centuries.

At the same time, Yale Law School's Oscar M. Ruebhausen Fund has been extraordinarily generous in supporting this project, permitting the expedited publication of this book and allowing me to engage in wide-ranging debates about its implications with thinkers and doers in the United States and beyond.

INTRODUCTION

An Existential Question

What should I make of my life?

Through most of human history, almost nobody took this question seriously. They didn't have to. The overwhelming majority of men and women were illiterate peasants who lived their entire lives without ever leaving their place of birth. Instead of taking responsibility for defining the shape of their individual lives, each existed as an "I" who passively accepted the social identity imposed upon them by their tightly knit communities – typically numbering no more than a thousand inhabitants. As soon as they became aware of their social surroundings, they knew it would be very difficult to hide anything important from local busybodies. By the time they became young adults, it was unthinkable for them to declare their independence from the patterns of social life in which they had been socialized – even when they found them oppressive.

If they insisted on challenging the status quo, their village counterparts would treat them as pariahs or even threaten their lives. If they did not rapidly and publicly admit the error of their ways, they would find it tough to engage in the successful operation of their farm or trade, as this frequently required the cooperation of their contemptuous neighbors.

Worse yet, it would be virtually impossible to begin a new life elsewhere. They would have to leave behind the community and local property that served as their principal source of wealth. When they arrived in another closely knit community, they would enter as a stranger whose weird behavior would encounter greater hostility than they had experienced in their original home.

Given these realities, premoderns were stuck with the social identity imposed from birth by their tight-knit communities. If "I" had been assigned the status of a lowly servant, I would have no choice but to accept my fate and deal with my humiliations as best I could.[1]

Nor could I take the path that seems obvious to us today—fleeing to a big city in search of new opportunities for self-realization. As late as 1800, only four cities in Western Europe had 200,000 inhabitants—with Paris (550,000) and Naples (430,000) topping the list. Despite the great cathedrals and mansions dominating the skyline, the residents of these cities treated impoverished newcomers with deep suspicion, which is precisely why so few of them arrived.[2]

In capital cities there was always a king or prince who asserted his dominion over the surrounding countryside. But these aristocrats typically lacked the bureaucratic and military resources required to act decisively when tightly knit communities mistreated or murdered members who insisted on defining their own meaning in life. So-called sovereigns exercised little actual power, other than to insist that each agrarian community recognize their dominion by paying them an annual tribute of goods and services. If community members complied, they could be confident their overlords would allow them to brutally suppress local deviants in blatant violation of the law books found in the monarch's far-away capital. When communities defaulted on their tribute payments, their putative governors often found it hard to compel compliance, encouraging further acts of defiance.

Similarly, tightly knit communities would typically reject strangers even if they shared a common faith in the nature of ultimate reality—as expressed by Buddha or Confucius or Jesus or Mohammed or Moses or Socrates or some other spiritual leader. The real-world meaning of their lives was based on their success in fulfilling the expectations of people they had known since childhood, and the mere fact that strangers shared common ideals did not make their concrete patterns of speaking and doing any less strange, given the very different forms of meaningful engagement into which they had been socialized from infancy.

It would take a shattering series of cultural, economic, and political revolutions to break the stranglehold of tightly knit communities.[3] For present purposes, it is enough to consider only one of these decisive transformations: the Industrial Revolution.

By the eighteenth century, mass production techniques were already encouraging the development of factory towns that enabled families to escape their local communities with increasing confidence. By the 1830s, the rise of the railroad was enabling millions of Westerners (on both sides of the Atlantic) to say goodbye to their old-time neighbors and build better lives for themselves in a distant city.

Yet if they were to succeed in fulfilling their hopes, these newcomers had no choice but to revolutionize the experiential foundations of their very existence. Once they moved to the city, they would no longer encounter the same familiar faces in the same familiar places. Instead, they would live very different lives at home and at work. While their family was still demanding displays of love and thoughtfulness, their fellow workers were demanding competence and cooperation. The fragmentation of their time into different spheres of inter-subjective engagement required them to confront a paradigmatically modern predicament. Since their disparate sets of "sphere-mates," as I will call them, expected very different things, they would devote time and energy to developing very different aspects of their character. Their loving expressions of thoughtfulness at home would be treated with bewilderment if they tried to hug their fellow workers on the assembly line, and vice versa. They encountered similar, but different, challenges in constructing meaningful relationships with next-door neighbors from very different parts of the country, as well as in establishing serious friendships with people they casually encountered in everyday life.

Since each set of sphere-mates had very different expectations for meaningful performance, they would predictably make demands on your time and energy that seemed reasonable from their point of view. But taken together, you might be utterly unable to satisfy all of them for one simple reason: as a human being, you need at least five or six hours of sleep each night to sustain your existence in a satisfactory fashion during the rest of the day. As a consequence, you will regularly fail to live up to the expectations of your different sphere-mates *for reasons that don't make sense to them.* Your systematic underperformance, moreover, will increasingly alienate them, and they may well turn their backs on you if you cannot somehow reconcile them to repeated disappointments. A fundamental fact of human existence – the finitude of your waking life – confronts you with an inescapable predicament now that your days are split into different modes of face-to-face engagement, with different sphere-mates seeking your cooperation in achieving different forms of mutually meaningful self-realization.

There is no way out of this existential predicament of modern life, which I will call the "dilemma of inter-spherical commitment." Consider, for example, a tragic scenario that has shattered the lives of countless modern men and women over the course of the twentieth century. For purposes of this thought experiment, I would like you to put yourself in the shoes of somebody named "Bewildered" who is about to go home from work when the boss orders him or her to stay on the job and work overtime for several hours to meet a crucial deadline. As a practical matter, Bewildered has no choice but to comply with this demand– and encounters a grim reception upon returning home. Not only have "I" arrived too late to have dinner with my family, I've arrived too late to help my kids with their homework.

My kids may well forgive me at first. But if I keep on working overtime, they will increasingly resent their failure to receive the loving help they need in responding to the demands of their schoolwork–after all, many of their schoolmates tell them how much their parents help them out in solving their classroom assignments. As a consequence, a time may come when I open the door to say hello only to find that my kids turn their backs on me and deliberately exclude me from their ongoing activities. Worse yet, my spouse whispers to me that I will make the situation worse if I insist that my kids allow me to join in their fun and games.

I respond by pretending that nothing is wrong. Rather than risking an angry confrontation, I leave my spouse playing with our kids in the living room and go into the kitchen to eat the dinner leftovers by myself–emerging from this self-imposed isolation only when I see my spouse send the kids to bed in the normal way.

When my partner returns from the bedroom, I explain why I had no choice but to comply with my boss's demands. My spouse may well respond reassuringly that he/she "understands," and the two of us spend the rest of the evening together in ways that reassure each other of the depth of our relationship.

But as I return to business the next day, it's all too clear to me that my boss will be making many more demands for overtime in the future, and that I am facing the prospect of a bitter breakup at home when I arrive late the next time and the next time and the next. Yet if I fail to meet my employer's deadlines at work, my boss may well crush my hopes for career advancement—and may even fire me, forcing me to search desperately for a half-decent alternative.

How to resolve this inter-spherical predicament?

Rather than finding it surprising that so many modern men and women have been overwhelmed by this question, we should find it remarkable that many others manage to resolve their ongoing dilemmas in ways that enable them to sustain both their careers and their marriages in a deeply meaningful fashion. Yet even if your marriage breaks up and your career breaks down, your failed efforts to maintain them tells you something very important about yourself: that "I" am somebody who is struggling to make sense of *my life as a whole,* despite the fact that I will *inevitably* disappoint many of my very different sphere-mates in my effort to construct a meaningful life for myself in the modern world.

This ongoing struggle has been vastly complicated by the proliferation of additional relational opportunities over the twentieth century. For example, my athletic abilities may have led my neighborhood soccer league to ask me to join one of their teams in competing for the local championship, but my neighborhood childcare center may call upon me to devote myself to the care of youngsters who have been abandoned by their parents. At the same time, my fellow citizens may urge me to join a nationwide effort to challenge an entrenched form of social injustice.

Each of us can say yes only to a few of these opportunities. Yet the more time and energy we devote to these additional spherical projects, the less time we have to dedicate ourselves to our job and family and friends – and our repeated absences may well provoke more moments of bewildered alienation.

People in the premodern era understood themselves very differently. Locked within their tightly knit communities, they were in no position to view themselves as *self-determining* human beings for the simple reason that their communities gave them no such choices but treated them as deviants if they ever asserted themselves as an "I" who could legitimately question the patterns of living assigned to them at birth.

Yet readers of this book have long since abandoned the tightly knit communities of their ancestors, which leaves them with two choices. They can hope they will be lucky enough to avoid bewildering existential tragedies in their own lives – and make desperate last-minute efforts to avoid breakups if they nevertheless arise. Or they can spend some time trying to gain a perspective on the fundamental predicaments of modern life and construct their spherical relationships in ways that self-consciously take their dilemmas of commitment into account.

In urging you to take the second course, I will be following the path marked out by a series of great existentialist thinkers of the twentieth century – beginning with Edmund Husserl's breakthrough contribution in the early 1900s, which provided a framework for a dynamic intergenerational debate between writers like Simone de Beauvoir and Maurice Merleau-Ponty and Jean-Paul

Sartre (to name the authors who have most influenced my own approach).

These thinkers and doers, however, were not content to insist on the centrality of the predicament posed by the fragmentation of modern life into a host of competing spherical commitments – and the endless struggle for self-definition required as a result. Given the fragility of these multi-spherical engagements, they urged us to confront a clear-and-present danger to our personal integrity that is inextricably embedded in the very structure of contemporary existence. To see their point, consider that your sphere-mates are deeply familiar with your activities in only one of your modes of engagement – your kids and spouse might never even meet your fellow workers, and vice versa. As a consequence, when you confront their inevitable disappointments, you are constantly tempted to minimize their alienation by misrepresenting the reasons for your failure to fulfil their expectations.

When you arrive late to work, for example, you might ask your business associates to excuse the delay since "I had to take care of my sick child until my spouse could take over the task." But in fact your kid was perfectly fine – and you were delayed because you had been celebrating your friend's birthday until three in the morning, making it impossible to get out of bed on time. Nevertheless, your fellow workers find this excuse entirely credible: they express sympathy rather than annoyance when you finally show up – precisely because they don't see your children on a face-to-face basis, as they would in a tightly knit community. In short, you have managed to evade responsibility for your breach of your sphere-mates' expectations by *transforming your work life into a lie.*

This stripped-down example only gestures toward the profound ways in which twentieth-century existentialists confronted their contemporaries with the pervasive danger of self-betrayal built into the structure of their lives. The source of modern inauthenticity is the sheer impossibility of escaping a fundamental feature of the human condition – that I only have 18 or 19 hours available to me between the time I wake up and the time I go to sleep. As a consequence, the physical isolation of each set of sphere-mates from their counterparts gives me constant opportunities to minimize their disappointments by misrepresenting the character of my extra-spherical relationships in ways they can't observe in face-to-face fashion.

Worse yet, if I choose to deal with the oppressive character of some – or all – of my spherical relationships in a totally honest fashion, I confront a second danger. The political elites that currently dominate the government may view my displays of authenticity as challenges to the legitimacy of a system that requires me to work overtime to sustain my family's economic well-being, at the cost of destroying the meaningfulness of my intimate relationships, and they will do all they can to destroy my life if my denunciations of the status quo come to their attention.

This is the point at which leading thinkers of the twentieth century called upon their fellow citizens to take decisive action to reform the prevailing system of domination in the name of existential justice. Simone de Beauvoir's great work of 1949, *The Second Sex*, serves as a paradigmatic example of this call for creative forms of political organization in the struggle against continued subordination. At the time it was written, entrenched forms of gender domination enabled macho men to brutalize women at home and humiliate them at work if they did not "voluntarily" accept their continued subordination in either of these spheres of modern existence. Moreover, Beauvoir did not simply join with other leading feminists in denouncing these abuses as fundamental violations of the egalitarian ideals of the French Revolution. She provided a compelling account of the systematic failures by the police and the labor movement to respond to the real-world protests of the women brave enough to raise their voices against their oppression, thus enabling the men in their midst to continue firing them from their jobs and brutalizing them at home. Beauvoir's move – from abstract ideals of equality to real-world acquiescence in their betrayal – profoundly influenced the direction of the feminist movement in the postwar era.

Yet she did not content herself with this achievement. *The Second Sex* extended its real-world analysis to people who understood their gender identities in ways that defied the traditional male/female dichotomy. Her book provided an extended analysis of the ways in which the modern separation of home and work enabled transgendered people to hide their loving relationships within the privacy of their homes – but only if they were willing to act as "normal" guys and dolls at work and in many other spheres of engagement. Beauvoir considered this form of gender domination no less oppressive than those that had previously preoccupied feminist activists. She called on the movement to form a united front with gays and lesbians in a broader campaign for existential justice. This is precisely why her book continues to serve as a landmark three-quarters of a century after its original publication. Rather than focus on the obvious differences between each form of gender domination, her existential analysis encouraged the construction of a broad-based liberation movement united by a common understanding of the inter-spherical dynamics of their different-seeming predicaments.

At the time de Beauvoir published her book, in 1949, she understood her work as part of a much larger debate – involving Merleau-Ponty, Sartre, and many others – over the existential implications of the ongoing struggle by modern men and women to create meaningful lives for themselves out of their fragmented spherical existences in time and space. Yet her writings are the only ones from that era that continue to influence real-world debate. Even in the academy, the great existentialist works of the past have been pushed to the periphery of sustained attention.

Instead, starting in the 1960s, the rising generation of serious intellectuals increasingly took a very different approach to social justice, which, by the end of the Cold War, had decisively displaced existentialist concerns at the center of earlier debates. Under the new paradigm, it was considered a big mistake to look upon one's real-world struggles against domination and self-betrayal as a crucial source of insight into the principles of justice that should guide efforts at reform. Instead, the new generation approached the question of social justice through a thought experiment that invited them to look upon the modern world from an Olympian perspective. To be sure, the intellectual leaders of this movement disagreed on the precise design of this decisive thought experiment, with breakthrough books by Jürgen Habermas and John Rawls playing key roles in driving the debate.

Rawls asked his followers to put themselves behind a "veil of ignorance" in which they would not know what place they would occupy in society before they began to bargain over the terms of the social contract that would govern their power relationships. Habermas asked them to imagine themselves in an "ideal speech situation" where they could debate the nature of universal principles of human dignity that should apply at all times and places throughout the world.

There are important differences between these thought experiments, which I will explore in a later chapter. The point of this book, however, is to challenge the basic premises of these exercises in self-transcendence – and call on my readers to reconstruct an existential approach to social justice. This is especially important because the debates inspired by these alternative paradigms moved far beyond the academy. They influenced the shape of real-world reform. By the end of the Cold War, a new generation of progressive political and legal leaders were recommitting their countries to social justice, but redefining it in contractarian or dignitarian terms. This was true of Bill Clinton no less than Nelson Mandela, Tony Blair no less than Mikhail Gorbachev, Helmut Kohl no less than Luiz Inácio Lula da Silva, and many others.

Over the last 30 years, however, their brave new worlds have collapsed, leading to escalating bewilderment and despair at the future of democracy. In calling on my readers to join me in reinvigorating an existentialist approach to social justice, I don't suggest that this paradigm shift will be enough to rebuild the foundations of a strong constitutional democracy over the next generation. Nevertheless, it will focus attention on a crucial aspect of the problem: the remarkable way the high-tech revolution has been transforming the pattern of everyday existence during the same period in which the worldwide crisis of democracy was taking place.

There has been lots of fine work dealing with the internet's sweeping impact on social and political life. But an existentialist approach puts the spotlight on an aspect of the problem that has been insufficiently appreciated: the danger that our current practices on the internet will destroy our face-to-face relationships – at home, at work, and in many other spheres that are important in building a meaningful life for ourselves.

To see my point, consider a couple of variations on my not-so-hypothetical case involving the disappointments confronting parents when they arrive too late to help their kids with their homework. Suppose, once again, that Bewildered stays in the kitchen and leaves it to his spouse to get their alienated children ready for bed. At that point, Bewildered enters the living room to express his gratitude, but this effort is interrupted by a text on his phone: his boss wants to discuss issues involving his overtime work. He goes to his laptop to respond and finds himself embroiled in two hours of intense discussion of a series of documents displayed on the screen. When the give-and-take finally ends around midnight, Bewildered looks up to see his spouse reading a book, but when he suggests that it's time to go to bed, she no longer pretends that everything is OK. Instead, she bursts into tears and angrily confronts him about their lack of time together.

When Bewildered returns to work the next day, he is determined to change his working conditions to reduce the danger of a family breakup. He asks his boss for a meeting to talk things over, and she replies that she is happy to do so. When Bewildered arrives for his half-hour appointment, however, the conversation takes a disappointing turn. As he begins with a brief survey of possible solutions to the overtime problem, he sees his boss constantly glancing at her laptop as urgent requests for attention keep distracting her. Their meeting quickly degenerates into a disjointed series of one-minute sound bites in which his boss announces one or another possible "solution" but doesn't really listen to Bewildered's replies. The conversation goes nowhere, and Bewildered leaves her office frustrated and angry. He not only faces more last-minute overtime demands from his boss but must deal with an increasingly estranged family when he finally gets home. Nevertheless, he must confront the fact that he only has 18 hours a day to construct a meaningful life for himself—and that the internet can make it even more difficult, both at home and at work, to engage in successful efforts to resolve the inevitable inter-spherical dilemmas of modern life.

This book invites you to confront the implications of this postmodern predicament. For the first time since humanity emerged on this planet, we are shifting endlessly from physical to virtual reality—trying to live two lives at the same time. In emphasizing the extraordinary perplexities generated by our dual existence, I do not suggest that we should throw away our cellphones and march back into the twentieth century. The internet can vastly enrich our lives as well as destroy them. The challenge is to define the real-world contexts in which the prospect of self-destruction posed by our double lives is a clear and present danger —and consider whether our battered democracies are strong enough to take steps that can decisively reduce the tragic dynamics unleashed by the high-tech revolution of the twenty-first century.

I will divide my confrontation with these questions into three parts. The first part, the longest, begins by recognizing that the Bewilderment breakdowns I have described greatly oversimplify the ways in which we respond to danger signs of inter-spherical conflict in real life. What is more, these predicaments will change dramatically over each person's lifetime. When a young couple first commits to marriage, their dilemmas are very different from those they will face if they decide to have children. If they manage to stick together long enough to see their children emerge from school as young adults, they must struggle, once their kids leave home, to redefine the terms of their intimate relationship. If they reach the age of 80 or 90, they confront different dilemmas in helping each other respond to the challenges of physical and mental decline. During each phase of life, the internet offers different prospects for enhancing face-to-face relationships – or betraying them.

The same is true of their efforts to sustain a meaningful relationship to their careers and to fulfil their responsibilities to friends, fellow citizens, and other significant sphere-mates. If we are to take seriously the double life predicaments posed by our brave new world, it is not enough to speak in broad generalities. We must take these complexities with high seriousness.

Easier said than done.

I will consider it a success if part 1 builds a provisional framework that can help you in your own confrontation with these issues. Moreover, I am greatly encouraged to see that, during the years I've been struggling with this manuscript, some of these existential predicaments have been insightfully discussed by other writers, albeit from different angles, setting the stage for a new and vibrant debate.

In this book, part 1 sets the stage for a more fundamental question. Even if the internet revolution has a profoundly destructive impact on many face-to-face relationships at vulnerable stages of life, these bewildered people can respond by turning to the internet to try to construct fulfilling relationships in virtual reality in an effort to fill the void left by the breakdown of their real-world commitments to their family, fellow workers, friends, and other sphere-mates. Yet if they manage to find meaning in a more intensive immersion in virtual reality, are they missing crucial aspects of face-to-face relationships that can *never* be experienced in their virtual encounters?

If the answer is yes, the postmodern predicament takes on a truly tragic aspect – stripping countless men and women of a profound dimension of human experience. If the answer is no, at least the people abandoned by their real-world counterparts can seek consolation by deepening their virtual engagements.

Part 2 tries to persuade you that the answer is yes, and that the existentialist debates of the twentieth century provide a precious resource in defining fundamental aspects of human experience that are threatened by our postmodern effort to escape the dilemmas of real-world existence by endlessly clicking into virtual reality. In contrast, if we continue down the path marked out by Habermas and Rawls, their paradigm of self-transcendence will blind us to the insights required to address this crucial question – regardless of how we then try to answer it.

In making my case, however, I must confront an existential problem of my own. In my academic career I have spent many hours trying to understand the breakthrough books written by leading existentialists of the twentieth century – since they are written in a style of French and German that is notoriously difficult to understand. Unfortunately, the English translations of these works are even tougher to comprehend. Luckily for me, I have a good command of both French and German, so I can confront these textual obscurities without puzzling over the English translations. Nevertheless, given the complexity of their arguments, my own interpretation of their enduring significance will inevitably be controversial, especially since I am trying to deploy their twentieth-century insights to diagnose twenty-first-century predicaments that none of these writers actually confronted during their lifetimes. As a consequence, if you find part 2 especially interesting, you should try to spend some time puzzling over the original texts that I have appropriated for my own purposes.

I will take the same approach in dealing with Habermas, Rawls, and other leading defenders of the paradigm of self-transcendence. They too have made many – sometimes contradictory – arguments in their ongoing efforts to vindicate their paradigm. Since I have engaged in a sustained critique of their basic premises in other writings, most notably *Social Justice in the Liberal State,* I will only briefly summarize their arguments here. Instead, I present a series of real-world scenarios that invite readers to appreciate how the Habermasian and Rawlsian paradigms of self-transcendence blind us to crucial aspects of our existential predicament as we shift endlessly from virtual to face-to-face reality, and back again.

Part 3 argues that, once you adopt the existentialist paradigm, you will begin to understand the worldwide crisis in constitutional democracy in radically different ways. I begin that part with a chapter that emphasizes the dark side and conclude the book by taking a grimly optimistic view of the prospects for long-term reform.

To emphasize the short-run dangers, part 3 begins with an existentialist critique of the reformist path marked out by two thinkers whose writings have been most influential in shaping internet developments over the past two decades: Cass Sunstein and Richard Thaler. Within a decade of its publication in 2008, their book *Nudge* had sold more than a million copies – and it has inspired worldwide efforts to put its teachings into practice.

Yet I will try to convince you that these well-meaning reforms are propelling the world in precisely the wrong direction – legitimating the power of Silicon Valley billionaires to organize the internet in ways that encourage vast numbers of real-world people to destroy crucial face-to-face commitments that they can never hope to replicate through online relationships. While there is a growing worldwide reform movement to curb the abuse of power by the Silicon Valley power-elite, movement leaders have nevertheless failed to take these dangers seriously—despite *Nudge*'s devastating impact on real-world relationships, like marriage, that are central to the struggle for a meaningful existence. Now is the time for reformers to reconsider their embrace of well-intentioned, but profoundly counterproductive, measures like those advanced by Sunstein and Thaler.

The existentialist paradigm offers a more affirmative opportunity: to focus on real-world problems that confront *every* modern man or woman under postmodern conditions and to propose bipartisan initiatives that cut across traditional left-right divisions. To be sure, any serious reform will inevitably be controversial, since it will disrupt traditional expectations and entrenched economic interests. But at least on some occasions, it may well be possible to frame reforms that will bring citizens together rather than split them apart—and yield especially large gains for impoverished and stigmatized groups.

My final chapter tries to persuade you that my hopes for constructive change are not mere utopian dreams. To make my case, my proposals build on real-world initiatives that have in fact gained strong bipartisan support in the recent past. Rather than providing a rapid-fire survey of these recent political efforts, I will focus on three significant initiatives that seem particularly promising in encouraging postmodern people to recommit themselves to the project of democratic citizenship in the internet age.

None of these proposals will make a big difference in the short-term struggle against the worldwide assault on democracy by demagogues with dictatorial ambitions. That will require the mobilization of millions of activists who are already committed to Enlightenment principles – and their ongoing effort to defend the shattered democratic institutions that their particular country has inherited from the recent past. At the same time, however, they must look beyond the current crisis and try to formulate a broad-based program that could inspire many of their bewildered fellow citizens to join them in a serious effort to achieve decisive real-world reform through democratic means.

In advancing my three-part program in the concluding chapter, my aim is to show the different ways in which the three different initiatives deal with the complexities of the postmodern predicament explored in parts 1 and 2 of the book. Rather than suppose that readers will find my discussion completely convincing, my aim is to provide them with perspectives that encourage them to join the reform debate and search for better alternatives in the years ahead.

After all, no serious democrat supposes that there is a magic solution to the real-world struggles for power and meaning that surround them in the twenty-first century. The real challenge is to present realistic alternatives that will enable rival political leaders to engage in thoughtful debate before their fellow citizens go to the polls and decide which path their country will follow over the next few years, at which point, there will be a moment for democratic reappraisal at the next election.

But before we can take this hopeful scenario seriously, we have a long road ahead of us.

PART I

MODERNITY

Chapter 1

THE PRIORITY OF THE PRESENT

Nobody spends all of life dreaming about the future or musing about the past. Moments of solitary reflection may have great value, but we spend most of our time in more active forms of engagement. Modern men and women cut up their days into distinct temporal frames: I wake my children and send them off to school, meet with fellow workers on the job, go to lunch with friends, and then move on to other spherical collaborations before returning home for the night.

These spherical time frames are structured in a fashion that can't be adequately expressed in clock time. Rather than measuring them in minutes or hours, we mark out our spherical encounters holistically. Suppose, for example, I am meeting a few friends for lunch at a restaurant. When we sit down at the table, we remember that some of our past lunches have been deeply rewarding while others have been dull – or worse. But we don't suppose that the meaningfulness of our current lunch can be assessed on a minute-by-minute basis. Instead, the relevant temporal frame is *lunch as whole.*

Suppose that "lunchtime" begins at 12:30 and ends at 14:00. If I make a remark at 12:35, it may have a very different significance by the time our lunch ends, depending on the comments it provokes from tablemates at 12:58 and 13:46. Our lunchtime experience can only be assessed as a totality, from the moment I greet my friends at the restaurant to the moment we say goodbye and go our separate ways. Modern men and women live out their daily lives in a series of "here and nows" framed by their current spherical engagements.

Call this the priority of the present. The existential challenge is to reflect on the way it shapes the dilemmas of modernity and postmodernity. For starters, consider the way the priority serves as the very foundation of modern *self*-understanding. It is not enough to make a good-faith effort to engage with my lunch partners or other sphere-mates in a manner that makes sense to *me.* My self-presentation must also make sense to *them.* In short: *mutual recognition by sphere-mates* is the foundation of *each individual*'s personal identity in the modern world.

I will explore the crucial role of mutual recognition through a number of scenarios in which sphere-mates confront predicaments generated by breakdowns in the particular "here and now" in which they find themselves. As my argument proceeds, it will become clear that the pathologies provoked by different kinds of breakdown depend on the particular sphere in which they occur. To clarify some fundamentals, however, this chapter will present variations on my lunchtime-with-friends scenario, deferring lots of important questions until later.

Breakdown Scenarios

As I sit down to join my friends for lunch, I find them laughing at each other's jokes, gossiping about goings-on, and discussing the menu. Instead of joining in, I say absolutely nothing and stare silently into space. After a while, my friends ask, "Is something troubling you, Bruce?"

Their expressions of alarm arouse me from my zombie state. I explain that before I met them for lunch, my boss humiliated me in a way that shattered my hopes for success in my career. After this brief explanation, I again lapse into impassivity—traumatized by this shattering event. How will my friends respond?

With shock, and then increasing alarm as I am so nonfunctional that I cannot even order lunch or respond further to their questions. By hypothesis, none of my lunchmates are my spheremates at work, so my news has taken them entirely by surprise. At best, they will count it a success if they can get me to walk silently out the door without any of the other diners at the restaurant noticing that something weird is going on. Under this scenario, my friends manage to call a taxicab and get me home so that my family can help me to once again engage in the shifting spherical competences required by a socially competent adult in the modern world.

Consider, however, an even worse-case scenario—in which my friends' efforts to arouse Bruce from his restaurant silence only succeed in generating alarm from diners at neighboring tables. At some point the restaurant owner orders my friends to stand aside as he expels me from his place of business and watches me stagger down the street—with my friends taking desperate measures to prevent the police from taking notice of my disorderly conduct.

These cases are extreme but not hypothetical. Tragedies like this occur throughout the world every day. They suffice to dramatize my claim that "I" cannot exercise control over my own body unless I behave in a fashion that my sphere-mates recognize as appropriate in the particular "here and now" in which we find ourselves.

Nevertheless, mutual recognition is only a necessary, not a sufficient, condition for successful meaning-making in the modern world. Suppose, once again, that I have just suffered from a shattering experience at work, but when I meet my friends for lunch, I respond very differently. Instead of staring interminably into the void, I have relatively little difficulty telling my friends about the terrible episode that has just destroyed my hopes for a successful career.

But I find their reactions bitterly disappointing. Rather than showing sympathy for my predicament, they use my confession as an occasion to boast of their own job-related successes. When I suggest that I expected a very different response from my so-called friends, it only provokes escalating antagonism as our meal proceeds. Yet these acts of mutual humiliation proceed in a "civilized" fashion. My friends and I don't act in ways that alarm other diners to the point where we are kicked out of the premises. We finish our lunch, pay the check, and leave. Nonetheless, it is clear to *us* that our friendship is in danger: if friends don't support one another at moments of crisis, are they really friends in any meaningful sense?

Here is where the priority of the spherical "here and now" assumes truly existential significance. Suppose that, toward the end of our lunch, we make an effort to save our friendship. While drinking my coffee, I may apologize for precipitating the disastrous episode: "My friends, I'm to blame for making such a mess of our lunch. I shouldn't have blurted out all my troubles at the very beginning of our time together. Rather than dominating the conversation from the very start, I should have invited your sympathies in a more thoughtful fashion." Better yet, perhaps my sphere-mates respond in ways that suggest forgiveness. Better still, perhaps some of my friends apologize for reacting so unsympathetically, and I accept their apology.

Or perhaps there is no effort at reconciliation, and we walk out the door in despair. Once we say goodbye, we lose our existential capacity to reshape the meaning of our lunchtime experience.

This is the key point: our jokes, angry disagreements, and our efforts at reconciliation, happened – and that is that. Our lunchtime "here and now" has come to an end. Each of us spends the rest of the day in very different spherical encounters: I go back to work, somebody else goes home to take care of the kids, others race off to the sports stadium to cheer for their team. These different engagements generate different lived experiences – from deep despair to profound satisfaction to something in between. But none directly implicate the state of our friendship.

Moments of Reflection

When we move on to other activities, we won't forget our terrible lunch together. While we must take care to perform competently within our current sphere, we often get a chance to think about extra-spherical matters without seriously undermining our performance in the "here and now" we presently inhabit. During these moments, some of us may reflect on the enduring significance of our lunchtime breakdown. By the end of the day, different friends may take different views of the episode. Some may emphasize the extended period of bitter controversy; others, the last-minute efforts at reconciliation.

Moreover, each friend's initial view of these exchanges may change over time.Suppose, for example, that I tell my spouse about the episode at dinner, and our conversation leads me to change my own perspective on the fiasco. To be sure, he or she wasn't present at the restaurant. Nevertheless, my partner knows me intimately and may be personally acquainted with at least some of my friends. So my inter-spherical conversation at home can provide new insights into my spherical predicaments at the restaurant.

Each friend may well end up telling him/herself a very different story about the lunchtime breakdown. Yet these *self-narrations,* as I will call them, only serve as a prologue to the next critical turning point in their mutual relationship—when the friends agree, once again, to get together for lunch.

As I greet my friends at the restaurant for our next lunch, none of us may mention our previous disastrous experience. Nevertheless, we may each be telling ourselves different stories about its significance. "I" may blame you; "you" may blame me; both of us may blame a different so-called friend. Nevertheless, despite these disparate self-narrations, one thing is clear to all of us: the last lunch revealed the fragility of our friendship. The crucial question is whether we will use our current "here and now" to repair our relationship, or whether our present encounter only serves to raise the question: *Are we really friends at all?*

Even if nobody puts this question into words, we will soon be answering it existentially. Suppose we once again spend our time engaging in egocentric assertion at each other's expense. The repetition of these now-familiar scenes of self-aggrandizement will further undermine our spherical engagement, dramatizing the fragility of our relationship. Even a last-minute effort at mutual reconciliation will seem much more problematic the second time around.

In contrast, the tablemates might leave the restaurant with renewed confidence in their friendship—but only if they engage with one another's concrete interests and problems in ways that express serious concern. If they merely profess "undying friendship" while continuing to squabble, these expressions of commitment will only dramatize the disintegration of their relationship where it really matters—in the "here and now."

The Problematics of Commitment

I have portrayed my "civilized breakdown" scenario as a three-stage affair. An initial spherical crisis provokes a period of individualistic reflections on the fragility of the group's friendship, which is then tested in another mutual confrontation in the living present.

Yet this tripartite scenario is repeated endlessly in the course of any real-world relationship. There will inevitably be times when friends disappoint one another—leading to periods of reappraisal and face-to-face efforts at reconstruction. Some friends may find that their moments of disappointment are rare and insignificant, making it relatively easy for them to reinvigorate their spherical relationship when needed. Others will find that the need for mutual reassurance grows more frequent even as the expectation of success diminishes, leading them to decide that it doesn't make sense to "waste more time" trying to redeem their spherical commitment to one another.

Even the best of friends must reckon with the intrinsic fragility of their existential relationship. They cannot know what the future holds—and whether some disaster will overwhelm the patterns of mutual concern that currently prevail around the lunch table. The best they can do is to reinforce the *credibility of their commitment* through successful efforts to resolve their dilemmas of mutual recognition generated by their ongoing engagements in the "here and now."

The problem of credible commitment is at the core of the modernist predicament. It arises from two features of modern existence. The first is the primacy of the present: to have any hope of a meaningful life, we must confront the imperative demands of the "here and now." The second is that in our daily lives, we constantly engage with different sets of sphere-mates, generating ongoing inter-spherical dilemmas in fulfilling the competing demands of our very different partners.

It will require a lot more work to construct an adequate framework for confronting the postmodern predicament. But this chapter will be a success if it convinces you of what I call my "linkage thesis": together, these two fundamental aspects of modern life make it *existentially impossible* for us to absolutely guarantee our future fidelity to our current sphere-mates.

To establish this thesis, I have stripped down my argument to its barest essentials. I have focused on a single spherical relationship: friendship. Yet this mode of meaning-making differs from other forms of spherical engagement in many ways. Even if I have managed to persuade you that my linkage thesis is plausible, it will take a lot more work to convince you that it is convincing.

Chapter 2

THE STRANGER

Friendship, work, family. Each sphere of engagement raises special challenges as we try to construct meaningful lives. Yet they have one important thing in common. I get to know my spheremates personally through our ongoing engagements. Even when fellow workers have the same official status, I don't treat each the same way. I may try hard to avoid provoking Worker A's many anxieties; with Worker B, I find it easier to have a frank and friendly discussion of our job-related responsibilities. This is even truer of my family and friends – or teammates on my neighborhood soccer club.

Yet modern men and women are also obliged to deal with lots of people impersonally. Even here, however, their relationship to strangers is highly dependent on spherical context.

A couple of examples. When I go to the polls on Election Day, I cast a secret ballot. If an election official asks me whether I voted for Candidate A or Candidate B, I will rightly denounce her effort to compromise my voting rights. When I am shopping in a shoe store, however, it would be downright weird if I expressed outrage when a salesperson asks me whether I want Commodity A or Commodity B. How can the store do business with me if I won't say what I want to buy? My angry refusal to answer the salesperson's question might lead her to wonder whether I was having a mental breakdown.

Our daily decisions as consumers and citizens play constitutive roles in defining "what I really think is important" and "who I really am." Yet we cannot engage in these forms of self-definition solipsistically. Although I may not know sellers or voters personally, "I" cannot arbitrarily decide how to deal with them. If I hope to engage in meaningful acts of self-definition, I have no choice: *subjective* self-understanding requires the mastery of the prevailing modes of *mutual spherical recognition*, including the complex patterns of stranger-stranger engagement that are necessary for competent everyday performance.

I may come to regret the decisions I make as a voter or consumer and try to redefine the way I discharge these roles in the future. Yet these efforts at *intra*-spherical redefinition are only part of a larger project of *inter*-spherical equilibration that serves as the framework of modern existence. My choices as a consumer may provoke disappointment from family members or other sphere-mates, who were hoping that I would bring back very different commodities. My political commitments may generate lots of conversations with my friends—which may eventually lead me to modify my political identity or perhaps to find new friends.

It is one thing for me to tell myself that I have achieved a relatively stable form of holistic self-definition, but I will be deluding myself unless I can sustain the credibility of my commitments to the sphere-mates who currently serve as the focal points of my existence.

In the chapters that follow, I will explore the complex demands of self-definition imposed by the fact that in the twenty-first century we are encountering a new breed of stranger—people we confront virtually, not physically. Although these new forms of encounter generate shattering new challenges, they build upon the already complex ways in which modern men and women collaborate with strangers in the physical world. Yet even these forms of face-to-face engagement are a relative novelty in the history of human existence. Until the nineteenth century, the mass of humanity lived in tightly knit communities where encounters with strangers were exceptional and viewed with profound suspicion. Newcomers risked their lives if they challenged local patterns of face-to-face interaction, yet it was tough to adapt quickly enough to avoid pariah-status if the stranger was born and raised within a different tightly knit culture.

The modern world reverses this traditional pattern. "Normal" people can no longer treat strangers as deviants; they must instead understand themselves as strangers in many daily contexts. Strangerhood is such an entrenched feature of our existence that it is hard for us to gain perspective on its distinctive demands.

My aim in this chapter is to present a stripped-down scenario that invites you to consider the legitimation of strangerhood as a defining feature of modernity. Once we gain a deeper historical perspective on our contemporary situation, the next chapters will explore the complex interactions between consumerism, citizenship, and other forms of strangerhood that play a significant, even dominant, role in our efforts to define a meaningful life for ourselves.

Stranger Self-Restraint

I will begin with a stripped-down scenario that asks you to assume a role familiar to almost everybody. Wherever you live, you will often find yourself functioning as a pedestrian – walking down the street on the way to some destination. When operating in this mode, you expect to encounter other pedestrians who are also on their way somewhere.

This is a classic case of stranger-stranger engagement – in which "I" find myself sharing the street with people I have never met. Nevertheless, I cannot walk down the street however I like. As a competent adult in the "here and now," I must conduct myself in ways that will not alarm or annoy my fellow pedestrians or, in the most extreme instances, attract the attention of the police.

What makes my responsibilities as a stranger even more demanding is that acceptable modes of pedestrian behavior differ dramatically from place to place. Flamboyance that might be acceptable in Rio de Janeiro may seem outrageously alarming on the streets of Tokyo, while what counts as non-weird in my hometown may be dramatically different from what is expected in either of these places. If I'm not walking in my hometown, I had better find out about the particular modes of non-alarming behavior in alien territory before I start travelling down the streets in the "here and now" in which I find myself – otherwise I risk being identified as a weirdo.

So even an activity as seemingly straightforward as walking down the street is a remarkably complex existential exercise. Nevertheless, I would like to persuade you that there is one form of behavior that is viewed as illegitimate throughout the world, regardless of where you happen to be.

To see my point, suppose a couple of fellow pedestrians suddenly block your path and ask you to spend a few minutes in a conversation dealing with a subject of great importance. Suppose, moreover, that they might be right in predicting that you will find the encounter worthwhile if you allow it to continue. Nevertheless, their street-corner intervention raises a fundamental question: up to this moment, you have been sharing the street as strangers, yet these anonymous others are now trying to establish a personal relationship with you, although you have not given the slightest indication that you want this.

For all they know, you may be on your way to an urgent engagement with some significant sphere-mate. Their unexpected intervention may prevent you from getting to your appointment on time. Yet they are asserting unilateral authority to transform a pedestrian encounter into a personal relationship.

If they can legitimately intervene, other strangers could do so as well. Their cumulative intrusions would radically destabilize your efforts to live out your own life on your own terms. You could not even rely on your friends to meet you for lunch—since their walks to the restaurant might be disrupted by different interlopers. If you somehow managed to make it to the restaurant on time, you might be sitting at an empty table, denied the opportunity to deepen your friendship with one another.

Strangers must remain strangers until both sides mutually express an interest in a more personal relationship. This principle does not merely apply to strangers who intend to do me harm—in any of the complex ways elaborated in criminal and civil law. It extends to strangers who are trying to enrich my personal life—and might even succeed if given the chance. Nevertheless, despite their good intentions, they must confront the fact that their fellow strangers are awake for only 16 or 18 hours a day and must therefore make hard choices about how to spend their time in the most rewarding way, given the competing demands of their friends and families, schoolmates, workmates, and co-religionists—as well as many non-pedestrian forms of collaboration with strangers. This principle of stranger self-restraint is, in short, nothing less than an *existential precondition* for the pursuit of a meaningful life in a modern society.

Even when this precondition is satisfied, there is no guarantee that "I" will make wise decisions on how best to deal with the inter-spherical demands on my limited time and energy. Once I take advantage of the opportunity to have a series of lunches with my friends, for example, my repeated disappointment with their responses to my personal predicaments may lead me to turn my back on them.

But it is one thing for me to look for new associates to fill the void left by my alienation from old ones and quite another for strangers to impose themselves upon me, even if they think they can solve my problems better than I can. If such interventions were legitimate, it would strip me of my capacity to search for fulfilling relationships *on my own terms.*

Call this the principle of stranger self-restraint—and it is an existential precondition for living a meaningful life in the modern world. As this book proceeds, I will try to identify other building-block principles, culminating in the shattering internet challenges that currently confront us as we try to live in virtual as well as physical reality.

For now, it's important to take a step-by-step approach and consider the relationship of stranger self-restraint to our more personal commitments to friends and family and schoolmates and workmates. Given the multi-spherical demands of our daily lives, occasions will inevitably arise when the principle of stranger self-restraint points us in one direction, but our personal loyalties point us in the opposite direction. How to resolve this dilemma?

There are two possibilities. On one hand, each of us may claim the authority to make our own trade-offs on a case-by-case basis. Call this the individualistic solution. On the other hand, the fundamental structure of modern society may require all of us to deal with these conflicts in the same way—at least on certain critical occasions. Call this the uniformity solution.

My next task is to persuade you not only that the uniformity solution is required but that we must sometimes uphold our responsibilities to strangers even when they conflict with our most important personal commitments.

A shocking conclusion, I grant you. Yet consider an everyday scenario that is commonplace throughout the world. Once we think it through, we can consider its larger implications.

Suppose you are running down the sidewalk to get to an urgent meeting with the most important person in your life. Earlier that day, you learned that your lover was going through a terrible personal crisis and was contemplating suicide. You have dropped everything to rush to her side.

As you are racing down a crowded street, however, someone pushes you, and you trip and fall to the ground. As you tumble downwards, you hit another pedestrian—who also falls and breaks her ankle. While you yourself are lucky enough to avoid injury, the accident victim angrily demands that you accept responsibility for the damage you have caused her.

But you refuse, explaining that you had no choice but to fall on her and that the person who is truly responsible is the one who pushed you to the ground—generating the chain reaction that led to her injury. When you explain this chain of events to your injured counterpart, however, she denounces your efforts to escape responsibility and shouts to passersby to call an ambulance to come to her assistance and also get the police to the scene and arrest you for assaulting her.

Your past experience suggests that the police will be arriving within a few minutes. In the meantime, you have two options. You can run away from the accident site before the police arrive, or else you can wait to tell them your side of the story.

Which do you choose?

If it were up to me, I'd leave the scene immediately. Once the police arrived, it could take an hour or more for them to interview all the witnesses. Even if they were persuaded that I wasn't to blame for the accident, my lover might have killed herself in the meantime. The very thought would be intolerable. Here I am engaging in bureaucratic mumbo jumbo with the police while my lover's life is in danger.

One thing should be clear: the principle of stranger self-restraint does not require me to stay. Despite the chaotic conditions prevailing on the street corner, it remains true that I have never previously encountered my aggrieved counterpart. And I have absolutely no interest in getting to know her better. It is she, and she alone, who is insisting that I engage in a more personal (if antagonistic) conversation with her once the police arrive. If anyone is violating the principle of stranger-restraint, it is she, not I—by unilaterally transforming our impersonal relationship into a more personal encounter. So long as the decision is left to me, I would certainly seize my opportunity to leave the scene and come to the aid of my lover.

Yet throughout the entire world, I am required to wait until the police arrive. If I flee, I have committed a serious criminal offense—even if I wasn't to blame for the underlying accident. My legal duty to the police trumps my spherical duty to my lover.

To be sure, I may well defy the law and run to my lover as the street-corner bystanders shout out their outrage. Speaking for myself, I hope I would do so. What is more, depending on the local laws, it might be possible to obtain a pardon once the tragic character of my predicament was brought to the authorities' attention.

For now, I am more concerned with the general principle than particular exceptions. Why is it that, throughout the modern world, I have a legal obligation to respect the demands of the police more than to respect the claims of the people who are most important to me?

The Rise of the Police in the Breakthrough to Modernity

Begin by putting my street-corner dilemma in historical context. Before the 1820s, nobody in human history would have had to decide whether to flee the site of an accident before the police arrived—because police did not yet exist. We owe their creation to the French. After the defeat of Napoleon in 1815, the restored monarchy was determined to prevent another mob from reenacting the seizure of the Bastille that had led to the overthrow of Louis XVI. Until that time, even an urban center like Paris—whose total population of 550,000 made it Europe's largest city—relied on the tightly knit communities within each neighborhood to maintain public order.[1] But given its fears of renewed revolution, the monarchy created a para-military organization called the "police" to defend divine right against the continuing threat of overthrow by "the mob."

In taking this step, the king's ministers recognized that it was necessary to transform their new recruits into a disciplined force.

Otherwise, if there were renewed unrest, the street fighters hired as police could easily join the revolutionary agitators rather than suppress them. At the same time, this task could not be assigned to the standing army, since the presence of troops on the streets of Paris would make the city feel like a conquered province and further undermine the Restoration's already problematic legitimacy.

The monarchy was determined to create a distinctive institutional identity for its new "police force." Unlike the army, its members would understand themselves as a new breed of professionals confronting the distinctive challenges involved in calming the daily flare-ups of Parisian life. Officers would be taught to resist the temptation to respond to disorder with lethal force. Their training would also require them to move beyond their subjective intuitions in imposing law and order. Instead, the police would have special skills designed to deal with the characteristic urban problems they would confront daily.[2]

To put it mildly, understandings of "professional" police conduct have changed dramatically since French *gendarmes* started patrolling the Paris streets—and postmodern conditions will require further sweeping reforms in the future. But our contemporary debates should not obscure the profound significance of the recent rise of policing as a world-historical reality.

To put the point in terms of my breakdown scenario: for almost all of human history, disputes arising from street-corner accidents were resolved in premodern fashion. My sidewalk confrontation would occur within the context of a tightly knit community, and my outraged victim would call upon neighbors to punish me for my breach of local norms. If I tried to leave the scene, nearby residents would respond to my antagonist's calls for assistance.

Upon their arrival, my fate would depend on my relative standing in the community. If I had a good reputation and my opponent was a well-known troublemaker, I could expect my neighbors to accept my side of the story and impose sanctions on the troublemaker. But death might well await me if I were a total stranger passing through the community on my way to "somewhere else." With the exception of visiting members of the nobility, interlopers were always viewed with suspicion – even if they made good-faith efforts to conform to local mores. But when, as in a street-corner collision, aggrieved insiders accused strangers of outrageous conduct, interlopers would be lucky to flee with their lives before the insider's neighbors could kill them.

It is a mistake, then, to view the rise of the police in the 1820s as merely one of the countless contingencies marking the dawn of the modern age. It was a necessary institutional precondition for the rise of the modern world – in which men and women have the fundamental right to construct personal relationships with spheremates that make sense *to them*, without immediate reprisal from the community of their birth. Parents and neighbors might react bitterly to the choices you make as an adult, but the police will prevent them from using physical force to punish you for betraying the parental values that shaped your early existence.

This assumes that you live in a country with an effective police force. When a nation collapses into anarchy in the twenty-first century, its citizens confront an even grimmer prospect than their premodern counterparts. While residents of tightly knit communities did not choose their identities, they could count on their neighbors to defend them against the assaults of outsiders. But when the police collapse in the current era, traditional communities have typically disintegrated as well, leaving the community without either form of criminal deterrent.

Putting these breakdowns to one side, even relatively effective police departments notoriously fail to enforce the law impartially. Throughout the world, officers impose oppressive cultural, economic, religious, and racial domination on stigmatized groups. They often seem more concerned with enforcing the social hierarchy than enforcing the law. Given their crucial role, fundamental reform of the police is an urgent matter of existential justice.[3]

Many of my readers don't have to worry about these abusive practices because they occupy a socially dominant position and know the police will treat them relatively fairly. But they cannot responsibly blind themselves to these discriminatory practices. The integrity of the police force serves as a crucial institutional presupposition of their own individual search for a meaningful life. Suppose, for example, that after leaving school and getting a job in a distant city, you meet someone and fall in love. When you tell your parents of your decision to marry your lover, they emphatically disapprove of your choice and do all they can to induce you to abandon your partner and choose somebody who conforms to their traditional values.

In this scenario, the distinctive character of your sidewalk predicament emerges – even for those who have escaped face-to-face forms of police brutality. If the police did not exist, you would never have had the opportunity to escape your closely knit community and explore other places that offered you the opportunity to find somebody like your lover – for the simple reason that, before the rise of the police, your arrival at another closely knit community would readily provoke your expulsion or death. It follows that if I run away from the scene of my accident before the police arrive – even if it is to rush to my lover in her hour of need—*I will be repudiating a key institution that made my love possible.*

At the same time, however, if I wait for the police, and my lover commits suicide in my absence, I will be destroying the very meaning of my life. An impossible situation!

Yet something like this happens regularly on street corners around the world: people cause unintentional injury while urgently trying to perform some unselfish act. Hopefully, you and your loved ones will manage to avoid such tragedies. Nevertheless, you should not ignore them as you reflect more generally on your duties as a citizen of a modern state. Otherwise, you will be engaging in an *existential self-contradiction,* refusing to join with your fellow citizens to take action that supports the very institutional conditions—in this case, police integrity—that make it possible for you to *take responsibility for the meaning of your own life* in the real world of the twenty-first century.

In this crucial respect, your relationship to citizenship stands apart from countless other relationships that the modern world makes available to you, including encounters that made it possible for you to meet the love of your life. Even if your most precious commitments are destroyed by tragedy, it remains *for you* to decide how to respond.

In contrast, if you choose to ignore your citizenship obligations, you are engaging in an existential self-contradiction. By handing the task of government to others, you will have saved precious hours that you can devote to matters of personal significance—and this may well enable you to gain greater success over the course of decades. Nevertheless, it is your *democratic* responsibility to take part in the collective effort to assure the very conditions of your freedom to define yourself on your own terms.

To be sure, my not-so-pedestrian scenario only serves to make this point in very abstract terms. I have yet to consider any of its concrete implications for democratic practice. It is enough for now to emphasize the need for serious people to take their citizenship seriously—and not merely view their vote at election time as if it were a momentary diversion from the important things in life.

My next chapter takes the next step in this direction by comparing citizenship to a role that everybody recognizes to be of fundamental importance. While it is easy to trivialize citizenship, only fools would deny that their activities as consumers are crucial to their ongoing efforts at self-realization. But once again, although we take this status for granted in the twenty-first century, it was unknown until modern times. How to account for its central significance? Why does it seem so much more important in everyday life than democratic citizenship?

Chapter 3

CITIZEN V. CONSUMER

Despite their obvious differences, your activities as a consumer have one basic similarity to your activities as a citizen. When you walk into a store or into a voting both, you are engaged in a stranger-stranger relationship. When you hand money over to cashiers at the supermarket, you aren't interested in getting to know them personally – this is even truer when you deal with a computer on-line.

Similarly, when you vote for a candidate, you cast a secret ballot. If vote counters spy on you and find out how you vote, they are assaulting your fundamental status as a citizen. While we take the secret ballot for granted, it strongly contrasts with other paradigmatic acts of democratic citizenship – most obviously, your freedom to speak publicly on matters of political importance. You have a fundamental right to state your views, even if they are based on serious factual mistakes; but you have an even more fundamental right to lie to pollsters when they ask how you voted.

The reverse is true when you are dealing in the marketplace. You can't lie to sellers about your financial status, and they can't misrepresent their products to you. Indeed, this chapter argues that dominant understandings of "consumer protection" require far more honesty than do personal relationships.

This claim, to put it mildly, is counterintuitive. But once we track its historical development, we will be in a far better position to consider the very different fate of democratic citizenship in the twenty-first century. Lots of political scientists and constitutional thinkers have advanced a host of different approaches to the "political polarization" destroying faith in democracy throughout the world. But they haven't asked the inter-spherical question I am raising here: how can we account for mass *alienation* from democratic citizenship during an era of mass *commitment* to integrity in consumer relationships?

My answer: it is precisely the vitality of consumerist self-understanding that is encouraging people to suppose that it is perfectly legitimate for them to treat democracy as if it were just the site of another marketplace—in which it is *perfectly legitimate* to treat political influence as a commodity that can be *appropriately* bought and sold in response to the changing demands of competing political parties and movements.

There is nothing inevitable about the commodification of democratic life in the twenty-first century. Rather than engage in neo-Marxist denunciations of bourgeois democracy and call for a radical revolution, I hope to encourage a thoughtful debate over the real-world institutional reforms that will reinvigorate the sphere of citizenship under postmodern conditions.

The path to realistic reform will depend on the particular dilemmas confronting the particular countries in which you are particularly involved—and I will only take up these issues seriously in part 3. The place to begin, for now, is by reflecting on the remarkable way in which the rise of consumerism over the twentieth century has reached the point where it poses a profound threat to the very credibility of democratic citizenship.

Consumer Loyalty v. Personal Commitment

Let's start with a typical case from everyday life. You go on the internet to buy toothpaste, which ShinyTooth Inc. is only too happy to provide. You are not personally acquainted with anybody working for the firm, but that doesn't bother you. Even if you haven't done business with ShinyTooth before, you can check its reliability on an appropriate website. Having done so, you have only one serious objective in mind: to determine whether the firm is offering you the best price for its toothpaste, or whether a different toothpaste of comparable quality is cheaper.

You can only be sure if you search the marketplace and thoroughly compare price against effectiveness. But you have lots more important things to do with your time. So if your market intuitions tell you that ShinyTooth's price doesn't seem "too high," you give it a try. If you like it, you may develop brand loyalty to the firm and not waste your time searching for a better buy.

Yet this form of *brand* loyalty is categorically different from your *personal* loyalties in other spheres of life. Given the increasing significance of one's status as a consumer, it is important to analyze this difference.

Begin with a test of your brand loyalty to ShinyTooth. As you scroll the internet, you accidentally come across an advertisement from ToothWizard offering a competitive toothpaste for less money. When you accept the offer and start brushing, you find that it does a better job than ShinyTooth and tastes just as good.

Since ToothWizard is cheaper, it would be silly to let your brand loyalty to ShinyTooth stop you from switching immediately to ToothWizard. After all, you were "loyal" only because it seemed like a good deal for the money, given the limited time you were willing to spend exploring the toothpaste market. Now that ToothWizard has brought its cheaper product to your attention, why remain faithful to ShinyTooth?

In contrast, personal loyalties have a dual temporal aspect. They are not merely based on forward-looking assessments of future options. They are grounded in backward-looking understandings of the enduring meaning of past relationships.

Suppose, for example, you are a member of a volunteer soccer club in your neighborhood, and a rival team asks you to join them instead. Their offer is a lot better than anything you can expect from your old club. You are presently playing a minor position on defense, and the rival team wants you to be its star goalie.

Despite the obvious attractions of this offer, you confront a dilemma. Over the past few years, you have built close friendships with your teammates as you struggled together on the playing field. If you switch sides, you will regularly encounter your old teammates in league competition. Whenever you manage to block one of their goals, your opponents might give you a kind of grudging respect – "you were never that good when you played with us" – but it might come with an undercurrent of resentment, given the many years in which your old teammates significantly enriched your life.

Deciding whether to transform yourself into a star goalie isn't as easy as it first appeared. Are you willing to betray your old teammates for your personal advancement?

Maybe yes, maybe no. Perhaps the prospect of athletic excellence is so important to you that you regretfully say goodbye to your pals in your search for self-realization. Or perhaps you stay in your minor position as a substitute midfielder and hope your team gives you a starring role in the future. Whatever you decide, you cannot escape the existential character of your choice: if you stick with your sphere-mates, you affirm your identity as a person who puts personal loyalty over stardom; vice versa if you join the other side.

This existential question simply doesn't arise when you are a consumer deciding whether to stick with ShinyTooth, now that ToothWizard is giving you shiny teeth at a lower price. On this scenario, I can think of only one reason to remain loyal. Perhaps brushing with ShinyTooth reminds you of a better time in your life, before your once-happy marriage ended in a divorce. In those days, you emerged from your morning tooth-brushing ritual to join your spouse and kids around the breakfast table, enjoy each other's company, and talk about your plans for the day. While you may often recall these happier times in the abstract, brushing with ShinyTooth is one of the few real-world experiences that permits you to relive the past—if only for a moment—and help compensate for your present loneliness.

Yet this scenario reinforces my point. It is only if I transform my use of a commodity into a backward-looking experience of a past *personal* relationship that it makes sense to refuse ToothWizard's better offer. Otherwise, absent some concrete reason, such as cheaper price or better taste, brand loyalty to ShinyTooth looks like a bizarre form of commodity fetishism.

The Rise of Consumerism

In emphasizing the one-dimensional temporality of consumerist decision-making, I don't want to minimize its importance. To the contrary, it will play a key role in my contrast with citizenship self-understanding in the next chapter. Even though your activities as a citizen– like those you undertake as a consumer–involve lots of people you don't know personally, they do *not* display the one-sided temporality exemplified in the ShinyTooth case. Instead, your past political commitments do indeed play a fundamental role as you join with your fellow citizens to shape the future course of your democracy.

To gain perspective on this crucial difference, I will proceed in step-by-step fashion, beginning with the historical dynamics that have propelled consumerism to its present prominence. I will then turn, in the next chapter, to consider the very different dynamics at work in the case of citizenship.

It was only in the middle of the nineteenth century that merchants began opening up so-called department stores–offering commodities to any consumer who had the cash to buy them. Before then, traveling peddlers occasionally entered the tightly knit communities of the premodern world to sell things that local butchers or bakers couldn't provide, but they were careful to act in a fashion that would not provoke hostile reactions to their intrusions into the neighborhood. Even in urban centers, people generally dealt with neighborhood merchants on a first-name basis. To be sure, they had one great advantage over their country cousins: cities were centers of trade, where one could find sellers of exotic goods obtained from faraway places. Yet these sellers typically obtained their goods through very particular supply chains based on extended family ties or similar arrangements.

Only a tiny elite could enjoy an experience similar to those modern-day consumers take for granted. Big-time merchants in Paris or London or Vienna built large mansions to display a rich selection of luxury goods acquired through a variety of supply chains, and they invited members of the elite to enter the premises to consider their purchasing options.

But you had to gain the merchant's explicit permission before you were allowed to enter his mansion. It was easy, of course, for a well-recognized member of the elite to use his or her personal connections to obtain these invitations. But aggressive up-and-comers would find it tough to gain admission, since the arriviste's entry onto the scene might discredit the merchant's respectability in the eyes of established buyers. So this quasi-consumer experience was very much an elite privilege, not a fundamental aspect of modern life.

It is easy to mark the moment the consumerist revolution began – and once again, the breakthrough took place in Paris, only a decade after the rise of the first police force. Le Bon Marché opened its doors in 1838 – and its great success inspired entrepreneurs in Europe and the Americas to open their own department stores over the next generation.[1]

It couldn't have happened without the Industrial Revolution, which massively increased the supply and variety of commodities – creating enormous profit-making opportunities for entrepreneurs opening their doors to vast numbers of new purchasers, who were abandoning their rural communities in search of a better life in big cities. Yet these technological breakthroughs were necessary, but not sufficient, conditions for the mode of consumer understanding that we take for granted today.

Even under the old regime, Paris was full of commercial enterprises that were open to anybody wanting to buy one commodity in particular – sex. While macho men of all classes were endlessly entering these "dens of iniquity," they entered these places in a quasi-covert manner that recognized they were defying divine command in treating women as mere objects of consumption. Just as the church had condemned these adulterous exercises in sexual ecstasy for centuries, it might well have denounced the department store for its sinful "celebration of earthly delights" that would lead mankind yet further away from the path set out by God's law.

Yet this didn't happen. The department store had little trouble establishing itself as a sphere of human freedom rather than licentiousness. Consumers entered these monuments of commodification with self-confidence, not anxiety—while church leaders focused on other matters and governments affirmatively attempted to facilitate these novel modes of encounter.

Consumerist forms of engagement gained further momentum as rural areas gained access to improved postal services over the following decades, allowing the vast majority of the population, which still lived in the countryside, to act as consumers by purchasing commodities through mail-order catalogues. By the beginning of the twentieth century, almost everybody was playing the role of "consumer" in leading nations on both sides of the Atlantic—as well as in advanced economies in the rest of the world. With the rise of the internet, rural residents of less developed economic zones are joining the crowd—deploying their cellphones to move beyond their tightly knit communities and operate as competent consumers in the postmodern marketplace.

Once it became entrenched in ordinary life, consumerism became a foundational legal status in the aftermath of World War II. Consumer protection law responds to the distinctive dilemmas each of us encounter as we engage in this sphere of stranger-stranger relations. As we have seen, consumers generally can't spare the time required to search through the entire marketplace to get the best deal for commodities. Without effective legislation, this permits sellers to exploit our ignorance in their efforts to maximize their profits. Since lots of consumers have experienced occasions on which they were induced to pay more for lower-quality goods, they provided broad support for political movements in support of "consumer protection" legislation. Significantly, these laws don't apply when buyers are merchants, who are expected to be as market savvy as the sellers they encounter in the marketplace. They aim to protect ordinary consumers from sellers who would otherwise manipulate their buyers' "imperfect information" in illegitimate ways.[2]

A second aspect of this legal effort is even more significant. The problem arises when merchants, invoking their "freedom of contract," refuse to deal with stigmatized groups of their fellow citizens while inviting all other consumers into their stores. These selective forms of discrimination are banned by consumer protection statutes, and in many parts of the world, they are understood as assaults on foundational constitutional commitments to human dignity.

To see why, suppose you were lucky enough to live in a place like Scandinavia, which guarantees you a generous economic safety net against misfortune as well as the educational resources required for a fair chance at success in adult life. Even in such places, everybody is forced to confront tough inter-spherical decisions as they struggle to make sense of their lives. Some people will devote a great deal of their time to high-paying jobs; others will settle for more modest careers and devote their energies to the needs of their family and friends; and so forth.

Despite their safety net, however, lots of people will make economic decisions that turn out badly over time, to the point where their treatment as consumers in the marketplace undermines fundamental principles of existential justice. To see this pathological dynamic at work, look upon it from the vantage point of a Mr. or Ms. Moderate Income – or ModInc. (For stylistic reasons, I'll be changing ModInc's gender from paragraph to paragraph, switching "him" to "her" and back again.)

When he walks into a department store, ModInc finds himself surrounded by consumers with lots more money than he possesses. I will begin with two familiar cases that don't involve assaults on his standing as a self-defining human being – but will set the stage for a third, tragic, scenario.

In case 1, ModInc walks into a SuperGadget store offering a technology called Wonder that will vastly expand her access to the internet. But the store is charging $1000 for Wonder. As ModInc considers her low supply of cash, she sees a fellow consumer, HighInc, hand over $1000 to the SuperGadget representative at the sales counter – and leave with Wonder in his knapsack, looking forward to a dramatic expansion of his internet freedom. Despite the temptation to follow HighInc's lead, ModInc reluctantly concludes that, given other pressing priorities, she can afford only $500. She asks the sales clerk to ask his boss to make an exception and sell a Wonder for half price. The clerk summarily rejects her offer, saying he "won't waste the boss's time" with "such a ridiculous request." A demoralized ModInc leaves the store without Wonder. Nevertheless, despite her disappointment, SuperGadget hasn't lowered her standing as a consumer by insisting that she pay the $1000 price it is charging all other consumers for Wonder.

In case 2, ModInc continues to walk down the street and is delighted to come across a second high-tech store, MiracleNet, offering a really great bargain. Its display window announces that, for this day only, it has slashed the price of Wonder technology to

$500. ModInc runs into the store, hands over his cash, and emerges with his own Wonder machine in hand. Not only does his internet future look bright, but he looks back to his experience at SuperGadget with great pride.

It's hard to measure the extent of her self-satisfaction – call it *X* – as she congratulates herself on her refusal to follow HighInc's lead and hand over $1000. But for purposes of my argument, *X* will suffice as a benchmark as we turn to consider my tragic third scenario.

In case 3, ModInc lives in a country that hasn't enacted consumer protection legislation. In this scenario, when he walks into SuperGadget, he no longer has the chance to have his $500 offer for Wonder rejected by the store clerk in a face-to-face encounter. Instead, he confronts a large sign on the front window telling him that SuperGadget refuses to deal with members of his ethnic or gender or racial or religious group. Shocked, he scrutinizes the sign further to study the company's explanation for its decision.

It assures her that the firm's employees would be perfectly happy to do business with the pariah group. The problem is that a significant percentage of SuperGadget's customers are so prejudiced against the despised minority that the company's profits could drop if the firm began selling its products to people like ModInc. After stating these hard truths, SuperGadget's sign concludes with an expression of sympathy: "We very much hope that the day will dawn when we can open our doors to everyone – but we urge our disappointed customers to recognize that the reason we're in business is to make money in the 'here and now.' "

ModInc walks to the entrance to confront an armed guard blocking his way – and demands to meet with SuperGadget's management team to urge reconsideration of the firm's decision. The guard rejects his request and threatens him with physical harm if he doesn't stop blocking the entrance for other customers.

As a consequence, she has no choice but to go down the street to try her luck at MiracleNet, which, as in case 2, has announced its special one-day sale. When she arrives, she finds that the store continues to serve all consumers. She rushes in and buys Wonder for $500, and looks forward to a bright new future on the internet, but she leaves the store asking herself new questions: Although I got a great bargain at MiracleNet, will this be the last time they let me in? Will I be forced to roam the streets begging stores for admission? What will be my fate if all merchants find it in their profit-maximizing interest to say no?

In the premodern conditions that prevailed until the nineteenth century, these questions were un-askable. Almost everybody remained trapped within their tightly knit communities. Two centuries later, the opposite is true: continuing access to the marketplace is a necessary condition for survival. If firms can legitimately close their doors on impoverished or stigmatized groups, they would be stripping these people of their fundamental status as self-defining individuals searching for meaning in the modern world.

This was precisely the point of the famous sit-ins inspired by leaders like Martin Luther King Jr.—where civil rights activists occupied lunch counters to demand service on equal terms with whites. When their offers to buy coffee or hamburgers were rejected, they refused to leave, requiring firms to call in the police to seize them and bring them to court, where they would be convicted for criminal assaults on law and order.

Despite the Supreme Court's decision in *Brown v. Board of Education* in 1954, the justices refused to deal decisively with this issue. Indeed, the court even contented itself with very slow, and reversible, steps toward serous desegregation of all-white schools.

But King was not content to mobilize his movement to protest the continuing stigmatization of black children by school systems throughout the country. He was demanding the extension of egalitarian principles to the marketplace – leading massive protests against state governments and federal courts that continued to uphold the fundamental right of property owners to decide whom they would recognize as legitimate customers. The massive sit-ins by civil rights activists, moreover, provoked massive counter-demonstrations by militant defenders of the status quo. Meanwhile, rival political leaders in Washington, D.C., issued competing pronunciamentos on the key issues – while the system of checks and balances led, at best, to ambiguous and interstitial legislation.

It was only the assassination of John F. Kennedy in November 1963 that broke the logjam. Lee Harvey Oswald's bullet propelled Lyndon Johnson into the White House. In contrast to his fellow southerners, Johnson had been a strong supporter of civil rights since the very beginning of his political career. Yet without the massive street demonstrations mobilized by leaders like King, he would never have been in a position to gain the swing congressional votes he needed to include a provision in the Civil Rights Act that unequivocally barred the owners of hotels, restaurants, and other public accommodations from discriminating "on the ground of race, color, religion, or national origin." The mobilization of a broad-based coalition of activists was also crucial in enabling Johnson to gain congressional authorization for the construction of a nationwide system of enforcement that could prevent racist politicians in the states from sabotaging the act's antidiscrimination principle.

Even these springtime triumphs on Capitol Hill, however, did not assure a decisive victory. Indeed, in the short term, they helped propel Barry Goldwater to victory in the Republican primaries. The Arizona conservative made the repeal of the Civil Rights Act the centerpiece of his campaign to oust Johnson from the White House: "In your heart, you know he's right!"

It was one thing for white liberals to say, "No, Barry, you are wrong." It was quite another for black activists to engage in the hard work required to convince their intimidated neighbors to go to the polls, and face the further prospect of retaliation if Goldwater managed to win the presidency. This grassroots effort to get out the vote would never have succeeded were it not for the bitter experience of existential injustice that had led millions of black activists to take their democratic citizenship seriously in the course of the preceding decade.

When the polls closed, Johnson defeated Goldwater in a nationwide landslide that exceeded Franklin Roosevelt's triumph over Alf Landon in 1936. No less significantly, the Democrats won two-thirds majorities in the Senate as well as the House, making it impossible for hard-line conservatives to filibuster further egalitarian initiatives and consolidating the principles of the 1964 act into the foundations of American law for the foreseeable future.

This was the point at which commercial enterprises could no longer legitimately close their doors to stigmatized groups – even if these exclusions could be justified on profit-maximizing grounds that were otherwise central to the operation of a market economy. Instead, each and every consumer had gained the fundamental right, as a modern man or woman, to enter *any* commercial enterprise and demand that their owners deal with them in a respectful fashion.

They had won this *individual* right, moreover, only through the ongoing efforts by millions and millions of Americans to take their responsibilities as democratic *citizens* seriously. Without their long-term commitment of time and energy to the civil rights movement, this fundamental reorganization of the marketplace would not have occurred. It is a big mistake, then, to view this economic transformation as if it were the product of Adam Smith's "invisible hand." To the contrary, this fundamental reorganization of the economy was rooted in a broad-based commitment to democratic citizenship. This was also true in many other parts of the world.[3]

To be sure, these ideals were never fully realized even at the best of times – and they are currently under assault around the world by authoritarian demagogues aiming to re-create a social order in which massive numbers of consumers will once again be treated as pariahs. I will return to the implications of this counterrevolution in later chapters. For now, I want to put the citizenship achievements involved in reconstructing the marketplace into broader perspective – by comparing them to the larger effort to achieve real-world democracy in the modern, and postmodern, world.

Chapter 4

DEMOCRACY V. PLUTOCRACY

At the dawn of the twenty-first century, the destruction of the Berlin Wall seemed to be the culmination of a half century of democratic triumph. There were great leaps forward in apartheid South Africa, caste-ridden India, as well as postwar Germany and Japan. Indeed, military dictatorships were retreating before grass-roots movements in Latin America and elsewhere. Meanwhile, the European Union seemed well on its way toward the construction of a vast Continental democracy extending from the British Isles to the Russian frontier.

Over the last two decades, the rise of demagogic dictatorships has shattered democratic self-confidence. Despite the prevailing gloom, however, I hope to convince you that the prospects for democratic revitalization are better than they appear. But to make my case, let's begin by reflecting upon the fundamental ways in which the rise of the modern, and postmodern, world has revolutionized the very nature of citizenship.[1]

Begin with the basics: committed democrats confront a political situation radically different from the one their counterparts faced in classical Greece and Rome. During its moment of glory, the Athenian republic consisted of 30,000 citizens linked together in dense face-to-face networks. If Citizen Beta didn't know Gamma personally, he typically had a friend who knew him well enough to give him a sense of Gamma's character. Rome was also governed on a face-to-face basis after its inhabitants overthrew the monarchy in 509 BCE.

This is precisely why the ancient republics failed to sustain themselves after their military leaders conquered vast regions inhabited by millions of aliens. In both cases, creative statesmen made repeated efforts to sustain their face-to-face democracies within the vast domains they had gained through force. But they ultimately failed, enabling military strongmen to govern the Athenian and Roman empires as autocrats.[2]

When Enlightenment revolutionaries in France and the United States looked back on the ancient world, they were painfully aware of the failure of these great experiments in republican self-government. As Madison put it in *Federalist Ten*, "The instability, injustice, and confusion introduced into the public councils, have . . . been the mortal diseases under which popular governments have everywhere perished." The first *Federalist* begins with Alexander Hamilton's plea "to the people of this country, by their conduct and example, to decide the important question, whether societies of men are really capable or not of establishing good government from reflection and choice, or whether they are forever destined to depend for their political constitutions on accident and force."[3]

At the Constitutional Convention of 1787, everyone agreed that it would be foolish to take classical models of face-to-face democracy as their starting point. Instead of talking directly to one another, Americans would express their will by voting for representatives. At this point, however, members of the Convention began to disagree over the best way to prevent elected representatives from abusing their power while in office—and how they should deal with the vast numbers of Blacks and Native Americans whom the Convention refused to recognize as self-determining human beings.

Yet despite agreeing on the centrality of the ballot in the constitutional system, the Founders understood the practice of voting in a way that radically differed from modern understandings. Citizens didn't cast secret ballots on Election Day as they do in the twenty-first century. In the early republic, they announced their votes in public. Madison and many other leaders of the founding generation defended this practice by arguing that secret balloting encouraged voters to consider their selfish private interests when making their crucial contribution to the democratic process. Only if voters announced their choices in public, they insisted, would they stand up for the candidate who would best maintain the "permanent interests of the community" against assaults on the public good by self-aggrandizing leaders of political "factions."[4]

These views remained dominant for a surprisingly long time despite strong opposition by committed democrats—who rightly emphasized that public voting enabled those in power to punish citizens for supporting candidates who challenged the status quo in the name of social justice—depriving so-called democracies of their significance for the overwhelming majority of citizens.

Nevertheless, it was not until the 1850s that reformers gained their first real-world victories for the secret ballot. This breakthrough into modernity didn't take place in America, France, or another center of Enlightenment civilization. Instead, the great leap to modern citizenship took place in faraway Australia, which had been seized by the British to serve as a penal colony for those who committed crimes within the United Kingdom. Between 1788 and 1868, more than 150,000 felons, including about 25,000 women, were transported to the "other side of the world."

As these convicts began to have families, their imperial overlords allowed them to engage in limited self-government. Within this distinctive context, public voting seemed inappropriate. One could hardly expect the residents of Australia's penal colonies to display their proud dedication to the general interest through public voting. Instead, an individual's announcement of support for a candidate would invite sneers of contempt from fellow-felons who backed rivals.

Through the 1850s and 1860s, the secret ballot was adopted in one penal colony after another.[5] But the precedents created by felons didn't have an immediate impact on the rest of the English-speaking world. Not until 1872 did Britain institute the "Australian ballot." Americans waited until the 1890s to adopt it on a nationwide basis.[6]

The Europeans arrived at the same destination about the same time but by a different route. During the early years of the French Revolution, the Constitution of 1795 explicitly guaranteed the secret ballot to all citizens.[7] But once Napoleon Bonaparte swept away the revolutionary republic, he also swept away the secret ballot—and it came to be systematically deployed in practice in France and the rest of Europe only during the second half of the nineteenth century. By 1900, however, it was recognized throughout the West as an indispensable precondition of collective self-government. A century later, nobody disputes its centrality. Current efforts by would-be dictators to falsify vote counts only testify to the significance of the twentieth century's break with the face-to-face precedents established in Greece and Rome. Regardless of their disagreements on many other matters, everybody takes it for granted that the *only* democratic way for citizens to choose their leaders is by going into the voting booth and casting a secret ballot. Government-by-strangers is an indisputable existential premise of contemporary democratic practice.

While I thoroughly endorse this principle, it represents only a first step toward a real-world system in which citizens can contribute meaningfully to the democratic enterprise.

Taking Citizenship Seriously

Why only a first step? For starters, voters can't join with their fellow citizens in a common project of self-government if they haven't taken the trouble to understand the basic issues raised by the election.[8] To be sure, since my ballot is secret, nobody can find out that I haven't the slightest idea why I am voting for Candidate A rather than B or C. But it is one thing to fool them; it is another thing to lie to myself. This book is about how each of us understands the meaning of his or her *own* existence under modern conditions.

Before I can understand myself as a citizen, I have no choice but to inform myself sufficiently so that I can confront the basic question posed by any election: should the citizenry retain the present government or replace it with political leaders urging a new course?

Some elections involve relatively minor critiques of the status quo; others, much larger changes. Whatever the stakes of a particular election, one thing is clear. If individual voters are to engage in meaningful acts of citizenship, they must have easy access to mass media that permit *opponents* of the present government to voice their objections to the current leadership. If dominant elites can keep their critics on the sidelines and transform the media into mouthpieces for the status quo, citizens can't realistically cast informed ballots, and they cannot act as a credible source of democratic authority.

Once again, no serious democrat questions the principle of adversary contestation, as I will call it. Yet current discussions typically focus on only one side of the problem: the opportunities the internet provides charismatic demagogues to mobilize their followers for totalitarian takeovers. Given the grim repetition of this scenario recently, the final part of this book will give this demagogic danger the attention it deserves. At this early stage of the argument, however, it is more important to focus on how the internet revolution has reshaped each person's self-understanding as a democratic citizen. As you and I consider our responsibilities as voters, we confront a straightforward but fundamental question: does my endless clicking onto the internet make it easier or harder to make an *informed* decision when casting my secret ballot?

I will explore this bottom-up question from two angles. I will begin by challenging the prevailing pessimism by emphasizing the enormous contributions the internet revolution is making to informed and responsible voting on Election Day. I will then look at the ways in which the communication breakthroughs of the twenty-first century do indeed make voters more vulnerable to charismatic demagogues. This bottom-up approach will lead me to emphasize the fundamental ways in which this technocratic form of democratic alienation structurally resembles the postmodernist dilemmas explored in previous chapters.

But first things first.

Turn the clock back to the 1990s and consider the formidable obstacles confronting reformers trying to gain an electoral victory over the political incumbents currently governing the United States. The challengers' chances to speak to voters were in the hands of a small number of television and radio networks, newspaper editors, and movie producers. The executives at the top of these pyramids played a crucial role in organizing public debate – and if they were not persuaded to give the reformers a serious opportunity to reach the electorate, their candidates' chances of winning on Election Day would depend on grassroots organizing.

Nowadays, critics of the status quo no longer need to pass through this old-fashioned obstacle course to reach the broader public. They can produce their own internet podcasts and videos for potential voters and coordinate them with efforts by committed activists to convince constituents to support their challenge to their entrenched rivals. If this campaign begins to mobilize a larger following, traditional media are obliged to take notice.

Incumbents can counter these critiques by flooding the internet with their own appeals to the electorate. But this only serves to energize debate on both sides and raise citizens' sense of the stakes involved in the election.

What is more, the contending candidates must make their case before the most educated citizenry in history. If, for example, we turn the clock back to the America of 1960, only 4 percent of blacks and 8 percent of whites had graduated from college by the time they were 25. By 2020, 28 percent of blacks and 45 percent of whites had gained college degrees. No less remarkably, black college graduates gain advanced university degrees at about the same rate as whites.[9] By 2020, this meant that 1.5 million blacks had earned post-graduate degrees – with more gains coming as the rising generation replaces their grandparents. Overall, 10 percent of black Americans currently possess a doctorate, master's, or professional degree – a higher share than the percentage of whites who had simply managed to graduate from college in the 1960s. Many nations have made similar, or even more impressive, educational breakthroughs over the past half century.[10]

In emphasizing this transformation, I don't mean to downplay the deeply entrenched forms of humiliation and poverty that continue to crush racial, ethnic, religious, and other minorities in their struggle for a meaningful life. While the 28 percent graduation rate of black Americans is remarkable, 45 percent of their white counterparts are gaining a similar success, and 16 percent are earning post-graduate degrees, as opposed to 10 percent of black men and women. These disparities provide compelling evidence of the continuing existential injustices that force impoverished and stigmatized youngsters to drop out of university for lack of cultural and financial support. Nevertheless, the formidable achievements of blacks and other minorities serve as a powerful rebuke to those who predict the death of democracy in America.

I don't deny, of course, that charismatic demagogues will use the internet to mobilize their followers for an all-out assault on the democratic way of life. But more and more citizens now have the analytic skills required to expose their lies and emotional appeals and to soberly compare demagogic critiques with those advanced by more responsible challengers to the politicians currently in office.

Still, many people pay little attention to the vibrant debate going on around them – and vote for candidates without bothering to seriously consider their positions. Worse, many will undoubtedly vote for candidates they would have opposed had they spent more time on their citizenship responsibilities. This may lead them to regret their voting decisions when candidates they support win the election and then disappoint their ill-considered expectations—especially when it turns out that the candidates have dictatorial ambitions.

Nevertheless, backward-looking regret is common in many other spheres of modern life. Is there anything about current electoral practices that poses a truly distinctive threat to twenty-first century democracy?

The answer leads me down the counterintuitive path I warned you about at the beginning of this discussion. Paradoxically, it is the secret ballot itself that makes us vulnerable to demagogic appeals. To see why, put yourself in the position of a radically disengaged citizen. Suppose I have a college education that equips me for a thoughtful assessment of the competing candidates. Nevertheless, I am really busy trying to do a good job at work, as well as responding to the demands of family, friends, and teammates on my neighborhood soccer club team. As a consequence, I simply can't spare the time required to confront *any* of the key campaign issues in a thoughtful fashion. Nevertheless, when Election Day arrives, I care enough about my country to go to my polling station and cast my ballot.

I now confront a distinctive existential predicament. On one hand, by casting my ballot I am joining my fellow citizens in a common project of democratic government. On the other hand, I have failed to play a constructive role in this project—since I am voting with no sense of what the candidates stand for. The entire point of my participation at the polls is to join my fellow citizens in a collective effort to choose leaders who will help shape the nation's future. Yet, for all I know, I am casting my ballot for candidates whom

I would emphatically reject if I had taken the time to consider at least one or two key issues raised during the campaign.

By showing up at the polls, I am simultaneously embracing and repudiating my role as a democratic citizen *at the very same moment* I am casting my ballot. In short, I am engaging in an existential self-contradiction. I should emphasize that this self-contradiction arises even if I happen to vote for candidates supported by a majority of responsible citizens who have taken the trouble to take the issues seriously. The fact that they have taken their citizenship responsibilities seriously does not change the fact that *I haven't.*

Nevertheless, despite the ease with which citizens can betray their own self-understanding in casting their ballots, secret voting is far superior to the public voting system that previously governed democratic practice in the nineteenth century. As we have seen, before the rise of the Australian ballot, citizens voting against the political establishment faced the prospect of physical assault and economic retaliation. It took real courage for citizens to brave these very real dangers to cast their public ballots for a political party aiming to change the course of their country's future. In contrast, the secret ballot permits citizens to play this crucial role in a fashion that makes sense within the multi-spherical framework of modern life.

With the rise of the internet, moreover, public voting would have an even more devastating impact. During the nineteenth century, political bosses were required to make face-to-face contact with employers to convince them to fire you if you were brave enough to vote the "wrong way." But in our brave new world, the dominant political party can use the internet to spy on you, disrupt your spherical activities at their most vulnerable moments, and arrange for thugs to assault you when you least expect it.

As a consequence, a return to open voting would yield a parody of democracy in the postmodern world. In this scenario, electoral officials emerge to announce that the governing party has been reelected by an overwhelming majority, without any *visible* sign of coercion or manipulation that made this landslide possible. When opposition candidates nevertheless dispute the legitimacy of the election, the triumphant despots dismiss these charges as "demagogic nonsense" – and increasingly, it will be nearly impossible for genuinely independent journalists to point to face-to-face facts that demonstrate that the autocrats are wrong. In short, despite the failure of large numbers of voters to meet their own standards of citizenship responsibility, the secret ballot will be absolutely necessary to sustain the *credible* functioning of postmodern democracy.

This, in turn, leads to some puzzling conclusions. Although credible democracy requires a secret ballot, it also supposes that citizens will devote the time and energy required to think before they vote, and many will fail to do so. Sometimes this won't lead to a big problem – in these cases, ignorant voters don't swing Election Day results away from candidates who have gained the support of more thoughtful voters. But sometimes it will lead to the triumph of political parties that would never have won the election if more people were taking their citizenship seriously.

In some cases, the leaders of these political parties will be charismatic demagogues; in some cases, boring do-nothings; in other cases, sensible statesmen. But in all cases, they would not have gained their position if their constituents had been more conscientious – and this failure will predictably generate very real problems of legitimacy and stability in the coming decades. We will be returning to these predicaments in part 3, where I will be advancing real-world reforms that might serve as constructive responses to these postmodern dilemmas. But for now, I have said enough to make a larger point about the need to gain a multi-spherical perspective on our postmodern predicament.

Plutocracy in America

At best, this chapter has thus far made a useful contribution to two already vibrant discussions of the rise of consumer protection and the secret ballot over the course of the twentieth century. Yet there are no comparable efforts to consider how these two different forms of strangerhood interact with one another in postmodern life. Once we do so, we confront new questions: Is an individual's self-understanding as a consumer potentially at war with his or her self-understanding as a citizen? If so, how can this danger be reduced, if not eliminated?

To frame an answer, consider three ways in which the two spheres differ from one another.

The first is *differential anonymity*. This deals with the manner in which strangers present themselves to one another as voters and consumers. I vote in secret, but when I go into a store, I must pay the cashier for anything I want to buy. If I tried to sneak out without paying, I would destroy my standing as a responsible adult. In contrast to the total secrecy surrounding my vote, merchants know exactly what I have chosen and how much I paid for it.

The second involves *differential forms of self-understanding*. When I cast my ballot, I am trying to decide which candidates possess the character and advance the proposals that will best serve the political community over the next electoral cycle. Some politicians focus their campaigns on small changes in the status quo; others ask voters for a mandate for fundamental reform.

Rivals will also predictably frame their appeals in ways that serve my private interests. Nevertheless, this shouldn't be enough to determine my decision. I have an obligation to seriously consider whether I should vote for a candidate who supports a war that I think is required for national survival – even if it may require my children to risk their lives in the armed forces. Putting such crises to one side, candidates will often call upon me to back proposals that I believe to be in the public interest even though they will increase my taxes. If they persuade me of the merit of their policy initiatives, I will betray my citizenship responsibilities if I vote against them on "pocketbook" grounds.

When entering the marketplace as a consumer, I understand myself in an entirely different fashion. It is up to me to use my money in the way I think best. In defining my own self-interest, I may keep the interests of my family and friends in mind as I make my decisions, or I may spend my money to support my public-regarding concerns.

But I would be shocked if a cashier told me to put my purchases back on the shelf – because I should spend my money on different goods that would be better for my family or friends or society as a whole. When entering the store, I was assuming the role of consumer, and the cashier has absolutely no authority to transform our stranger-stranger relationship into a personal affair. This would be true even if the cashier were personally acquainted with my intimate partners; by giving such advice, he or she would be stepping out of their role as cashier and wasting my time in a pointless confrontation. If the cashier persisted and refused to take my money, the managers of the firm would rightly impose serious sanctions on their employees for their extra-spherical activities.

A third difference – involving *differential modes of commitment* – is no less fundamental. As both a citizen and a consumer, I am constantly faced with hard choices, but the way I resolve them is different. When I believe that an election has particular importance for my country's future, I have a responsibility to increase the level of my political engagement and spend more time considering the issues before I vote – and maybe go further and join an activist effort to convince fence-sitters to agree with my view of the public interest. If I don't back up my beliefs with action, I am betraying my own sense of citizenship responsibility: telling myself that my country is at a crucial turning point while acting as if nothing special is going on.

In contrast, I experience no similar anxieties when operating as a consumer. To be sure, the deals that I make depend on my income and wealth. If I'm rich, I will go to different merchants, and buy different things, than if I'm poor. Yet even if my poverty is largely due to membership in a stigmatized social group, merchants have no right to deny me access to the commodities I am desperately searching for. When acting as a consumer, it's up to me to decide how to spend my money.

This will sometimes require tough decisions. Middle-class consumers may have to choose between buying a car for the family or saving for their children's college education. Impoverished consumers may be forced to decide which products will permit them to avoid starvation. The rich and powerful will have opportunities that many others can barely imagine. For present purposes, the existential situation of the broad middle class – between the super-rich and the desperate poor – is of particular importance. In making their tough decisions in the marketplace, consumer protection laws limit the power of profit-maximizing firms to manipulate them with misleading advertising. It won't prevent them from making choices they will come to regret. Nevertheless, when "I" enter the marketplace and hand over my money to merchants, they must treat me *as a responsible adult with the capacity to define the meaning of life on my own terms.* Putting tough choices to one side, I experience this affirmative form of mutual recognition on countless occasions in daily life.

This isn't true when it comes to citizenship. Instead of constant reinforcement of my sense of consumer sovereignty, I will fail to discharge my democratic responsibilities if I cast my ballot without taking the time to seriously consider the merits of the candidates and the issues raised by the election. Indeed, if I repeatedly fail to live up to my sense of citizenship responsibility, I may well give up entirely and fail to show up at the polls at all.

Citizen alienation will escalate further as a consequence of another fundamental feature of democratic government: its guarantee of free speech to a broad range of political parties and candidates. This commitment is very different from the consumer-protection guarantees that protect buyers from systematic misrepresentation in the marketplace. As a consequence, voters will confront a flood of self-serving propaganda by rival candidates that further escalate their predicament as responsible citizens.

Since World War II, modern constitutions have confronted this threat and have taken a variety of steps to reduce, if not eliminate, the clear and present danger—and part 3 will be building on these initiatives in ways that take into account the distinctive challenges posed by the internet. For the present, however, it is more important to recognize that the United States, with its ancient constitution, has failed to fill this gap. Consider a plutocratic practice that has so entrenched itself in American politics that it is called, without embarrassment, "the money primary." Presidential hopefuls make pilgrimages to mega-billionaires to beg them for enormous campaign contributions before the first official primaries take place. The winners of the money primary gain an enormous advantage over their rivals, yet these bargaining/begging sessions are kept entirely secret from the public.

This means that primary voters, in casting their secret ballots, can't know where rival candidates really stand on the issues of the day. While they say one thing in public, they may have promised their favorite plutocrats something very different in private. Even worse, the candidates who fail to gain plutocratic favor might well have gained a far bigger vote if they had received the mega-billions provided by the super-rich. But their campaigns can't get off the ground since they won't have the cash to compete with the winners of the money primary. As a consequence, plutocrats may veto candidates who could well have won the general election if they had been provided with a fair share of campaign resources in the Democratic or Republican primaries. Since there are more super-rich conservatives than liberals, it also puts Democratic candidates – whoever they turn out to be – at a systematic disadvantage in the final vote count. Rather than challenging the legitimacy of these practices, however, the Supreme Court has transformed them into fundamental constitutional rights.[11]

In contrast, leading European democracies not only forbid plutocrats from intervening in the electoral process but enforce these prohibitions against powerful politicians who violate them. In 2017, for example, the Italian judiciary upheld the criminal conviction of Silvio Berlusconi, who had repeatedly served as the country's prime minister, for illegally paying millions of euros to induce members of parliament to support his effort to gain yet another term in office. In defending his conduct, his lawyers argued that the constitution's guarantee of "freedom of parliamentary activity" exempted his deal from criminal prosecution. But the courts decisively rejected the notion that legitimate parliamentary activity included "the transfer of money . . . resulting in the sale of Senators." Though Berlusconi managed to avoid spending time in jail, this judicial condemnation seriously weakened his support among voters. French presidents Jacques Chirac and Nicolas Sarkozy suffered comparable blows to their public standing when legal proceedings revealed that they had been selling their political influence in the course of their careers.[12]

These judicial demands for democratic integrity serve as dramatic transatlantic contrasts to the Supreme Court's successful effort to entrench the money primary into the Constitution of the United States. At the very least, they suggest that there is nothing inevitable about the court's grim defense of plutocracy in America.[13] Nevertheless, before a decisive change can plausibly occur, it won't be enough for committed democrats to come up with a realistic reform program that would operate effectively in the complex federal system that serves as the framework of twenty-first-century American politics. Even if leading reformers could reach a rough consensus on a plausible set of statutory initiatives, plutocratic defenders of the status quo will predictably flood the media with massive sound-bite campaigns denouncing even the most thoughtful reforms as reckless assaults on the sacred principles laid down by our Founding Fathers.[14]

These plutocratic defenses, moreover, will be designed by high-paid consultants who will use the most advanced computer models to make their sound bites seem plausible to different segments of the mass public. In order to come out ahead, reformers must somehow convince millions and millions of their fellow Americans to take their citizenship responsibilities seriously enough to engage in an ongoing discussion of the crucial issues raised by the debate.

It is not utterly utopian to suppose that such a collective conversation is a real-world possibility. After all, 40 percent of Americans have gained college degrees by the time they reach the age of 25, and many others have sufficient schooling to consider the key questions in a thoughtful fashion – both on the internet and in face-to-face conversation.[15] Nevertheless, it is precisely their day-to-day success as consumers that will make it tough for them to take these issues seriously.

For two reasons. On the one hand, the hours they spend as consumers restrict the time that remains available for Americans to shift into citizenship mode to consider the complex questions raised by the money primary. On the other, their experience as consumers will give them a misplaced sense that it is OK for billionaires to market their favorite politicians in the same ways that major corporations advertise commodities like toothpaste or cars. After all, commodity advertising often provides useful information that potential buyers would have otherwise ignored – especially when consumer protection laws effectively safeguard against blatant misrepresentations. If this is true when choosing between competing automobiles, why isn't it equally true when choosing between competing candidates for the presidency?

Reformers have answers to this question, but they can expect many Americans to respond skeptically when they first hear them, since it challenges their intuitive responses based on their day-to-day experiences as consumers. As a consequence, critics of the money primary confront a more formidable challenge than many other reform movements that don't encounter the same degree of initial skepticism. Nevertheless, there are encouraging signs that their challenge to the plutocratic status quo is mobilizing the active support of increasing numbers of American *citizens*.

Only time will tell whether this citizen movement will continue to gain momentum, to the point where a reform-minded president and Congress will be in a position to enact decisive legislation and encourage the Supreme Court to reverse course in the light of the very different course taken by European democracies. After all, such "switch-in-time" scenarios have occurred on many previous occasions in American history.[16]

Nevertheless, these past transformations occurred under very different conditions from those we face in the twenty-first century. This book confronts the complexity of our multi-spherical existence under postmodern conditions – emphasizing how the competing demands of different spheres can both enhance and undermine our overall struggle to live a meaningful life. As our spherical investigations proceed, I will also be suggesting how these inter-spherical demands will shape the struggle by the rising generation to take citizenship seriously. This analysis will prepare the ground for my concluding effort to persuade you, in part 3, that it is far too soon to despair at the future of democracy in the twenty-first century.

Chapter 5

MEANINGFUL WORK

In addition to transforming democracy into plutocracy, does consumerism threaten the possibility of meaningful work?

My answer, once again, is yes – but the inter-spherical dynamics are very different. There is nothing problematic about an employer paying employees for their labor. If you don't get cash for your work, you don't have money to buy things as a consumer – and you and your family end up starving. The existential rationale for paid labor could not be more straightforward.

The consumerist threat comes from a different direction. When you go to a store, you are under no obligation to buy anything. As far as you and the merchant are concerned, it is up to you to decide whether the goods on display are worth the asking price. If nobody wants to pay for the commodities offered by a firm, its owners can't force people to hand over their cash. They must change their product in ways that satisfy consumer demand or go out of business.

My employer can't treat me like that. I am not a commodity. When I go to work, I am involved in a joint enterprise with my fellow human beings. We may succeed or fail in our effort to produce worthwhile goods and services. But we will succeed or fail together.

I may have only a small role in this collective effort. Nevertheless, my fellow workers, including my bosses, cannot legitimately treat me as if I were a modern-day serf or slave, bowing down humbly before their commands. Nor am I a machine to be commanded by a flick of the switch. They must engage with me in ways that enable us to recognize each other as collaborators confronting a central dilemma of modern existence: the struggle to achieve a meaningful life through meaningful work.

It is crucially important, of course, for me to get a weekly paycheck, since this provides me with the money I need to meet my needs and those of my family, friends, and other sphere-mates of great personal significance. But these are *extra*-spherical benefits generated by the thousands of hours I spend on the job. To make my work time a meaningful part of my life, I require something more than a paycheck. Yet bosses are typically in a position to use their power of command to treat employees as mere instruments in the firm's pursuit of profit maximization. When underlings raise work-related problems, employers don't use their questions as an occasion to treat them as collaborators in a joint project but as disloyal "troublemakers," and they threaten to fire them if they keep on suggesting that they may have better ideas. Worse yet, if a boss does fire a troublemaker, it will be difficult for that person to find a decent job elsewhere, once potential employers learn the reason that he or she has been thrown into the ranks of the unemployed.

It is all too easy, then, for my current employer to get me to sign a contract in which I "freely" authorize my bosses to treat me in a purely instrumental fashion. Once I have consented to my servitude, don't the principles of "freedom of contract" authorize my bosses to deal with me in the same top-down fashion they treat machines – and unilaterally determine how I can spend my work time for years to come?

Since the Industrial Revolution, this has been the key question organizing the struggle for meaningful work in the modern world. During the nineteenth century, the labor union movement was the dominant force through which workers struggled for the right to bargain collectively over the terms and conditions of their employment. More recently, a second path to meaningful work has gained prominence. Over the course of the twentieth century, workers have increasingly relied on their membership in "professions" rather than "unions" to establish meaningful workplace identities.

In this chapter I will invite you to compare these two forms of workplace identity. I won't try to tell you which is better. My aim is to investigate the existential premises organizing these different modes of spherical self-presentation – and thereby provide a framework for more thoughtful debate in the struggle for meaningful work in the postmodern era.

Before proceeding, I want to emphasize that for all their differences, unionism and professionalism share a common aspiration. They refuse to be satisfied by an employer's abstract expressions of concern with employee welfare and instead demand that the workplace be organized in a fashion that requires bosses to respect their employees as meaningful collaborators in the everyday dynamics of production.

Organizing the Work Force

Up to now, I have been describing the commodification problem in abstract terms. Here is a more concrete thought experiment that I hope will clarify the existential stakes.

Suppose that whenever a company's workers make even trivial mistakes, their boss humiliates them in front of their peers. This repressive response is not a symptom of one boss's aggressive temperament but a deliberate company policy, emerging from a study by a special team of experts. After a rigorous cost-benefit analysis, the experts determined that systematic humiliation would sometimes lead anxious employees to make more serious mistakes than they otherwise would. But it would also make them redouble their efforts to escape their bosses' outrage by avoiding many other blunders. Overall, a strategy of frequent humiliation would make operations more efficient and generate bigger profits for the firm's owners.

In a breakthrough humanitarian gesture, however, the owners have decided to add a "browbeating bonus" to every worker's paycheck, so that they can share in the profits of the new policy. This bonus allows them to enhance their engagement in other spheres of life – to buy tickets to the soccer game or get drunk at the neighborhood bar with boozy companions. Nevertheless, during their time on the job, these workers will continue to be treated worse than computers and machines, which are incapable of feeling humiliation or intimidation. Those who refuse to go along will be fired. While the threat of unemployment, together with their browbeating bonus, may lead workers to shut up and accept their pay checks, they will have been transformed into the modern equivalent of premodern serfs. Rather than spend their work time as fellow participants in the firm's collective effort to produce valuable services, they will be bowing down before their bosses in an environment that mocks the crucial role of work in modern self-understanding.

In the real-world development of trade unionism during the nineteenth century, employers saw no need to offer a browbeating bonus to transform their workers into serfs. They ruthlessly exploited their employees' weak bargaining position to maximize their firm's profits, firing troublemakers who entertained the mistaken notion that they could legitimately challenge their boss's treatment. It is at this point where the modern labor union entered world history. Despite profound ideological disagreements with one another, the entire union movement proceeded on the basis of a common premise: it denied, as a matter of principle, that employers could impose working conditions on workers without their collective consent. I emphasize this point because it is does not loom large in historical accounts of the union movement. This enormous literature mostly emphasizes ideological struggles between different parts of the movement – since different ideologies triumphed at different times, with profoundly different consequences. Socialist movements, for instance, have insisted that nationalization of major enterprises is the only way to assure worker recognition as empowered collaborators in production. More market-friendly movements limited their demands to mandatory collective bargaining over wages, hours, working conditions, and retirement pensions. Yet another path has been carved out by corporatists, who demand that workers share decision-making power on corporate boards of directors.

For our purposes, however, it is more important to emphasize the *anti-commodification principle* that all three movements had in common: workers have an *existential* interest in demanding that their bosses treat them as collaborators in a common project rather than as commodities whose sole function is to maximize their firm's profits.

I invite you to view this principle within a larger multi-spherical framework: as we struggle to construct meaningful lives for ourselves, the sphere of work plays a crucial role in our efforts at self-definition. As we leave school to encounter the world of work, some of us will define career paths that lead to a deep self-fulfillment; others will remain directionless or confront a series of disappointments. In all cases, however, the search for self-realization in work is a fundamental feature of modern existence, and the unionization movement has been a key institutional vehicle through which workers have expressed their demand that power elites recognize this existential imperative.

It is particularly important to emphasize this principle at a time when the union movement is reeling from decades of real-world setbacks. These defeats have led many serious advocates for social justice to give up on the unionist enterprise and look entirely to other spheres for improvements in the lives of oppressed and humiliated people.

Yet this would be a tragic mistake when these very same people are confronting a new assault on their existential standing as workers. The high-tech revolution is transforming millions of them into robot-like humanoids whose work time is consumed by responding to computer commands that they must obey and cannot challenge, since the computer programs don't permit them to reach a human boss to raise job-related problems. They thus find themselves in a postmodern predicament that is more serf-like than those faced by nineteenth- and twentieth-century workers. At least those people had the grim satisfaction of confronting their bosses in face-to-face protests – even when their efforts to gain mutual recognition ended with their dismissal. In the twenty-first century, millions live in a world where a computer cuts off their paychecks when they disobey its algorithmic commands – without even allowing them to demand recognition as meaningful collaborators in the sphere of production.

The challenge is to learn from the past and reinvigorate the existentialist commitments of the union movement for the postmodern age. This is especially important when the computer revolution is creating new opportunities for self-determination by workers who manage to travel a second historical pathway to meaningful work, which has generated much more dynamism in the contemporary world: professionalism.

Modern Professionalism

Somebody is a "professional" if their job not only requires on-the-job training but also demands the study of a scholarly discipline. While professionalism is a familiar form of life in the twenty-first century, it is a relative newcomer in world history.[1]

Putting academics to one side, only three groups had organized themselves as professions in premodern Europe.[2] The first were clerics, who interpreted the word of God to the masses; the second were jurists, whose understandings were rooted in the classic texts of Roman law; the third were doctors, whose work was organized by principles based on the teaching of Hippocrates in ancient Greece.

Of these three, only physicians confronted a real-world test of their learning, and until the nineteenth century, they were obliged to confront its tragic limitations. In cases of serious illness, they would spend hours trying to ease the pain of their patients, but they could do little to cure the underlying disease. While the Hippocratic Oath required doctors to "do no harm," they were not in a position to help their patients to survive.

This began to change in the 1820s. Path-breaking physicians began taking advantage of scientific breakthroughs to perform primitive surgeries on patients previously considered hopeless. These interventions caused excruciating pain, but they sometimes led to successful recoveries, inaugurating a new era for an ancient profession. Doctors were actually lifting patients from their deathbeds to continue their lifelong struggle for meaningful existence. The same thing happened in law. The Prussian and French Civil Codes of 1792 and 1804 required the legal profession to cast aside the teachings of the past and confront the challenges of modernity. The revolutionary transformations of the clergy began much earlier, with the Protestant Reformation of the sixteenth century, and I will discuss its historical development later.[3] For now, it's more important to emphasize the nineteenth-century breakthroughs taking place in spheres of work where the notion of "professionalism" had been entirely absent.

The military led the way in this radical transformation. Before the French Revolution, the key to success on the battlefield was the wise use of practical judgment – a talent acquired through battlefield experience but for which there was no formal academic training. The Napoleonic Wars, however, shattered the status quo. Although he was finally defeated at Waterloo, Bonaparte's remarkable series of military triumphs convinced European governments to require future officers to attend military academies. An aristocratic background was no longer sufficient qualification for a commander: one had to attend a military academy and master "scientific" doctrines based on Napoleon's strategic insights. Only through these doctrines could one hope to crush rival armies led by commanders who had also gained their professional education from government-sponsored military schools. At the same time, professional engineers began to demonstrate that they, not traditional guilds, had the expertise required to build the bridges and roads essential for industrial development.[4]

The second half of the century witnessed further breakthroughs. Before then, gentlemen went to college – if they went at all – to reflect on the lessons of classical Greece and Rome. Increasingly, however, universities became the site of scholarly efforts to develop "sciences" of economics, sociology, and politics that would illuminate the dynamic transformations of the contemporary world. Once scientifically trained graduates obtained their doctorates, moreover, they were welcomed into Europe's burgeoning bureaucracies as "professional" civil servants.

European governments were not interested in recruiting these graduates merely to affirm their commitment to the Enlightenment; they had become convinced of the need for a professional bureaucracy to impose order on the militant labor movements threatening violent revolution. The rise of the police might suffice to deter everyday criminals from engaging in everyday crimes, but it couldn't protect established regimes against calls for revolution. While nothing could guarantee the stability of the status quo, a professional civil service was essential if governments hoped to resolve socioeconomic dilemmas while keeping most workers loyal to the existing system.[5]

The British developed distinctive variations on these Continental themes, and the Americans made their own contribution at the dawn of the twentieth century. Until then, up-and-comers did not suppose that they should go to a great university and gain a graduate degree in business administration before launching their careers. Real-world success depended on entrepreneurial insight, social connections, wealth, and luck—as well as ruthless determination to drive competitors out of business. It took the Panic of 1907 to sweep away the self-confidence of the ascendant power elite. When stock prices suddenly dropped by 50 percent on Wall Street, President Theodore Roosevelt convinced Congress to enact legislation creating the Federal Reserve Board—and President William Howard Taft then appointed governors who were convinced that the Reserve Board required the assistance of economists to prevent Wall Street speculators from causing future panics.[6]

Yet American universities were in no position to provide the "scientific" education that these presidents and Fed governors believed was required. The first "School of Finance and Economy," at the University of Pennsylvania, had only been founded in 1881, and its faculty initially contented itself with giving undergraduates a rudimentary understanding of the dynamics of the industrial economy.

With blinding speed, Harvard University began to fill this gap. In 1908, its Graduate School of Business Administration established a model that came to dominate business education in the twentieth century.[7] As early as the 1920s, MBAs were advising political elites in China, Germany, and India, as well as the United States—though the versions of political economy that served as their framework differed radically in the different capitals.[8]

On many other fronts, professionals don't tailor their "science" in the politically self-conscious fashion exhibited by schools of business and public administration throughout the world. Consider, for example, the professional training provided to doctors and nurses.

High-visibility health crises will sometimes provoke highly politicized controversies over treatment issues – as in the case of COVID. But in general, there is a remarkable international consensus that professionally run hospitals should protect doctors and nurses from political interference in their day-to-day operations.[9]

Yet professionalization has made no inroads in the production of cars and trucks on a postmodern assembly-line, where a very different consensus prevails. Throughout the world, workers depend on unions, not professional associations, to protect them from top-down subordination by their bosses. By contrasting the meaning-making premises organizing these two paradigmatic modes of production, we can gain a deeper insight into the dynamics through which professionalism has imposed powerful limits on top-down management during an era in which unionization has so visibly declined.

Unionization v. Professionalism

Begin by comparing an autoworker on an assembly line with a nurse dealing with patients in a hospital. Both are at the bottom of the pyramid of power prevailing in their systems of production – and, as a consequence, they will display some important similarities in dealing with their bosses.

Suppose that Nurse John Smith spends most of his time on a particular ward inhabited by a particular set of patients – and so knows them much better than Doctor Elizabeth Jones, who comes in daily to review their progress. As a consequence, Smith and Jones must engage in regular conversations if they hope to help their patients recover. Smith also needs to collaborate with his fellow nurses since they are jointly responsible for the patients' care.

Members of the nursing team must pass on those responsibilities to colleagues when they leave the hospital at the end of their working day—and join their family, friends, and other sphere-mates in radically different forms of meaning-making. To sum this up in a single word, Smith must display competent *teamwork* if he hopes to succeed as a caregiver.

The same is true on the assembly line. Worker Fred Skillful specializes in particular tasks as vehicles pause in front of him for a few minutes so he can install specific components. If he has trouble completing his task in the allotted time, he also resembles Smith in relying on teamwork to solve his problem—by collaborating with both his fellow workers on the assembly line and his supervisors who are responsible for its overall operation.

Smith and Skillful will both pay a big price if they consistently fail to solve their productivity problems. Their supervisors will be obliged to fire them from their jobs and replace them with workers who will succeed where they have failed. To sum up: it isn't enough for either Smith or Skillful to display teamwork in dealing with their colleagues; each must demonstrate real-world ability to solve problems if they hope to sustain a meaningful relationship to their working lives.

But if this is so, how is Smith's professionalism fundamentally different from Skillful's teamwork and success at the car factory?

The answer lies in the kind of training they need to get their jobs in the first place. To qualify for a job at the auto plant, Skillful does not need a scientific education at a university. Instead, he must convince his potential employer that he is physically fit enough to perform occasionally demanding work, will show up reliably and work hard, and can learn the tasks required on the assembly line.

He could, for example, qualify by presenting recommendations from past employers or passing performance tests at the auto company's training site.

Smith, on the other hand, must devote at least a couple of years to the serious study of medicine at his nursing school. Even this is not enough. Not only must he demonstrate his scientific competence on academic exams, but he must also spend time learning how to translate theory into daily practice. Once he is recognized as a qualified professional, however, he will have considerable bargaining power in dealing with the doctors and administrators above him in the hospital hierarchy.

Suppose, for example, that Smith has a specialized nursing job that requires him to diagnose patients who display symptoms of potentially dangerous cancers. When these people arrive at the hospital, he has the task of taking a series of X-rays to determine whether their problem is serious enough to warrant their admission as a patient for sustained therapy.

If Smith is to succeed in this job, his nursing school must provide the scientific background he needs to produce a series of X-rays that will provide an accurate view of each patient's cancer risk. His examinations will be quite time-consuming, since each individual must be x-rayed from different angles to permit a professionally competent decision on an issue with life-and-death implications. Nevertheless, given the large number of people with potentially serious conditions, the hospital's administrators frequently pressure Smith and his colleagues to do their screenings faster, and they add to this pressure by scheduling screening appointments closer together than Smith thinks is wise. How many minutes should suffice?

Insofar as Smith is concerned, the hospital's answer to this question not only has life-and-death significance to his patients but also will affect his own career. If he spends too little time with each person, he runs a risk of producing misleading assessments of each patient's cancer risk. Too many misdiagnoses will put him at risk of being fired from his job for incompetence. He thus has a powerful personal interest in the amount of time his bosses allow him to spend with each patient before moving on to the next person awaiting diagnosis.

In confronting their nurses' predictable demand for longer examination times, moreover, hospital administrators are constrained by the dynamics of professionalism. Medical schools have already considered problems in training their nurses for this particular specialty, and they have reached a consensus about it. They have established twenty minutes as the minimum time required for producing X-rays sufficient to serve as the foundation of a sound professional judgment. This consensus greatly empowers nurses in their dealings with hospital management. If an administrator tries to order them to see more than three clients an hour, they don't need to engage in high-visibility confrontations that would mark them out as troublemakers. They need only send word back to the nursing schools they came from, and their university teachers can be counted on to pressure their hospital administrators to respect prevailing standards. Given the virtual certainty of this scenario, it is unlikely that any hospital management would endanger its professional standing by requiring a speedup from its nurses in order to increase short-term revenue.

In contrast, consider the way top management of an auto company would deal with a similar scenario. Suppose a particular team of workers has the job of installing a particular piece of equipment into a vehicle before it moves onto the next stage of the assembly line—and that previously twenty minutes has been allotted to do so. As part of its regular reappraisal of the production process, however, its high-powered team of MBAs has concluded that the benefits of a speedup far exceed its overall costs—and that workers should be given only ten minutes to install their device.

Under this scenario, workers could only respond by organizing a labor union to protest against their bosses' refusal to deal with them as meaningful collaborators in the productive enterprise to which they were devoting such enormous amounts of time and energy. If management refused to take their union seriously, its leaders would have no choice but to call on members to go out on strike until management deigns to engage in good-faith collective bargaining on this crucial issue.

This scenario is the polar opposite of the one prevailing in the hospital case. In that setting, top management retreated at the very prospect of condemnation by the professional standard setters based in medical schools. At the auto plant, it is up to the workers to decide whether they are willing to accept the heavy burdens that a walkout would impose on themselves, their families, and their friends. They may well be unwilling to make the sacrifices required to go on strike, and humbly accept their role as modern-day serfs to their corporate masters.

My aim is not to tell them how to make such tragic decisions. To the contrary, I have been arguing that the need to confront inter-spherical dilemmas is an inevitable feature of the postmodern world—which is precisely why I am inviting you to reflect on the nonobvious ways in which professionalism can serve as a pathway in the ongoing struggle for existential justice.

But my contrast with unionism remains incomplete. Thus far, I have been treating professionalism as a three-part system of checks and balances in which top executives must be concerned with (1) university-based standards of professional competence; (2) nurses engaged in day-to-day practice; (3) their own commitment to professionalism as doctors.

Yet this triangle fails to emphasize the key role that hospital patients will also play in constraining the unilateral exercise of top-down power. To continue with my not-so-hypothetical scenario, when patients enter the X-ray room, they may well be full of anxiety, but they haven't the slightest idea whether it takes 10 or 20 minutes to do a professional job of obtaining a set of images that can serve as the basis for a thoughtful decision on their cancer risk. They are coming into the hospital precisely because it makes sense to put their future in the hands of serious professionals. As a consequence, if word leaks out that top administrators are violating these expectations, they can expect a furious reaction from the general public. After all, everybody recognizes that they may well confront a serious risk of death in the future, and that they typically will need serious professional help to deal with this risk in a constructive fashion. This means that hospital administrators will face a powerful backlash if they move forward with their speedup. If they nevertheless insist on ten-minute examinations, they could readily provoke a political campaign for decisive state intervention that would further constrain their discretion.

We have come, then, to a final paradox. *It is precisely because they know they are ignorant* that postmodern men and women put their trust in professionalism, throwing their support behind a powerful backlash against the most powerful hospital officials if they persist in demanding that their least powerful nurses violate professional standards.

To be sure, there are many real-world cases in which, despite the dynamics of this virtuous cycle, high-powered doctors abuse their authority in their dealings with people below them in the hospital hierarchy – and then use their superior positions to avoid punishment. These patterns of abuse certainly require careful study in the ongoing effort to construct realistic reforms.

Nevertheless, they should not divert attention from the fact that top executives in car companies don't face the same virtuous cycle in dealing with their workers – for the simple reason that people who want to buy a car enter an auto dealership with radically different spherical expectations. They deal with sales personnel as more or less market-savvy *consumers* who require accurate answers to their commonsense questions – not as if they were hospital *patients* who don't know the right questions to ask about their disease.

In dealing with workers on the assembly line, automobile executives do not confront anything like the virtuous cycle of protest by nurses, local physicians, medical schools, professional associations, and anxious patients that constrains hospital bosses. Instead, assembly-line workers must rely on the power of their labor unions to gain the mutual recognition that nurses typically take for granted.

Hospital workers may also need unions to negotiate working conditions beyond their basic professional requirements, and unions may well campaign for stronger principles of corporate responsibility. One of my aims in this book is to encourage these inter-spherical movements for existential justice – and I will return to this theme later. It is enough for now to emphasize the existential importance of professionalism in transforming work time into something more meaningful than a paycheck, especially since leading public intellectuals currently condemn professionalism as a curse of the postmodern age.[10]

No less important, I have been inviting you to place this mode of meaningful work within a more general framework that emphasizes the central role of stranger-stranger relationships in the modern struggle for self-definition. On the surface, it may appear that the way I act as a professional has nothing to do with the way I walk down the street, cast my ballot, or go about buying groceries. But all of these forms of engagement, and many others, involve me in encounters with people I don't know—and yet, even though we have never met, it is crucial for us to have been socialized into modes of engagement that are spherically appropriate. If I walk down the street in a weird way, my fellow pedestrians will give me a wide berth, maybe cross the street to avoid me, or if I'm being extremely weird, perhaps call the police. The same is true if I act weirdly at my polling place or supermarket or nursing station, but my modes of weirdness are very different in each sphere, as are the ways in which my more socially appropriate engagements can enhance the meaning of my life.

Yet throughout human history, the overwhelming majority of men and women lived in a premodern world in which these stranger-stranger relationships were entirely alien to their way of life. Today, they are of foundational significance for every one of us. Premoderns would also be bewildered by the freedom with which we define our more personal relationships with family, friends, neighbors, and soccer club teammates. So far as they were concerned, they had no choice but to conform to the entrenched mores of their tightly knit community – while for us, it is the commitments we *choose* to make in particular relationships that most crucially define "who I am."

This leads me to my next question. Since our ability to establish modern meaning-making relationships – with strangers and with friends – doesn't come "naturally," how do we go about learning how to make these crucial connections?

Chapter 6

BECOMING A PERSON

At the moment of your birth, you did not recognize yourself as an "I." You could not even distinguish the boundary between your physical body and your physical surroundings. It took months for you to recognize that the "outside world" continued to exist when you closed your eyes.

In early infancy, you were utterly dependent on your caregivers. Not only did they provide food and protection. They responded to your cries in ways that began to enable self-recognition. When you shouted into the void, they replied: "Is anything the matter?" "What do you want?" "How are *you*?" You were not yet able to respond by saying: I want you to do this-or-that. But the dynamics of intersubjective recognition were already under way.

Your caregivers asked their questions in Chinese or English or Hindi. You were not permitted to choose your native language. Instead, they encouraged you to channel your cries and giggles into patterns that made sense within the linguistic framework they imposed on you simply by surrounding you with it. As you moved beyond this prelinguistic phase, your caregivers' world of meaning continued to shape your own. Once you could engage in primitive conversation with your parents, they were in a position to fine-tune their influence over your developing self-understanding.

On the one hand, they began to channel your behavior-patterns with greater precision. As you started to crawl and stand awkwardly on two feet, they began teaching you the "right way" to eat or drink, dress or undress, speak to others: "If you want to be good, don't crawl under the table. Sit quietly while I put food on your plate." On the other hand, by teaching you to speak in ways they deemed appropriate, they made it virtually impossible for you to express some of your impulses in words: "Don't say your father is fat, short, and ugly. It's disrespectful."

Caregivers mixed these modes of behavioral and linguistic control into complex patterns as you tentatively began to take your first steps toward independence. When you walked and talked in ways that met with their approval, they would smile and express their support; when you failed, they would show their disapproval in subtle or not so subtle ways. If this dynamic of selective reinforcement turned out to be successful, you became a "good little boy or girl" by the time you reached three or four. At that point, you and your caregivers would be engaging in an ongoing exchange of *you*'s and *I*'s which expressed a concrete form of life that you all found meaningful.

But maybe you refused to play along. Even if you escalated your resistance, your caregivers couldn't give up. If they did, they would have failed to provide you with the cultural resources you would need once you left home to confront the many other adults seeking to engage you in the complex web of I-you-we relationships that await in modern society.

Caregivers sometimes fail to induce their wayward children to rechannel their energies in socially acceptable directions. If by the time youngsters reach four or five they are stigmatized as incorrigible troublemakers, they will be grievously disadvantaged in their later quest for a meaningful life. Special social responsibilities arise in these breakdown cases – and I will consider them at a later point. For now, it's better to begin with the standard scenario – in which an ongoing process of childhood education prepares a youngster for successful entrance into the larger society as a competent adult.

The process proceeds in two stages. An infant requires a great deal of cultural coherence to learn how to express its identity. If its caregivers talk to it in a different language each day, the result will be utter confusion. By the time it reaches the age of three or four, the child will emerge as a babbling nobody who can't talk to anybody about its desires or aspirations. If children are to begin to understand themselves as self-defining individuals, their parents must speak to them in Chinese or Turkish or Russian or Arabic or Hindi or English (or combine a small number of languages together).[1] Similarly, if caregivers tell young children "to behave themselves" in radically different ways on a weekly basis, they will quickly grow very confused. To put the point affirmatively: young infants require a *stable meaning-framework* if they are ever to speak and act as *socially competent* adults.[2]

Matters get more complicated as youngsters begin to express themselves as an "I" in a native language that they share with their immediate family. Their acquisition of language skills gives their caregivers an opportunity to socialize the child into the particular culture that defines the way the family should talk and act together when they are at home. Call this the culture of intimacy, and the child's growing confidence in its meaningful deployment is an essential precondition for further development. Nevertheless, it doesn't provide the cultural resources necessary for individuals to function as competent adults in the modern world.

Consider the problem of religious diversity. In the typical modern society, some caregivers invest time and energy training infants to appreciate the exemplary character of Jesus, while others point children toward Mohammed or Buddha, and still others repudiate the very notion that God can save your soul. Some of these children, when they become adults, will remain true to their elders' commitments, while others will expand their friendships and family ties across religious frontiers. Nevertheless, as modern men and women, they must be culturally equipped to collaborate meaningfully with people professing alien religious convictions – at work, in politics, and in other spherical zones.

This means that, if contemporary education is to be successful, it will turn out to be a two-stage affair. During the first phase, early caregivers provide their children with the cultural coherence and stability they need to understand themselves as *capable* of giving meaning to their lives. In the second stage, parents increasingly share control over their youngsters' time with professional educators, who are trained to provide them with the broader education they will require to deal constructively with the cultural diversity they will confront as adults.[3]

Organizing this curriculum is a tricky business. Educators must act with self-restraint in making their students aware of cultural possibilities that their parents find unacceptable. When children are seven or eight, their fragile sense of identity may collapse if they are regularly required to speak and act in radically different ways at school and at home. As they grow older, however, they will also grow more confident in their ability to act competently in different spheres—and so educators can then introduce them to the very different modes of spherical meaning-making they will be confronting as adults.

The Rise of Public Schooling

This complex mission has been a driving force in the rise of public education over the past two centuries. The first modern public schools opened their doors in the late 1830s—when the first police were patrolling the streets of Paris and consumers were entering that city's first department stores. With schools, however, the United States took the lead.[4]

At this time, America was becoming a magnet for millions of immigrants seeking a better life. Yet these newcomers were overwhelmingly illiterate and entirely unfamiliar with the practice of democratic government.[5] As citizens, they would be all too easily corrupted by politicians seeking to buy their votes. While reformers struggled against these abuses, they put a special emphasis on the newcomers' children. If they also grew up illiterate, corrupt practices would deeply entrench themselves in public life.

Such leaders as Henry Barnard, Catharine Beecher, and Horace Mann launched the Common School Movement for public education with the explicit ambition of training the rising generation for democratic citizenship.[6] In a remarkable series of writings, they insisted that an educated population was an essential condition for sustaining the Enlightenment project of republican self-government launched at the founding of the republic—and that without a state-sponsored educational system, liberal democracy would collapse.[7]

The writings of these educational leaders are well worth reading today. Yet their prospects of political success seemed bleak. Not only did their initiative require big tax increases, it also provoked passionate division along religious lines. Many of the new arrivals were Catholics from Ireland, Italy, and central Europe. Since the days of the French Revolution, the papacy had been profoundly opposed to the Enlightenment principles that the movement's leaders were celebrating.[8] American bishops therefore insisted that the rising generation of Catholic children be educated in Catholic schools.[9]

That is precisely what the Common School Movement was trying to prevent. It did not deny that Catholic and Protestant Americans were profoundly divided on matters of religious faith. Yet this was precisely why children of both faiths should be required to sit side by side in the same classroom and learn the principles of American government. By cooperating as youngsters in common schools, they would gain the skills they needed to join as citizens once they became adults—and refuse to allow their religious divisions to destroy America's democratic principles.[10]

Their opponents argued that common schooling would have just the opposite effect. Even if religious parents obeyed the state's command and "voluntarily" allowed their children to attend, the children would learn a different lesson when they came home. Their parents would remain free to denounce their public-school training and urge them to remain faithful to God in *all* walks of life. So far as the critics were concerned, forcing parents to send their kids to public school would alienate both parents and children from the entire project of democratic government—as well as generate a great deal of childhood bewilderment in the meantime. Rather than coerce attendance, it would be far wiser to allow parents to send their children to the school of their choice. This show of tolerance would allow Catholics and Protestants to fashion a mutually respectful understanding as Americans far more effectively than the common schoolers' demands for forced togetherness.[11]

This critique was especially powerful in an era when the anti-slavery movement was increasingly dividing the nation into bitterly contending political parties: wasn't it counterproductive to add fuel to the fire by splitting Americans along religious lines as well?

Despite the anxieties raised by these questions, Horace Mann successfully led Massachusetts to enact the world's first universal system of compulsory public education in the 1830s. Over the next decade, the Movement followed this with repeated political victories in state after state—though sometimes by very slim legislative margins.[12]

This first round of success only served to emphasize a second-round problem: when the youngsters entered their common schools, who would teach them how to deal with one another as American citizens?

At that time, teaching was not yet organized as a profession; youngsters were greeted by grown-ups who had the time and energy required to convey their particular notions of democratic citizenship. The resulting cacophony of voices was entirely unacceptable to movement leaders, who successfully campaigned for legislation to create a body of "superintendents" in each state to monitor the schools' quality—and intervene when schools fell short.[13] Yet this form of top-down control would fail unless these newly created officials received the special education required to supervise effectively. How, then, to fill this gap?

Under Mann's leadership, the Movement confronted this challenge in a remarkable fashion. It managed to obtain the necessary resources to establish special academies to train superintendents—and then rapidly expanded these academies to train local schoolteachers to redeem the promise of citizenship for the rising generation.[14]

Despite their unprecedented aspirations, the practical objectives of common schools were more modest. Students were required to attend only up to age 11 or 12. Secondary schooling remained a luxury, and university education was virtually unknown. The focus was on teaching everybody to read and write and giving them a basic sense of the constitutional tradition, whose future would soon be in their hands.

Nevertheless, it was a breakthrough of truly existential significance, especially when judged against the baseline established in the premodern era. Before the nineteenth century, almost all children lived in tightly knit communities and would be punished severely if they didn't conform to entrenched community practices. Whatever their limitations, America's schools pointed to a very different possibility, one in which youngsters joined together as citizens to construct a democratic community based on mutual respect.[15]

The Bigger Picture

America's breakthrough was not only important in itself. It vindicated one of the great themes of Enlightenment thought: the "discovery of childhood" as a distinct phase of human life.[16]

Jean-Jacques Rousseau played a crucial role in this development. In 1762, he published his great philosophical novel, *Emile*—in which he rejected the notion that children should obediently travel the path to maturity laid down by their parents. *Emile* advanced a radically different vision. Childhood should be understood as a unique moment of human liberation, during which each of us must be given the opportunity to define our own aims. Unlike the Enlightenment philosophers, who defined self-awareness in highly abstract terms, Rousseau showed Emile confronting real-world dilemmas designed by his tutor to test and encourage his growing capacities. At each stage of the boy's psychological development, the tutor has the same objective: to place him in carefully framed situations that help him more clearly recognize the distinctive character of his own feelings and aspirations. By the end of the novel, Emile emerges with a self-confident sense of what he really wants in life.[17]

The book was an extraordinary success upon its publication, provoking a vibrant debate in which different commentators elaborated very different existential pathways to Rousseau's destination: autonomous self-definition. A generation later, this debate helped shape the agenda of the French Revolution. If France's great republican experiment had not been destroyed by Napoleon, Paris in the 1790s—not Boston in the 1830s—would have been the scene of the modern era's first educational breakthrough.[18] Instead, it was only in the 1870s that the French Third Republic was able to launch a nationwide project of public education, which, like the American effort, sought to give the rising generation the cultural resources required for democratic citizenship.[19]

The French example helped inspire similar movements in Great Britain and the Continent, generating complex patterns of success and failure. By 1900, students in both the Old and New Worlds were attending schools taught by increasingly professional teachers, and as adults, they joined their fellow citizens in casting secret ballots to safeguard their crucial role in the project of democratic self-government.

These educational initiatives were shattered by Hitler and Mussolini—but they were not forgotten. Their central ideals played a key role in redefining the aims of public education after World War II, not only in Europe and the Americas but throughout the world. While vast regions were declaring their independence from the West, leaders like Nehru were insisting on the overriding importance of nationwide compulsory schooling if their countries were to avoid another Holocaust.[20]

These leaders saw, however, that it would not be enough for the rising generation to develop the skills, and understand the principles, central to the effective practice of modern citizenship. The catastrophes of two world wars had destroyed the integrity of countless tightly knit communities throughout world. If the children of premodern parents were to prepare themselves for meaningful work in the modern economy, they would need extensive preparation before they could meaningfully define their employment opportunities. The past half century had opened up vast new spheres for self-definition than had been available at the dawn of the twentieth century.

This meant that the postwar curriculum moved far beyond Horace Mann's precedent-shattering insistence that students remain in school until the age of 11 or 12. At the very least, graduation from secondary school was necessary before teenagers could responsibly confront the challenges of modern life. Moreover, as children advanced beyond primary school, their secondary education should increasingly invite them to define their own course of study around their own interests and abilities. Many would choose to focus their energies on vocational training programs that would provide the skills required to find meaningful work in an increasingly high-tech economy; others would devote themselves to academic programs, ranging from science and engineering to philosophy and the performing arts. Even when they graduated, at 17 or 18, increasing numbers would find a university education essential to making life-defining choices.[21]

This "infant-child-evolving adult" pattern imposed a heavy burden on taxpayers. When they failed to deliver, the rich sent their kids to private schools while countless children received third-rate public educations, especially if they came from impoverished families at the bottom of the socioeconomic hierarchy.

Despite these systemic forms of educational domination, some stigmatized individuals managed to construct meaningful lives for themselves – while some of their upper-class counterparts only succeeded in making themselves miserable. Nevertheless, the successes and failures of particular individuals should not blind us to the systematic character of the injustice imposed on socially subordinated children as they struggle to define their own lives. It is a profound existential injustice – and I will return later to discuss its reform. For now, it will serve as a concrete example of the need for a more sophisticated approach to the postmodern predicament.

Existential Justice

I will confront the problem of existential justice from different directions. The *universal* perspective focuses on the challenges that all of us face in defining a meaningful life for ourselves in the real world of the twenty-first century. The *egalitarian* perspective focuses on the forms of hegemony confronting postmodern individuals who begin life in a subordinate socioeconomic position.

While both are fundamental, the egalitarian perspective is more important. As we have seen, it is existentially impossible for the socioeconomic elite to isolate themselves from encounters with fellow citizens as they walk the streets, deal with employees, and engage in many spheres of postmodern life. Unless the power elite takes egalitarian justice seriously, it can't realistically expect its subordinated competitors to engage in a common effort to deal with the universal aspects of their joint predicament—in which case, the postmodern world will degenerate into brute struggles for power.

So long as the priority of egalitarian justice is respected, however, real-world reforms may also serve universalistic objectives—as in the case of hospitals that I discussed in the last chapter. Public schools resemble hospitals in providing a site where teachers can combine professionalism and unionism to campaign for reforms that not only improve educational opportunity for impoverished and stigmatized youngsters but also provide the middle classes with new opportunities for self-definition. I will explore real-world examples of such breakthroughs in part 3.

For the present, consider how the juxtaposition of universal and egalitarian perspectives illuminates the compelling claims raised by children whose tragic experiences during their early years have utterly disabled them from emerging as competent adults.

Consider, for example, the terrible situation of youngsters who have been bombed out of their homes during recent wars in the Middle East, Asia, and sub-Saharan Africa, and who find themselves dumped into refugee camps without family members to care for them. By the time they are three or four years old, these abandoned children are desperately looking for compelling role models, and not finding them. They are often in despair at their failure to define anything resembling a personal identity in the cultural chaos that surrounds them.

This is a condition of existential bewilderment that most of us find almost impossible to comprehend. It is precisely why it is important to make the effort, especially since American military interventions have been principally responsible for these tragedies during the past generation. As citizens of the United States, we have a special responsibility to the innocent infants whose lives were shattered by American bombs during our country's "war against terror." Even if you believe that these interventions were legitimate efforts to prevent even worse catastrophes, the fact is that the United States and its military allies have done virtually nothing to assist these children. The Russian invasion of Ukraine is contributing further to this tragedy, but I cannot join the protest against Putin's war crimes without reminding my fellow citizens of America's failure to respond to the most fundamental requirements of existential justice.

Chapter 7

POSTMODERN LIFE CYCLES

In the last chapter I considered the revolutionary transformation of the nature of childhood over the last two centuries, and the responsibilities these changes imposed on parents, teachers, and citizens to prepare children for adult life. A comparable redefinition of adulthood is now under way, also with revolutionary implications. The great engine generating this transformation is modern medicine, where recent breakthroughs have led to enormous increases in life expectancies. This expansion is transforming our understanding of the characteristic challenges of postmodern existence.

To see why, recall that young adults in the 1950s could expect to live only into their sixties – even if they were born in the richest parts of the world. Like it or not, they found themselves in a race against time. If they didn't get married by twenty, they might not have time to raise a family and celebrate their children's successes as grown-ups.

The same was true of their work life. If they failed to commit themselves to a career in their twenties, this nondecision would haunt them throughout their lives. Even if they later poured a great deal of time and energy into their jobs, they would confront age-mates who were already ahead of them in their chosen careers. Not only would these age-mates earn bigger paychecks, but latecomers would increasingly be surrounded by younger and younger associates at the lower ranks – and frequently find themselves humiliated by the superior performance of younger people on jobs on which these old-timers had been working for years.

To be sure, if they acted decisively in their early twenties, their initial commitments to spouse and career might well turn out to be bitterly disappointing. But to remain in limbo and defer these crucial decisions would be losing a "chance of a lifetime."

Things look different in 2020. In many parts of the world, 20-year-olds can expect to live until they are 90 – or longer, if medical advances continue at their present extraordinary pace. Africa is the big exception. There life expectancies remain in the 60-year range. But life expectancies of 70 years or more prevail in relatively poor countries elsewhere.[1]

This puts the rising generation in a very different position from their twentieth-century counterparts. As with their predecessors, the life choices they make in their twenties will have a sweeping impact on their capacity to realize their hopes for the first 45 years of their adult existence. But today's adults can look forward to the second half of their lives and confront the prospect of radical self-estrangement. Suppose, for example, that it were possible for a 20-year-old in 2020 to take a glimpse into the future and find that the person inhabiting their body between 2065 and 2110 does not share *any* of the beliefs, commitments, inclinations, or intuitions that defined their identity as a young adult. Indeed, if they met such a person in 2020, they would consider him or her a total stranger.

How should I respond to the prospect that "I" could well become such a person?[2]

It raises an unprecedented dilemma for the rising generation: "I" may well become radically estranged from the physical body I presently inhabit over the course of the second half of its 90-year existence. How should I respond to the prospect of this radical form of self-estrangement? As in the preceding chapters, my aim isn't to answer this question but to invite you to reflect on its basic presuppositions.

For starters, I should emphasize that radical self-estrangement is not an inevitable feature of twenty-first-century existence. Suppose, for example, a postmodern couple gets married in 2023—and their relationship manages to flourish throughout the entire 70 years of their adult life. For these people, the prospect of self-estrangement serves only as an esoteric philosophical speculation, not a predicament of their own existence.[3]

The same thing is true of young adults confronting career decisions in the 2020s. Some will find that their initial job choices will give them the skills they need to thrive in the high-tech economy of the late twenty-first century—and that their services will remain in demand long after the traditional retirement age of 65 or 70.

But it is equally apparent that many of today's 20-year-olds will face severe disappointment—even if they make their initial decisions in a mature and thoughtful fashion. Many couples who were deeply in love when they married in 2023 will find themselves in bitter conflicts, leading to divorce in 2033 or 2043. Some who made perfectly sensible job choices in their twenties will find that economic conditions take an unexpected turn during the next two decades, destroying their once-promising careers and requiring them to struggle to fill the void. Moreover, a misfortune in one sphere can undermine the other – unemployment might strain a marriage to the breaking point; family troubles can destroy work credibility – leading to an escalating bewilderment that provokes the disintegration of *all* the committed relationships that defined my personal identity when "I" was in my early twenties.

As the rising generation enters the adult world in the 2020s, almost everybody recognizes that they may well be confronting radical self-alienation in the second half of their extended lives, despite their grim determination to avoid it. Yet this is the first time in human history that this question has ever seemed of existential importance.

In calling it "existential," I mean to use the term in a special sense. To see my point, contrast the late-life predicament with the existential threat to humanity posed by global warming. I join my fellow environmentalists in warning that it may be impossible for humans to survive on this planet in the twenty-second century unless there are decisive cutbacks of air and water pollution in the very near future. This means that the collective decisions made in the 2020s by the world's governments do indeed have existential significance for humanity in 2100.[4]

But I am using "existential" in a different way. Even if humanity manages to avoid an environmental catastrophe, countless members of the rising generation will nevertheless confront dilemmas of self-estrangement as they enter the second half of their lives. Their existential predicament is personal, not collective – and this sets it apart from many other dilemmas that confront us in the twenty-first century.

It is by no means unique in this respect. We have already considered the personal predicament confronting orphaned children in refugee camps. These babies are without the cultural resources they need to understand themselves as self-defining human beings. In contrast, the present case involves young adults who can indeed define their real-world identities in the "here and now," but who will confront radical self-alienation in the foreseeable future. They are increasingly alive to the risk that they will hear cries for help emerging from their own mouths as if they were the shouts of a stranger. Both cases, however, raise the same question: should the rest of us, in our role as citizens, enable these lost human beings to regain the self-confidence required to function as competent adults in the postmodern world? This question is already being asked by escalating numbers of 80- or 90-year-olds who find themselves confined to senior-care centers where they are left to discover meaning in weekly bingo games and courses in "brain fitness."

Yet the future offers up even grimmer prospects. To clarify its distinctive dimensions, I invite you to compare three late-life scenarios, representative of ones that will arise with increasing frequency during the last decades of this century. All three stories begin in the year 2000. In each case, a recently married couple has a child. These children emerge into the modern world as self-defining adults in 2020. Over the next few years, they each get married and make a series of commitments, at work and in other spheres, which together define the foundations of their personal identity.

At this point the three scenarios diverge. In the first, the newlyweds of 2020 were both raised by super-rich parents, who have provided them with funds that enable them to buy a mansion in the richest part of town. Both partners, beginning in infancy, were propelled toward a place among the power elite. Their parents sent them to the most expensive day schools and preparatory schools and provided special tutoring, travel opportunities, and other experiences that enabled them to enter a top university and graduate in 2020 with a fancy degree.

Yet these privileged young adults have achieved these worldly distinctions at an enormous cost in personal anxiety. From infancy onward, parents and teachers have put them under intense pressure to "succeed" – pressures that only intensify as their elite credentials propel them up the socioeconomic pyramid.

These pressures intensify further when, upon marrying and having children, they find that their kids display the same anxieties that they had experienced as children. The young couple tries to deflect the high-pressure tactics imposed on their children by their schoolteachers. But these efforts prove unsuccessful, and their children succumb to the same intense competition to "succeed" that has increasingly led their parents to question the meaning of their own lives. As the years pass, one of the partners begins to drink and dope themselves into oblivion – losing their prestigious job, their spouse, and custody of their kids as their acts of self-destruction accelerate. At some point they lose the support of their own parents, who deny them their mega-inheritance, and become estranged from their siblings. By the time they reach 60, in 2060, they have abandoned all the commitments and relationships that defined their life in 2020. Some stagger meaninglessly through the world, but others have managed to reconstruct a radically different life for themselves. In my not-so-hypothetical scenario, they have quit drinking, found a steady job as a low-skilled worker, and come home to find a great deal of happiness with a sympathetic spouse – whose poor education makes it impossible to sustain their partner's super-educated modes of engagement in a credible fashion.

The same thing happens in my second scenario – but it begins in a ghetto neighborhood. The same day the baby plutocrat is born, a struggling black couple has a baby who manages to prosper in the stable and loving home they provide for the infant. As the child grows older, however, it begins to discover its transgender identity – which, if revealed to parents and schoolmates, would expose it to constant humiliation. In response, the child conceals its stigmatized identity from almost everybody and successfully gains a third-rate education from an underfunded public school before entering a racist and transphobic society in 2020. Nevertheless, despite living in a society marked by economic, sexual, and gender oppression, this person refuses to give up the struggle for a meaningful life – and as a young adult actually succeeds in finding a fulfilling job and building a loving relationship with a suitable partner.

Over the next decade, however, breakdowns occur on both fronts – leading to a decade of struggle to find a new loving companion and a job that will fill the enormous void at the center of day-to-day existence. But again, these efforts lead nowhere, and by the age of 60, this victim of economic, gender, and racial domination is in precisely the same existential situation as the person in my first scenario. Both find themselves impoverished and isolated as they despairingly confront the years of darkness that lie ahead in the second half of their adult lives.

Yet it would be a mistake to ignore the very different paths by which these two people reached their common destination. Young plutocrats had, from birth, enormous and utterly illegitimate advantages over their oppressed counterparts. To be sure, they were raised in cultural environments that put them under intense pressure. If these pressures hadn't been so remorseless, they might have been more successful in building meaningful lives for themselves. But the pressures were even greater on their counterparts in the second scenario—who not only began life in poverty but suffered systematic humiliation in their efforts to define their gender identity.

This is not to say that plutocrats cannot blame their parents and educators for driving them down a path to nowhere. But they cannot blind themselves to their own role in alienating their older selves from their younger selves. Many of their plutocratic counterparts also rejected the life course laid out for them but did so without leaving only destruction in their wake. Some refused to use their fancy degrees as springboards for careers perpetuating the plutocracy's domination and instead dedicated their time and energy to reforming the status quo.

The protagonists in my first scenario could have followed that example, but they didn't. They should recognize—however reluctantly—that they cannot place all the blame for their late-life crisis on their dead parents and teachers. They are also *personally* responsible for their own undoing.

This isn't nearly as obvious in my second scenario. It would seem plausible for oppressed ghetto residents to blame their second life crises *entirely* on the systematic degradations that surrounded them earlier in their lives.

Here is where my third scenario enters the story—with the aim of undermining such predictable efforts at self-exoneration. This time around, suppose that there were other black transgender children growing up in the same neighborhood as their second-scenario counterparts. After entering adult society, they also struggled successfully against these oppressive conditions and managed to establish loving relationships at home and meaningful work lives during the 2020s – only to have their sense of self-realization shattered by breakdowns during the 2030s.

My third scenario diverges from its predecessor at this point. Despite their early-life crisis in the 2030s, these bitterly disappointed people manage to reconstruct new forms of intimate relationship and reestablish thriving careers over the next couple of decades. By 2060 they are flourishing members of their community – loved by their family, successful at work, and broadly respected within their community. As they reach their sixties, they begin a campaign to assist elderly neighbors whose struggles for a meaningful life had been crushed by the pervasive injustices surrounding them.

Their campaign succeeds in creating a movement of activists who systematically make house-to-house visits to contact people shattered by late-life crises. In their efforts to reach out to their isolated neighbors, moreover, they encounter ghetto residents whose life stories bear an uncanny resemblance to their own. These people also managed to establish meaningful family and work lives in the 2020s but saw their initial successes break down in the following decade. But unlike the activists, they found themselves unable to define a new set of enduring spherical relationships and by the 2060s they were staring into the abyss.

Naturally, the leaders of the grassroots movement feel a special sympathy for their isolated and bewildered counterparts – and they make a special effort to extricate them from their postmodern predicament. It is by no means easy. Even with the aid of specially trained social workers, many of these alienated people cannot be encouraged to participate in renewed forms of meaningful engagement. But some do begin to respond, slowly and hesitantly, to these efforts and begin to reconstruct their lives in a series of meaningful spherical engagements.

Yet there is a paradox in their reemergence from darkness. While they will rejoice in their triumph over their postmodern predicament, their success also demonstrates that they cannot put all the blame for their previous breakdown on the humiliations and oppressions they suffered during the first half of their adult lives. If none of it were their doing, their reemergence into meaningful existence would be entirely inexplicable—since, by hypothesis, the prevailing system of domination hasn't significantly changed.

In short, my three scenarios invite you to move beyond my initial distinction between *collective* existential threats—like global warming—and *personal* existential dilemmas—like those confronting abandoned babies and bewildered seniors. These infants were deprived of the very possibility of entering the world as self-defining human beings. In contrast, the second-life scenarios involve two different existential dilemmas: structural, on the one hand; individualistic, on the other. In contrast to the plutocratic first scenario, both ghetto scenarios involve people who have been forced to struggle against structures of socioeconomic domination throughout their lives. Nevertheless, the second scenario involves individuals who have managed to succeed where their plutocratic counterparts have failed—and have responded to the breakup of their early adult lives by engaging in a relatively successful struggle to construct a new set of meaningful relationships. In short, despite their structural oppression, their individualistic initiatives have permitted them to succeed where the plutocrats have failed.

In contrast, the third scenario involves people who are like the plutocrats in their failure to deal with the structural imperatives imposed by their background, but they also have failed to display the individualistic capacity to sustain meaningful relationships that prevailed in the first of the ghetto scenarios—until a neighborhood movement for social justice managed to organize a group of social workers with the professional skills required to encourage further individualistic efforts by at least some of the bewildered members of the community.

Moving beyond the particular dilemmas raised by the dramatically extended lifetimes of the postmodern era, the distinction between social structure and individualistic effort provides an organizing perspective on all of the preceding chapters in the book, despite their different substantive concerns. The socioeconomic perspective focuses on structural obstacles to spherical self-realization—ranging from plutocratic domination of politics to subordination at work to stigmatization in other spheres of life. The individualistic perspective emphasizes the dilemmas of personal meaning-making—from the bewildered cries of abandoned infants in Syria to the self-destructive anxieties of 70-year-olds in the world's ghettoes.

If we hope to gain a deeper understanding of our situation, we should not focus on individualistic breakdowns at the expense of the structural injustice, or vice versa. We should integrate both in a larger effort to reflect on the postmodern predicaments that we all confront.

Easier said than done—and I will count it a success if this essay encourages you to confront the unprecedented challenges of contemporary life—and join your fellow citizens in the ongoing effort to revitalize democracy in the twenty-first century.

PART II

MY BODY, MYSELF

Chapter 8

UNCERTAINTY

Who am I?

One thing should be clear by now: you can't try to answer this question until you learn how to express yourself in a language that is intelligible to an increasingly diverse range of intimates and strangers. This is a necessary condition for a meaningful life in modern society.

But it's not sufficient. When we wake up each morning, we are immediately aware of our bodily surroundings without the need to say a word. Our spontaneous engagement with the "here and now" is a prerequisite for all our efforts at mutually intelligible communication.

Yet today we are increasingly turning our backs on face-to-face sphere-mates and search the internet for remote relationships that offer greater self-realization. This forces us to confront an unprecedented question: will my daily struggles for meaning in both virtual and physical worlds lead me to such self-contradictions that I no longer have any sense of who "I" am?

In part 1, I approached this question through scenarios that invited increasingly complex intuitive responses. Yet common-sense intuition is a problematic way to explore the unprecedented issues raised by our postmodern predicament—and here, the existentialist tradition of the twentieth century serves as an especially important source of insight. Leading thinkers gave very different answers to the fundamental questions of self-understanding raised by the destruction of the premodern world. But there was one point on which they all agreed: it is not possible to frame the problem posed by modernity without confronting the shattering implications of the scientific breakthroughs initiated by Werner Heisenberg, with his uncertainty principle, and Albert Einstein with his theory of relativity.

I will begin my second round of exploration by considering this revolutionary challenge.

The End of an Era

It took centuries for modern science to become a legitimate enterprise in the Western world. Galileo's effort to establish that the earth revolved around the sun was condemned as "heretical" by the Inquisition, and he was commanded to "abandon it completely . . . and henceforth not to hold, teach or defend it in any way whatsoever, either orally or in writing." Since Galileo was trapped in Rome at the time, he had no choice but to consent "voluntarily."[1]

Isaac Newton, born the same year Galileo died, was in a far safer position in Protestant Britain to help legitimate an Enlightenment understanding of the universe.[2] His formulation of the laws of motion and gravitation endowed them with a mathematical clarity that gave them the appearance of eternal truth. The great scientific breakthroughs of the nineteenth century only seemed to confirm Newton's mathematical mastery of space and time. Whatever their other anxieties, modern men and women were confident that scientists of the future would chart their relationship to the universe with ever greater precision.

Yet this era came to a decisive end at the beginning of the twentieth century—when Heisenberg's uncertainty principle and Einstein's theory of relativity consigned Newton's laws to the junk heap of history. At that moment, the problematics of self-location in space and time not only became a central preoccupation of existentialist philosophers. It also inspired the efforts by James Joyce, in *Ulysses,* and Marcel Proust, in *In Search of Lost Time,* to liberate their readers from the rigid Newtonian organization of space-time and explore radically different spatiotemporal forms of self-understanding if they hoped to make sense of their lives. The same was true of revolutionary representations of space/time in the paintings of Braque and Picasso, the sculptures of Brancusi and Nevelson, the music of Schoenberg and Shostakovich, and the modernist poetry of Eliot and Pound—to name only a few of the great efforts to fill the Newtonian vacuum with revolutionary revisions of humanity's effort to live a meaningful life in a radically uncertain world.[3]

For my purposes, however, it is more important to focus on self-consciously philosophical efforts to confront the dilemma of self-location posed by Heisenberg and Einstein. For existentialists, relativity and uncertainty raised a profound question of self-definition. Since science can't precisely locate any physical object in space and time, how can I confidently locate my own body in the world? Unless I can provide a thoughtful answer, I can only stumble meaninglessly through the so-called real world in which

I am fated to live out my life. How, then, to resolve this truly existential question?

Edmund Husserl took the lead by advancing a "phenomenological" path to an answer. To illustrate its distinctive character, permit me to offer up a humdrum example that usefully frames the post-Newtonian predicament – and its Husserlian solution.

First, the dilemma: suppose that, when you wake up in the morning, you vividly recall your experiences of the previous evening. Nevertheless, Einstein and Heisenberg have demonstrated that these memories of "the past" have no determinate relationship to your spatial and temporal location in "the present." How, then, to reconnect your recent self-recollections to your place in the physical world surrounding you?

Husserl's answer: you should take your spontaneous awareness of your bodily relationship to its immediate surroundings with high seriousness. After all, if you were not aware of the pillow beneath your head and the sun shining through the windows, you would be dead!

Husserl called his answer "phenomenological" because of the authority it gives to the *unmediated* awareness of phenomena in the "here and now." It is only this spontaneous form of self-consciousness that gives you confidence in your own real-world existence, now that Newton has departed from the scene. To be sure, once you get out of bed in the morning, your fellow workers and other sphere-mates may greatly value your powers of analytic thinking. Nevertheless, Uncertainty and Relativity tell you it is a fundamental mistake to suppose that your real-world existence can be established in a similar fashion. According to Husserl, I can establish my own existence with self-confidence only by recognizing the foundational significance of my *pre-theoretical* engagement with my immediate physical surroundings.

Husserl's phenomenology provided the basic framework organizing the entire existentialist debate over the twentieth century. Rather than attempt a comprehensive survey, I will focus on four leading thinkers whose work is particularly relevant to the approach I am advancing in this book. I will start with Martin Heidegger. Since his views require the complete repudiation of my own position, I will adopt a two-step approach to the arguments he advances in *Being and Time*. I begin by isolating the book's enduring insights into the existential challenges posed by modern life—and explore the ways in which they become even more relevant under twenty-first-century conditions. I then explain why, despite his insights, I cannot accept Heidegger's fundamental stance.

I will deal in the same way with three other existentialists who have greatly influenced my own thinking: Jean Paul Sartre, Simone de Beauvoir, and Maurice Merleau-Ponty. Each provides insights that enrich the existentialist analysis presented in part 1, but none has persuaded me to adopt their entire framework. So my dialogue with each of them will also take a two-step form—first identifying their key insights and then exposing the weaknesses in their arguments.

If my engagements with these four thinkers are successful, they will encourage you to explore the work of other twentieth-century existentialists—and their potential contributions to an understanding of our postmodern predicament. But for now, let's focus on Heidegger, Sartre, Beauvoir, and Merleau-Ponty and why their ideas are particularly relevant for a thoughtful confrontation with the precedent-shattering dilemmas of the twenty-first century.

Oneness?

Throughout part 1, I emphasized the need for modern men and women to sustain a complex web of spherical relationships if they hope to live a meaningful life. When I enter my workplace, I cannot talk to my boss as if he were a sales clerk in the supermarket, nor can I talk to my soccer coach as if she were the mayor, or to my neighbors as if they were my children. Instead, I must be constantly mindful of the sphere in which I am operating in the "here and now." Otherwise, I will have no hope of confronting the fundamental challenge of modern existence, which is to decide, within the limits of my waking day, whether my family or my job or my soccer team comes first when they make conflicting demands on me.

Of course, I might find myself so unequal to this challenge that the meaning of my life begins to fall apart. Even if I succeed in avoiding bitter breakups with my most important sphere-mates, I may still shift my relative commitments with such frequency that eventually I can no longer tell myself whether "I" really think my family or my job or my soccer team is more important to me—and thus lose all sense of who I am and what I really stand for.

Rather than ignoring the tragic situation of these bewildered men and women in part 1, I insisted that we cannot ignore their anxieties—and that fundamental principles of existential justice require us to respond constructively to the different ways in which their self-alienation expresses itself.

Martin Heidegger, however, would say that my appeals to "existential justice" are mere pompous professorial nonsense blinding me to a much harder truth: the very project of modernity makes it *impossible* to sustain our personal integrity as human beings.

In the phenomenological account advanced in *Being and Time,* the fundamental problem posed by modern society is precisely its demand that we deal with sphere-mates in different ways at different times. On Heidegger's view, the need to move from sphere to sphere in the course of daily existence transforms each individual's self-awareness into a series of disconnected fragments that deprives them of any understanding of "who I really am."

In *Being and Time,* Heidegger tells us that the path to integrity requires a totalizing repudiation of modernity itself and the adoption of a radically different stance to the world.[4] Each of us should wholeheartedly embrace *everything* that comes into our consciousness in the "here and now" – and refuse to engage in the complex forms of mutual understanding required by contemporary relationships. Instead, the only way to sustain a sense of self-fulfillment is to seek unity with your surroundings in the "here and now" at every moment of your existence.[5]

I will respond to *Being and Time* in a two-step fashion. I will first try to identify the valuable insights that Heidegger adds to my diagnosis in part 1 of the modern/postmodern predicament. Only then will I consider Heidegger's position on the merits. I will try to persuade you that *Being and Time*'s radical solution to the problem of self-fragmentation doesn't make sense in its own terms. Even if someone made a heroic Heidegerrian effort to live in complete harmony with the "here and now" until death, it would be utterly impossible to do so. Heidegger, in short, is caught up in an existential self-contradiction: it is impossible to live out the life that, according to him, is the only life worth living.

But first things first: the failure of Heidegger's radical vision should not blind us to the insights that *Being and Time* can contribute to a thoughtful encounter with the dilemmas we all confront in our ongoing struggle to construct meaningful lives for ourselves. I will make the affirmative case for Heideggerian oneness through a series of hypotheticals.

For starters, suppose you are on vacation and have taken a trip to explore the wilderness. (Heidegger himself invokes this scenario, but I will give it a contemporary spin.) Imagine that, before you set out on your hike, you have your cell phone in your pocket and you ask yourself: should I shut off my phone before I start down the wilderness trail?

The obvious answer is yes. If you leave your cell phone on, it will predictably disrupt your engagement with the wilderness. At any moment, your boss might call you, and even if you don't answer, the phone's buzz could lead you to worry about some business problem you've left behind. This would defeat the purpose of your hike, which is to immerse yourself in the natural environment in a way that permits you to open yourself up to the mountains looming before you and the birds soaring overhead.

Silent "modes of appreciation" occur in many different settings. I also shut off my cell phone when I enter a concert hall to join other music lovers in silently appreciating a Beethoven symphony. But it also explains why people watchers spend time in sidewalk cafes and silently enjoy the endlessly changing patterns of hustle-bustle on the street in front of them.

Heideggerian oneness comes to life in two other forms as well: mastery and togetherness. I will begin by exploring the significance of mastery with an example many readers will find familiar. Call it the "kitchen scenario." Suppose you are cooking dinner for your family, preparing their favorite stew for the evening meal. Since you've cooked the stew many times before, you don't need to consult a recipe to figure out the best way to proceed. You simply prepare the ingredients – wash them, slice them, coat the meat with flour, and so on – put them in the pot in the correct order with the right amount of water, turn on the flame, stir the stew when it needs stirring, take the stew out when past experience tells you it's cooked, and serve it triumphantly to your appreciative family.

From start to finish, you rely on your intuitions to achieve a sense of mastery over the pots, pans, and raw ingredients in your immediate surroundings. To put the point in Heidegger's terms, the kitchen has become your "clearing," and by relying on your intuitions, you are cooking in a way that profoundly enhances the quality of your experience.

Now consider the alternative scenario, in which you do in fact consult a cookbook before proceeding to each stage of culinary creation. Suppose, moreover, that despite your past experience, step-by-step deliberation enables you to produce a better stew than the one you could have created by following your instincts.

Nevertheless, the character of your experience would be very different. Your need to stand apart from your knives and cutting board and spice rack and ask "what do I do next?" is inconsistent with the sense of mastery you experienced when proceeding in harmony with your pots and pans.

Heidegger has another neologism – "tools" – to express his point in general terms. "Tools" are all the things I use to relate my body to the "clearing" that I inhabit in the "here and now." I achieve a sense of mastery when I use these tools to gain oneness with my clearing. I don't reach a similar sense of self-fulfillment if I have to pause and ask myself what I should do next – even if these periods of reflection yield a better stew when my family sits down for dinner.

Of course, when deciding how to cook the meal, you might choose to consult the cookbook periodically, thinking that it's more important for your family to enjoy their dinner than it is for you to gain a sense of oneness with your pots and pans. Nevertheless, I think Heidegger is right to emphasize that mastery permits a special – and intrinsically valuable – form of self-realization.

I have introduced mastery through a scenario that often arises in everyday life, but it is relevant in many other situations as well. For analytic purposes, the key point to recognize is that mastery scenarios arise in contexts that are fundamentally different from appreciation scenarios. To see why, return to my hike in the wilderness.

Suppose that after walking down the trail for a while, I decide to spend some time sitting on a rock and opening myself up to the glories of nature in a more relaxed fashion. As I look around my surroundings, I turn my attention to a particular tree. After staring at it for a while, I decide that it is an egregiously debased example of tree-ness, and that the wilderness would be a better place if it were cut down. So I take an axe out of my knapsack and throw myself into the task. I deploy my tool so skillfully that the tree thunders to the ground with remarkable speed – enabling me to gain the same sense of mastery in the wilderness that I achieve when cooking my stew for my family.

Nevertheless, the oneness displayed in mastering the tree is fundamentally different from the oneness gained earlier in my hike. During that period, I was silently appreciating the wonders of the natural world, not triumphantly correcting it by deploying my axe on the hapless tree.

Appreciation and mastery not only involve different forms of oneness. They arise in many places that don't resemble kitchens or forests or concert halls. I invite my readers to reflect on their own lives and consider whether and where they have gained these deeply fulfilling forms of self-realization. For now, let me introduce my third and final Heideggerian ideal type.

The word Heidegger invents for this third mode of meaning-making has no easy translation into English. He calls it *Mitsein,* literally "being-with," and I will call it "togetherness." Togetherness involves a special way of achieving oneness with people you encounter in the "here and now."

Consider this scene from a successful marriage. When a loving couple return home from work each evening, they spend time together in lots of different ways – laughing at each other's jokes, reporting their workday experiences, responding to their children's anxieties, deploring the outrageous conduct of their obnoxious neighbors, and so forth.

But sometimes their exchanges take a distinctive form. When I say something to my partner, she doesn't say something back. She simply runs her hands through her hair. This gesture is opaque to outsiders, but I have no trouble understanding it. It's obvious to me – but only to me – that she disagrees with what I just said. Rather than explain myself further, however, I respond by sipping my coffee in a fashion that she – but only she – immediately understands: I'm telling her that I'm no longer interested in defending the view she finds problematic and that I'm content to adopt her position on the subject.

In adopting this silent mode of engagement, I am not worried that further conversation will lead to an angry dispute. To the contrary, I am confident that we could reach common ground in a few minutes – since our disagreement involves a humdrum problem of no great importance. As a consequence, it seems more sensible to wordlessly signify my acceptance of her view than to waste more time on the matter. After all, there are lots more things to talk about!

At this point, my partner also has two choices. She can tell me how pleased she is that we reached an agreement on an issue that seemed to divide us. Or she can say nothing at all, act as if nothing remarkable has happened, and shift our conversation to another matter of common interest.

This is the point at which my scenario culminates in the expression of Heideggerian *Mitsein.* The loving couple has achieved a sense of oneness that does not rely on endless chitchat. They have so attuned their bodies to each other that they can affirm their togetherness without needing to say a word. Heidegger's contribution is especially significant here – since these togetherness-scenarios play themselves out every day in homes throughout the world. They are so common that their profound significance is easy to ignore. After all, countless individuals never find *anybody* with whom they can share this precious sense of oneness. Most manage to sustain rewarding relationships over time, but they never reach a point at which they can sustain a wordless sense of togetherness with even their most intimate sphere-mates. Even if they otherwise achieve great success in modern life, Heidegger suggests, something very precious is absent from their experience as human beings.

He is right. There is, however, a second basic way in which *Mitsein* experiences can arise. In these cases, the partners to the relationship don't express their wordless togetherness at the conclusion of a verbal disagreement. They simply reach out to one another spontaneously.

Suppose, for example, an intimate couple arrives early for brunch with some friends at a restaurant. They respond by sitting down on a park bench but don't spend the time talking about a practical problem. Instead, they spend their "free time," silently enjoying each other's company – until they get up, go to the restaurant, and join sphere-mates for a lively conversation. They are unlikely to think much about the contrast between these two experiences or to recognize the existential significance of their intimate capacity to enjoy a wordless sense of togetherness. Yet, once again, Heidegger is right to emphasize its significance.

Mitsein not only marks out a precious mode of being-in-the-world. It also enriches the two other forms of Heideggerian authenticity we have considered: appreciation and mastery.

Begin with appreciation. Suppose a couple decides to spend their vacation exploring the wilderness. They have two choices. They can hike down the trail *together* and wordlessly affirm their oneness with each other at the same time they are silently opening themselves up to their natural surroundings. Or they can take a more individualistic approach. Neither pays serious attention to the other's reactions but is content with silently appreciating the changing vistas surrounding them. They do not share their impressions until after their hike comes to an end.

Different couples will make different choices. The key point is that appreciation is not necessarily an individualistic experience. It can sometimes be greatly enhanced by togetherness. To reduce complications, I have been supposing that the two hikers are engaged in an intimate relationship throughout the entire year, living a meaningful family life at home when they return from their vacation to confront the challenges of postmodern existence.

But suppose you find yourself in a different relationship, say with a friend who shares your deep appreciation of the natural world but whom you otherwise see only occasionally. You decide to take annual vacations with one another to different wilderness areas to deepen your environmental understanding. Over the years, moreover, your explorations of the wilderness permit you to attain a *spherical togetherness* of a special kind. You no longer need speech to gain a sense of your sphere-mate's response to the sights and sounds of the forest that surrounds you. You have attuned your bodies to one another in a way that permits you to walk *together* down the trail.

This specialized but profound sense of oneness is a significant source of meaning in many spheres of life. Consider, for example, how two friends may go to a concert and express their togetherness as they sit side by side and silently absorb the familiar wonders of a Beethoven symphony. To make things even more interesting, suppose that you and your spouse typically go to concerts with your friend, and that all three of you achieve oneness in the concert hall before your friend says goodbye after the performance—while the two of you maintain your deep sense of intimacy upon your return home.

While loving relationships within the family serve as paradigmatic examples of *sustained* togetherness, postmodern forms of existence provide many opportunities for *spherical* togetherness—for those willing to engage their time and energy in cultivating deep face-to-face relationships. As the case of the Beethoven concert suggests, sustained and spherical forms of appreciation can combine in complex and deeply fulfilling ways.

The same is true when we expand our focus beyond appreciation to consider modes of mastery. But I will resist the temptation to explore them, since I have said enough to raise a fundamental question: do the increasingly disembodied forms of our postmodern existence on the internet endanger the face-to-face patterns of appreciation, mastery, and togetherness that have profoundly enriched the meaningfulness of twentieth-century existence?

I will return to this question in part 3. For present purposes, it's more important to call a halt to my search for common ground with Heidegger and explain why I reject his far more sweeping critique of contemporary modes of existence.

Being and Time contends that the entire project of modernity is misconceived. The ceaseless and conflicting multi-spherical demands of modern life, Heidegger writes, generate an intolerable form of alienation that requires us to split our sense of personal identity into self-contradictory fragments. Not only do we talk and act at home in ways that radically differ from those we adopt in other spheres of personal engagement. We also play a host of different roles when dealing with different sorts of strangers. As time moves on, this constant role-playing leads to utter confusion when we ask ourselves: who am I anyway?

According to Heidegger, no serious person can answer this question with self-assurance. So long as I endlessly move from sphere to sphere, I will fragment myself into a series of bits and pieces that will create a void at the very core my existence. The fundamental challenge is to confront the meaninglessness of modern life and repudiate its basic premises.

Being and Time calls upon us to give up endless role-playing in the search for self-fulfillment. Rather than deluding ourselves with the false promise of modernity, there is only one way to preserve our existential authenticity as human beings. We must unconditionally seek oneness with our immediate surroundings at every moment of our lives. This will enable us to *live at home in the world* without anxiety or doubt.

I disagree. Heidegger is wrong to look upon our ongoing struggles to define and redefine our aims in life as symptoms of an incurable spiritual dis-ease. They are, to the contrary, liberating responses to the economic, political, and social breakthroughs that have revolutionized the terms of human existence over the past 250 years.

Heidegger is perfectly right to insist that these competing invitations to meaningful spherical relationships will generate commitment dilemmas that inevitably provoke personal anxiety. Yet there are far better ways to respond to these anxieties than by trying to suppress them.

In taking this position, I am following down the path of a long line of existentialist thinkers in the twentieth century. The three who have most influenced me – Simone de Beauvoir, Jean-Paul Sartre, and Maurice Merleau-Ponty – also took the view that *Being and Time* was fundamentally misconceived. In advancing their critiques, moreover, each of them contributed insights that eluded the commonsense approach to postmodernity that I presented in part 1.

As a consequence, I will deal with them in the same two-step manner I deployed with Heidegger. I first try to identify their enduring insights and only then offer a critique of their efforts to construct convincing existentialist accounts of the dilemmas of self-definition generated by the modern world. I hope to persuade you that none of them provides an adequate framework for analyzing these dilemmas. Nevertheless, they provide precious resources for my own effort, in part 3, to develop an existentialist approach to the unprecedented predicaments we confront in the high-tech world of the twenty-first century.

Jean-Paul Sartre

I will begin with Sartre since, as its very title suggests, his great work *Being and Nothingness* presents itself as a decisive refutation of Heidegger's *Being and Time*. As with Heidegger, however, I will not try to summarize Sartre's extremely complex arguments in his extremely esoteric vocabulary but will give you a sense of his key points through a series of commonplace scenarios.

Permit me, then, to frame Sartre's critique of Heidegger by asking you to reflect on the moment when you wake up in the morning to find yourself at home in your bedroom. As the sun shines through your window, you quietly rest your head on your pillow and enjoy a few moments of peace before you get out of bed. Nothing could seem more natural. Yet so far as Sartre is concerned, your decision to get out of bed suffices to show how badly *Being and Time* misrepresents the human condition.

When you were resting on your pillow, you had *already* reached the precious oneness with your surroundings that, according to Heidegger, is the hallmark of truly authentic existence. On his view, once you attain this condition, you should never leave it: the paradigm act of self-alienation is to separate yourself from the "here and now."

Yet this is precisely what happened when you jumped out of bed. Moreover, you may well have done it without giving the matter a moment's thought. Rather than saying to yourself, "It's time to take a shower!," you simply propelled yourself into action. Such commonplace experiences suggest that, in fact, nobody lives a single day of their lives in truly Heideggerian fashion.

In Sartre's view, moreover, these everyday actions suggest something fundamental about human existence itself. Rather than wordlessly embracing our immediate environment, we are constantly dissatisfied with the status quo and are engaged in a continuous process of negation and reconstruction. Heidegger is simply wrong to condemn this dynamic as pathological. Instead, it represents the only real-world pathway to authentic self-definition. Whether I like it or not, I define who "I really am" by the features of my social situation that I am willing to repudiate over the course of my life.

Sartre's principles had radical implications for his conduct at the time *Being and Nothingness* was first published, in 1943. With the Nazis dominating Europe, there could be no denying that he confronted a system that ruthlessly condemned the mass of humanity to subordination and domination – and that even if Hitler were defeated, it would take a generational effort to dramatically transform the status quo. The only serious way to remain *true to yourself* was by denouncing these acts of subordination whenever you confronted them. If you chose to ignore them and proceeded with "normal" patterns of living, you would number yourself among the countless cowards who collaborated with the Nazis to sustain the prevailing system of existential injustice.

In short: Sartre joins Heidegger in calling on you to defend your sense of authenticity by repudiating "modern civilization," but he offers a very different reason for doing so. Heidegger contends that you must reject modernity to avoid fragmenting yourself into meaningless parts. Sartre contends that unless you reject the very foundations of the "here and now," you will transform yourself into a supporter of the existing system of oppression and domination.

I disagree with Sartre but not because I doubt the reality of deeply entrenched injustice. Nor do I deny that we currently confront a crisis of democracy that may lead to the consolidation of Nazi-like dictatorships – and where death-defying acts, like Sartre's publication of *Being and Nothingness,* may once again mark out the only real-world path to personal integrity. Nevertheless, I believe it is too early to give up in despair at the worldwide rise of dictatorship – and part 3 will advance a series of concrete reforms that could propel the progressive movement forward over the coming decade.

But for now, I have a different objective. Even though I reject Sartre's totalizing rejectionism, we can still learn a lot from his diagnosis of the modern predicament – just as we did from Heidegger's. In this spirit, I will isolate two modes of Sartrean negation which – like Heideggerian forms of togetherness – enrich our understanding of the dilemmas we encounter in our daily dealings with domination in the postmodern world.

The first of Sartre's insights involves the profound importance of self-sacrifice in the ongoing struggle for existential justice. Consider a case from the United States in the 1950s – a time when practices of racial domination were deeply entrenched in every aspect of southern life. In 1954, the Supreme Court repudiated segregation of public schools in *Brown v. Board of Education,* but it was perfectly obvious that southern governments would refuse to comply with the court's decree. Worse yet, armed groups of racist vigilantes throughout the South were murdering black men and women who were, in Sartrean fashion, responding to *Brown* by standing up against pervasive domination.

This racist backlash framed the meaning of Rosa Parks's remarkable act of self-sacrifice in Selma, Alabama, on December 1, 1955. After finishing her workday, she refused to give up her seat to a white man who demanded that she "sit in the back of the bus" in the section reserved for Blacks. By ignoring his command, she put her life on the line. Her white antagonist might have responded by pulling out a pistol and shooting her, following the example of other racist vigilantes.

Instead, she was immediately arrested by Montgomery's notoriously racist police force. Although she avoided abusive treatment at their hands, she was an obvious target for assassination once they released her from detention because the police had no interest in giving her special protection from racist thugs.

Yet Parks's display of bodily self-sacrifice inspired thousands of civil rights activists to join her in putting their lives on the line in the Birmingham bus boycott. Their example, in turn, greatly encouraged people throughout the country to join similar demonstrations against racial subordination. These collective mobilizations, climaxing in the March on Washington, were central to the Civil Rights revolution of the 1960s – and they call upon Americans of the 2020s to engage in similar sacrifices today.

If Parks had given up her seat, she would have joined the ranks of tens of millions of Black men and women who accepted – however bitterly – the humiliation they constantly encountered in everyday life. To put the point in terms of *Being and Nothingness:* the pervasiveness of racial domination left Parks with no choice but to confront death if she hoped to maintain her *existential authenticity* by standing up against the status quo.

Call this negation through bodily sacrifice. I should emphasize that Sartre took a similar step at a particularly vulnerable moment of his life. In 1939, at the outbreak of World War II, he was drafted into the French army, only to be captured and imprisoned by the Nazis after an early French defeat. He was then 35 and had not only marked himself out as a leading academic but had written a philosophical novel, *La nausée,* that became an instant success when published in 1938.

While confined in a Nazi prison camp, he devoted his time and energy to the study of *Being and Time.* Given Heidegger's notorious endorsement of Nazism and Sartre's position as a leading intellectual, the Germans hoped he would become the führer's leading intellectual apologist in France. They released him from captivity in 1942 and allowed him to return to Paris, then occupied by the German army. There he managed to complete *Being and Nothingness* in 1943, enabling the Resistance to publish his book at a time when German armies occupied most of Western Europe and were still fighting to control the East. For all Sartre knew, his public stand against Heidegger marked him out as a high-priority target for extermination in a France that might be under permanent Nazi domination. His decision to move forward despite this danger was a remarkable demonstration of authenticity in the face of death. In this respect, his publication of a complex philosophical text in 1943 resembled Rosa Parks's refusal to go to the back of the bus in 1955.[6]

Yet their lives took very different turns over the following decades. As a Black woman, Parks faced continuing discrimination. Despite the breakthroughs achieved by the Civil Rights and Voting Rights Acts of the 1960s, she confronted countless acts of face-to-face humiliation throughout her life.[7]

This was not true for Sartre. After Paris was liberated in August 1944, *Being and Nothingness* propelled him to the forefront of France's intellectual elite. In devoting himself to a wide-ranging critique of postwar practices, he was no longer crying in the wilderness but had assured himself a central place among the nation's white male elite. He never confronted the forms of face-to-face humiliation that continued to haunt Parks in the "here and now."

Turn next to a second form of Sartrean authenticity-through-rejection. Remarkably enough, Sartre himself provided a paradigm case of this ideal type at a later stage of his life—in 1964, when he received the Nobel Prize for Literature from the Swedish Academy. It is customary on these occasions for the honoree to travel to Stockholm to receive the prize at an elaborate ceremony, which begins with a series of tributes celebrating his achievements and reaches its climax with the winner bowing before the king of Sweden to receive the Nobel medal.

Some honorees had undoubtedly found this elaborate ritual more than a little embarrassing. Yet they had never allowed their modesty to deter them from accepting the prize—as well as the large sum of money accompanying it.[8]

Until Sartre. When news of his award hit the headlines, he did not issue a public statement but simply allowed a journalist to report his decision to reject the prize. According to the reporter, Sartre would not bow down before the king and his academy. To do so would be to celebrate a "Western Civilization" that, in his Marxist view, was perpetuating the capitalist exploitation of billions of people throughout the world.

The journalist reported, however, that the money associated with the prize confronted Sartre with a special dilemma. Sartre was "tortured" by the thought that if he accepted the award, he could give the money to Nelson Mandela's African National Congress, which "badly needed support" in its struggle against apartheid. Yet he refused to succumb to this temptation. On his view, his gift of "250,000 Swedish crowns" to the ANC would give Black South Africans the impression that "the West" was backing their liberation effort—when in fact the apartheid government was able to maintain its oppression only with enormous amounts of Western assistance.[9]

This point was decisive. Sartre could never allow himself to give Black Africans the impression that Western civilization was their friend when in fact it was their enemy.[10]

Whatever you think of the merits of Sartre's position, there is one thing you can't deny: his repudiation of the prize is entirely consistent with his views in *Being and Nothingness*. He refused to let others put him on a stage where he would be required to misrepresent *what he really stands for* in the "here and now."

The mode of authenticity Sartre exemplified in 1964 is different from the one he displayed in 1943. When he published *Being and Nothingness* in the middle of the war, there was a clear danger that the Nazis would hunt him down and kill him. In this respect, his decision was analogous to Rosa Parks's act of defiance in 1955. But in 1964, he did not put his life on the line by rejecting the Nobel Prize. His refusal of 250,000 Swedish crowns serves as a paradigm case of a second form of negation—the refusal to implicate oneself in the perpetration of injustice.

The two episodes differ in another respect as well. In 1943, Sartre expressed his opposition by publishing a book. In 1964, he said nothing at all—relying exclusively on deeds, not words, in turning down the award. Moreover, his deeds took a counterintuitive form. At the very least, many expected him to go to Sweden and refuse the medal in a face-to-face confrontation with the king. Instead, he took his stand by not showing up at all. To emphasize these differences, I will say that they involve negation by silent bodily disengagement.

Sartre's silent rejection of the prize became front-page news and significantly advanced the struggle against the West's support of the apartheid regime. Yet almost nobody has the superstar quality that makes their silent disengagement a matter that will provoke international attention. This leads to an obvious question: although Sartre's disengagement was indeed remarkable, does his second form of rejectionism offer a model for the rest of us?

I have become convinced that the answer is yes. Suppose, for example, you are living in a society with deeply entrenched prejudices based on race and gender. But you are determined to think for yourself on these matters and have established a committed relationship to a nonbinary lover of a different race – as well as rewarding friendships that also cross these forbidden lines.

When you go to work, however, you enter a very different spherical reality. Each day, your boss blatantly discriminates against employees on the basis of race and gender. Worse yet, his acts of subordination are entirely legal in the country you live in. Nevertheless, you manage to evade their impact simply because you are a male of the dominant race. As long as you keep your home life a well-guarded secret, you can develop your job-related skills within a flourishing environment.

This is precisely the strategy you adopt. Within a few years, your outstanding job performance gains the admiration of your fellow workers – and so you try to use your high standing to persuade your fellow workers to join an effort to reform your company's way of life. To your dismay, your efforts go nowhere. When you raise the issue in quiet conversations, most of your counterparts turn out to be true believers in the racist and sexist status quo – and many sympathizers are even too scared of reprisals to openly support a systematic revision of current practices.

You now confront a Sartrean moment of truth: Will you quit the firm and uphold your convictions? Or will you keep your mouth shut and continue to move up the company hierarchy? If you stick with the firm, you will remain free to express your outrage once you return home in the evening. Nevertheless, during the thousands and thousands of hours you spend on the job, you will be living a life that you yourself condemn as despicably racist and sexist. It is true, of course, that your ever-increasing salary will enrich the rest of your life, but a big paycheck cannot compensate for the self-contradiction at the very core of your existence. Every time you go to work, you will be playing the role of a dominant white male who treats his fellow workers with contempt for acting in precisely the same way you conduct yourself at home with your family. This means that *you will be living out a lie* in a sphere of life that will occupy a great deal of your time for decades.

To clarify the special character of this form of self-betrayal, compare it to the conflict between work and family obligations that was discussed earlier in the book. In these scenarios, I asked you to consider how you might reconcile your boss's insistence that you work overtime with your kids' insistence that you come home for dinner. Since you did not have the time and energy required to fulfil both demands, you also confronted a moment of truth. Whether you liked it or not, you had to decide which sphere was more fundamental to your self-identity. Nevertheless, your effort to define "who I really am" may not have required you to misrepresent yourself in either sphere of engagement. If, for example, you decided that your family came first, it might be possible to work out an arrangement with your employer that allowed you to continue a successful career with the firm. If you prioritized your career, you might be able to arrange your schedule in other ways that enabled you to spend enough time with your kids to sustain a loving relationship.

Of course, a tolerable inter-spherical equilibrium between home and work might not be achievable. Despite your best efforts, you might watch with despair as your colleagues turned their backs on you. Yet even under this bitter scenario, your life would still be anchored in at least one fundamental commitment—either to your career or to your family.

My Sartrean scenario, however, generates a very different multi-spherical dynamic – in which *both* your career *and* your family life may thrive throughout your adult life. When you go to work, your affirmations of white male heterosexual superiority help you advance your career. When you go home, your big paychecks permit you to provide greatly expanded opportunities for meaningful engagement with your kids, your friends, and your loving partner – especially if you manage to conceal the extent of your radically different conduct at work. In such cases, the only person who is aware of your self-contradiction is *yourself.*

Sartre has pointed out an important form of existential anxiety that would otherwise escape attention. Up to now, I have been emphasizing the foundational character of *inter*-subjective recognition in the construction of a meaningful modern life – both in your engagement with partners *within* particular spheres and in your struggle to sustain a satisfactory inter-spherical equilibrium *between* spheres. In contrast, Sartre is emphasizing the real-world ways in which you can betray yourself *without anyone else being aware of it.*

This is where Sartre's second mode of negation generates a second, if paradoxical, insight: even though your initial withdrawal may be silent, it can generate a larger dynamic that may contribute to a reform movement against entrenched injustice. To see this point, consider the likely reaction of fellow workers if you decide to walk out the door in despair at the racist and sexist features of their way of life. Rather than praising you for your courage, their loud expressions of outrage may bring the firm's racist and sexist practices to the attention of reformers who had previously been unaware of them – transforming the company into a target in their ongoing campaign for social justice, especially if a few fellow workers follow your example.

Over time, you and your fellow dissenters may well find yourselves playing a leading role in the reform movement. Your successful business careers have permitted you to develop a formidable set of organizational skills that can make a big difference in the effectiveness of activist campaigns. Moreover, other firms in the industry are unlikely to offer you a job – despite your record of outstanding achievement – now that you have gained the reputation of a troublemaker. Doesn't it make sense to dedicate yourself to a new career of public service on the local, regional, or national level?

Sartre's emphasis on the power of negative engagement is not limited to cases of racial and gender domination. His insights apply to a wide variety of cultural, economic, political, and religious forms of domination that prevail in different parts of the world. Each mode of domination creates different social cleavages. When the power elite singles out particular religions for humiliation, for instance, worshipers will include people of different races, genders, and incomes; the same will be true when a minority culture is a target of suppression.

If different groups begin to mobilize opposition on their own, their proliferation will have two consequences. On one hand, the power elite will pursue a strategy of divide and conquer, demonizing whatever groups pose the most immediate threat to their hegemony while seeking to pacify less formidable groups with small concessions. On the other hand, some opposition leaders will try to unite different social movements in a sustained struggle for a decisive transformation in the name of existential justice, which the existing regime will answer with an all-out effort at repression.

These confrontations will take different forms in the different socio-economic-political systems that currently prevail in Brazil or China or Europe or India or the United States. So far as Sartre was concerned, however, his Marxist understanding of history permitted him to strip away many of these complexities to define a relatively clear path to the triumph of the proletariat. Speaking for myself, I have never believed that the history of humanity is on a predetermined course – let alone that Marxists have discovered it. Nevertheless, even if you reject Sartre's historical determinism, he is right to insist that individual acts of disengagement not only play a crucial role in maintaining personal authenticity but also sometimes have a large impact on the course of political reform.

Simone de Beauvoir

Sartre tried to defeat Heidegger on Heidegger's terms. *Being and Time* insists on your bodily embrace of the "here and now." *Being and Nothingness* insists that integrity requires a never-ending struggle *against* the here and now. Simone de Beauvoir, however, challenges a premise that Heidegger and Sartre share. Both supposed that all of us have an intuitive command over our bodies as we confront everyday existence. She insists instead that if women are to achieve authentic self-understanding, they must repudiate the forms of cultural domination that have made men the masters of female bodies throughout the history of the West.

The Second Sex uses the same phenomenological methods marked out by Husserl to demonstrate the ways in which women are ceaselessly indoctrinated into passive acceptance of their gender inferiority from earliest childhood, when their parents pressure them to be "good little girls." Beauvoir elaborates the humiliating implications of the sexist stereotypes they confront in school and moves on to the remorseless social insistence on early marriage and motherhood, then to their second-class treatment in political and civic life, and finally to the tragic predicaments they face as they confront death.

No less remarkably, she confronts the foundational myths of Western civilization that serve as the basis for the particular practices that prevailed in 1949 at the time she published *The Second Sex*. She begins with Christianity and the way that Eve's betrayal of Adam sanctified male domination of women's bodies during the Christian era. She then argues that the scientific revolutions of the Enlightenment did nothing to liberate women but merely transformed the terms through which male domination was legitimated.

Beauvoir's principal target was Charles Darwin's *On the Origin of Species*. By the 1940s, generations of scientists had confirmed Darwin's hypothesis that humanity owed its existence to a process of "natural selection" through which males of various subhuman species used the female body to give birth to children who ultimately evolved into humans. In her view, Darwin's "survival of the fittest" merely served as the Enlightenment's substitute for Eve's temptation of Adam in sanctifying male domination over the female body.

It followed that women could not liberate themselves in the real world without engaging in a form of existential self-understanding that Heidegger and Sartre had ignored. They must recognize gender as nothing more than a historically contingent social construction. Beauvoir's insistence on cultural liberation from the prevailing myths, moreover, led her far beyond a critique of the "standard" forms of male domination that prevailed in postwar Europe. *The Second Sex* provides a stunning account of the ways the Nazis singled out Jewish women for especially excruciating forms of oppression during the Holocaust, and it goes on to elaborate the Nazi-like forms of violent domination imposed on Black women in America and elsewhere in the world.[11]

Even more remarkably, her breakthrough chapter "The Lesbian" confronted the existential tragedy faced by people whose self-understanding challenged entrenched male/female dichotomies, an issue ignored by even the most progressive writers of her era. "The Lesbian" remains compelling reading today—as Beauvoir shows how the biological essentialisms of Western science and religion transform LGBTQ individuals into criminals for acts of mutual intimacy in the "here and now."[12]

The Second Sex, in short, was a sweeping call to *all* victims of male domination to engage in a worldwide struggle for liberation. No less remarkably, it had a dramatic impact—both in the short and long term. Beauvoir's immediate target was the recently enacted French Constitution of 1946. Although it explicitly protected women against discrimination in broad spheres of economic and social life, it continued to authorize the criminalization of abortion.[13] Beauvoir urged her readers to repudiate this legacy of the sexist past, but she advanced her critique in a distinctive fashion. She did not analyze the issue in the traditional liberal language, emphasizing an abstract right of women to something called "individual liberty" or "human dignity." She made her case in phenomenological terms: Women, no less than men, understand themselves—first and foremost—as bodily creatures living in time. If they are to define themselves in an authentic fashion, they cannot be stripped of their power to control their own bodies as they struggle to construct a meaningful life for themselves.

Yet this is precisely what happens in the case of abortion—even if the woman has freely engaged in sexual intercourse at the time she is impregnated by her male partner. Her momentary act of consent should not be decisive if it requires her to bear the burdens of "motherhood" in a social world where "fatherhood" enables her male counterpart to escape similar responsibilities. It follows, according to Beauvoir, that women have an *unconditional* right to abort a fetus and thereby determine for themselves, in an authentic fashion, when – if ever – a commitment to motherhood enables them to engage in a self-enriching mode of being-in-time.

Beauvoir's existentialist approach led her to challenge the premises organizing the standard counterargument in the abortion debate. Opponents of abortion typically claim that fetuses are people with the same fundamental "right to life" as their mothers. Beauvoir is perfectly willing to agree that fetuses are human beings, but she insists that this does not suffice to transform them into autonomous people equivalent to their mothers. For a phenomenologist like Beauvoir, something more must be required before they can achieve this fundamental parity. The fetus must be able to define itself as an "I," separate from its surroundings, who can engage in an ongoing effort to establish a meaningful relationship to the "here and now." But until it achieves viability, it has no capacity to engage in this constitutive project of self-definition.

The fetus's mother is in a very different position. She is self-consciously confronting questions of the first importance: Should motherhood become a fundamental part of my life? Is this the time to take on its responsibilities?

If she tells herself "this is not the time for me to take care of kids," it is a category mistake for her opponents to argue that the fetus nevertheless demands its "right to life." The fetus is not yet in a position to understand itself as an "I" who can make value judgments. It is up to the mother, and nobody else, to determine the fetus's fate. Abortion opponents' claim to serve as the fetus's privileged spokespeople is utterly without existential foundation.

To see this point, compare a mother's abortion decision with another tragic choice she may be obliged to make. Suppose her doctors tell her that unless she undergoes a risky medical procedure, she may confront serious disabilities that will transform the shape of her future. But if she does authorize her doctors to go ahead with this procedure, there is a significant chance that they may be required to amputate one of her arms or legs. As in the case of the fetus, it is up to her—and only her—to make this life-defining decision. If somebody else intervened and stopped the medical procedure to preserve her leg's "right to life," this arrogation of authority would involve the same existential category mistake that antiabortionists make in asserting their right to protect the fetus's "right to life." In both cases, the interventionists seek to deploy the power of the state to strip people of their capacity to control their own bodies in their ongoing struggle to define who "I" am—even if this leads them to sacrifice a part of their bodies in their effort to live a meaningful life in the real world.

Beauvoir took the same existentialist stance when framing the more affirmative side of her feminist agenda. She called for the free provision of contraceptives so that women would not have to invade their own bodies to abort unwanted fetuses. When women did commit to motherhood, she called upon governments to provide nationwide systems of neighborhood community centers where specially trained educators would help raise the infants. This, she argued, was the only realistic way to provide women with the free time they required to pursue meaningful careers in business, politics, community service, or other spheres of special significance.[14]

Beauvoir's book has had an extraordinary long-term impact. It is no exaggeration to say that it is the twentieth-century equivalent of Karl Marx's *Communist Manifesto.* Both Beauvoir and Marx recognized that women and workers were the objects of different modes of socioeconomic domination in different parts of the world—and that liberation strategies that were realistic in one historical context might be utterly utopian in another. Marx would later claim to have discovered historical laws leading to the triumph of the proletariat much later in life—leading him to write *Das Kapital*—but his and Beauvoir's early writings had a more limited, though still fundamental, objective. Each called upon their readers to recognize that if they hoped to secure a meaningful existence for themselves, they had to have the courage to stand up to the powers that be—even at the risk of even graver forms of oppression.

Yet Beauvoir confronted a day-to-day reality that gives her work a dimension that cannot be found anywhere in Marx. After spending thirteen brilliant chapters urging her readers to say no to all forms of biological essentialism, she faces the grim reality that male partners will typically insist on sexual intercourse even when "their women" want to reject their power grabs. On many occasions, this feminist form of bodily removal will provoke physical abuse; even more frequently, the threat of violence will induce profound psychological submission to their male masters. *The Second Sex* responds with a lengthy cry of despair:

> Everything encourages [a woman] to be invested and dominated by foreign existences: and particularly in love, she disavows rather than asserts herself. . . . Men we call great are those who—in one way or another—take the weight of the world on their shoulders; they have done more or less well, they have succeeded in re-creating it or they have failed; but they took on this enormous burden in the first place. This is what no

> woman has ever done, what no woman has ever been able to do. . . . When finally it is possible for every human being to place his pride above sexual differences in the difficult glory of his free existence, only then will woman be able to make her history, her problems, her doubts, and her hopes those of humanity; only then will she be able to attempt to discover in her life and her works all of reality and not only her own person. As long as she still has to fight to become a human being, she cannot be a creator.[15]

If we were to recast this message in Marxist terms, Beauvoir is calling on "Feminists of the World to Unite and Win Revolutionary Victories in Political, Economic, and Social Life – but at the End of the Day, We Will Come Home to Our Husbands and Remain in Chains!"

I do not write these lines to minimize Beauvoir's achievement but to point out the limitations of her critical method. She is absolutely right to emphasize the need to say no to gender domination. Yet this is only a necessary, not a sufficient, condition for self-realization in intimate relationships. Before this can happen, the sexual partners must say yes to one another – and construct modes of credible commitment in which each of them respects *the other's* claim to bodily self-possession as they engage in sexual relations.

Beauvoir, however, refuses to move beyond rejectionism. In her view, Western culture is sexist to its core – and it is utopian to suppose that it provides resources for dissenting individuals to construct meaningful sexual relationships. It is this grim view that leads her to such a despairing conclusion.

Here is where Maurice Merleau-Ponty registers his dissent. While he recognizes the pervasive injustices entrenched in the status quo, he nevertheless believes it is possible to construct authentic relationships of mutual respect in the modern world. His intellectual breakthroughs, moreover, pave the way for my own efforts to reinvigorate existentialism in the twenty-first century.

Maurice Merleau-Ponty

Like Heidegger, Sartre, and Beauvoir, Merleau-Ponty begins by confronting the implications of Einstein's relativity and Heisenberg's uncertainty for modern self-understanding. Given the deconstruction of Newtonian certainties, we can no longer "relate to the things of the world . . . as a pure intellect trying to master an object or space that stands before it." We must instead rely on concrete encounters with our immediate surroundings, since it is the only aspect of existence we can really be certain about. At this point, however, Merleau-Ponty breaks new ground. He insists that the dynamics of mutual recognition play a crucial role in the ongoing effort at self-location: "I never become aware of my own existence until I have already made contact with others."

> Even young infants must learn to distinguish "between goodwill, anger and fear on the face of another person, at a stage when [they] could not have learned the physical signs of these emotions by examining [their] own bod[ies]." From the earliest moments of childhood, they can only understand themselves by engaging with the sounds and gestures offered up by the people surrounding them at home. Once they finally become socially competent grown-ups, each adult "will discover in his own life what his culture, education,

> books and tradition have taught him to find there. . . . The contact I make with myself is always mediated by a particular culture, or at least by a language that we have received from without and which guides us in our self-knowledge. . . . There is no 'inner' life that is not a first attempt to relate to another person."[16]

He elaborates his central thesis by exploring a predicament similar to the ones I asked you to consider at the very beginning of this book. In chapter 1, I presented a series of lunchtime scenarios in which friends struggle to sustain their friendship despite their escalating disagreements. My discussion was inspired by Merleau-Ponty's examination of an analogous case, involving an angry dispute with somebody he calls "Paul":

> When I reflect on my own anger, I do not come across any element that might be separated . . . from my own body. When I recall being angry at Paul, it does not strike me that this anger was in my mind [but] that it lay entirely between me who was doing the shouting and that odious Paul who just sat there calmly and listened with an ironic air.
>
> If Paul is my spouse, for example, the crucial question is whether we can manage to put this terrible incident behind us – and reestablish a relationship based on love and respect rather than anger and irony.[17]

This is the point at which Merleau-Ponty's emphasis on mutual recognition corresponds to my own efforts to understand the modern – and postmodern – predicament. As I have emphasized, we have only 16 or 18 hours each day to reconcile the competing demands of our children, friends, fellow citizens, employers, and other sphere-mates. We can neither expect nor achieve perfect clarity in any of our relationships – and must therefore make ongoing efforts at mutual collaboration if we are to achieve a clearer sense of who we are and what we stand for.

I follow Merleau-Ponty, moreover, in emphasizing that these relationships have been shaped by a legacy of profound injustice. If I am to understand myself, I cannot indulge the utopian supposition that my relationships with sphere-mates are somehow immune from the economic, political, and social domination that surrounds us. I must recognize that my fundamental spherical commitments are "never entirely exempt" from prevailing patterns of exploitation – and that I "can never" wholly liberate myself from the character deformations that distort my struggle to sustain meaningful relationships with my sphere-mates.[18]

Call this the problem of complicity – and here is where Merleau-Ponty makes a decisive break with Beauvoir and Sartre. He believes that his fellow existentialists are themselves engaged in an existential self-contradiction – refusing to confront the fact that their own personal identities are themselves products of the Western "civilization" they are denouncing. If they recognized that their own characters have been distorted from earliest childhood by the concrete patterns of domination prevailing in France during the early twentieth century, they would understand that it is impossible to isolate themselves from complicity with "the West," however brilliant their critiques. They can only gain an insight into their own biases by engaging with others in thoughtful conversation on this very question.

In making this effort, however, we confront a great danger: insularity. Given the pluralistic forms of life made available by modernity, it is easy to live in a social world that is isolated from people with very different convictions, people who pursue radically different forms of self-fulfillment. Only by breaking through these barriers can we hope for insight into the ways our own existence has been distorted by the pervasive forms of oppression that surround us. Yet given the sensitivity of such questions, it is tough to discuss them with strangers. Nevertheless, if we are to make an authentic effort at self-understanding, we must reach beyond our comfort zone and engage in serious conversations with people who are very different from ourselves.

This is especially important for elite intellectuals hoping to frame reform agendas for the coming generation. They can't gain influential positions without mastering the modes of discourse and self-presentation that are dominant within their educational systems. Otherwise, they would never get the outstanding grades and contacts needed to achieve positions of distinction. Yet these promotion systems are themselves rooted in entrenched injustices, making it particularly important for serious intellectuals to gain a sense of the extent to which their reform priorities are the product of an academic training that has cut them off from the real-world experiences of most of their fellow citizens. The only way to respond to this predicament, Merleau-Ponty insists, is to reach out to people from different social and economic backgrounds and take seriously what they have to say.

I very much agree – and it is especially important to listen to the critiques advanced by the relatively few thought leaders who emerge from the most oppressed classes in society. Yet even these remarkable individuals cannot claim to serve as unproblematic spokespersons for the oppressed groups from which they come – precisely because they have managed to overcome the obstacles that stand in the way of their peers. They are not immune from the disease afflicting their elite colleagues. They can never be sure how much their reform agenda is rooted in the life experience of the millions they have left behind and how much is based on their scholarly encounters with academic literatures favored by the university system that permitted them to gain their current high standing. The challenge, Merleau-Ponty tells us, is for all serious intellectuals to recognize their common predicament and search for constructive responses – rather than self-righteously denouncing one another as "sellouts" or "extremists."

This is my ambition in this book and I will make further efforts in the pages that follow. At present, however, it makes sense to focus on a key issue that Merleau-Ponty did not confront – since it became a serious problem only after he died, prematurely, in 1961. At that time, the computer revolution had not yet enabled social scientists to analyze power relationships in ways that rigorously explored the prospects for serious reform in a data-driven fashion. Nevertheless, Merleau-Ponty addressed analogous issues in physics and the other natural sciences, and he explicitly suggested that they also apply to scholarly efforts to treat social science in purely mathematical terms.[19]

His argument proceeds from first principles. Given the repudiation of the Newtonian paradigm by Einstein and Heisenberg, "the scientist of today, unlike his predecessor working within the classical paradigm, no longer cherishes the illusion that he is penetrating to the heart of things, to the object as it is in itself."[20] Instead, their impressive-looking equations are rooted in the special character of the scientists' work environment. When they leave home and arrive at the office, their "here and now" requires them to confront telescopes and microscopes and supercomputers.

As a consequence, they can use this equipment to see things that are invisible to the rest of us – since, when we leave home, we pay attention to very different matters. Indeed, it is precisely for this reason that post-Newtonian science can greatly enrich the multidimensional character of human understanding. Whenever I glance skyward, I am reminded that I am an inhabitant of a small planet in a vast universe – and that this relationship is becoming of increasing practical, as well as theoretical, importance. As a consequence, it would be foolish to suppose that the rise of relativity and uncertainty should lead astrophysicists to despair at the significance of their scientific enterprise.

To the contrary, it only makes it more important. During the Newtonian era, they supposed that their work with telescopes would only allow them to elaborate mathematical refinements of the eternal laws of motion. But now that they know that such laws *cannot* exist, it is only by building better telescopes, and analyzing their data more rigorously, that astrophysicists can hope to clarify our present uncertainties. Indeed, given the inevitability of indeterminacy, serious scientists "hope and expect that future generations will have better equipment which will reveal that their current equations require significant – and sometimes revolutionary – revision."[21]

This point is even more important in the twenty-first century, when social scientists have joined physical scientists in providing rigorous data-based answers to a host of important questions. To be sure, their problems don't involve the spatiotemporal organization of the universe but the struggle by the mass of humanity to define meaningful lives for themselves in the postmodern world of the twenty-first century. Nevertheless, these computerized forms of social science provide new sources of insight into the possibility of decisive reform of entrenched power structures that condemn billions to conditions of existential injustice. At the same time, however, they also permit entrenched power elites to seize control over the dominant computer networks in ways that systematically disrupt popular movements for real-world equality. To quote Merleau-Ponty once again, I will call on you to confront the rise of technocratic power in the postmodern age with "a special kind of courage."[22]

> We should no longer pride ourselves in being a community of pure spirits; let us look instead at the real relationships between people in our societies. For the most part, these are master-slave relationships. We should not find excuses for ourselves in our good intentions; let us see what becomes of these once they have escaped from inside us. There is something healthy about this unfamiliar gaze we are suggesting should be brought to bear on our species.[23]

This hope motivates the next chapter's effort to provide an "unfamiliar gaze" on the long and winding historical path that, after many centuries, is forcing us to confront the unprecedented predicaments of postmodernity.

Chapter 9

WHERE AM I?

The first decisive breakthrough to modernity was the invention of the printing press.[1] Before Gutenberg, many European monarchs lacked the education to read the classical writings that defined their civilization. Only a tiny corps of clerics and jurists could directly confront the handwritten texts memorializing the ancient words of the Bible or Roman law and write their own handwritten commentaries, enabling their learned successors to ponder and debate the words of Aquinas as well as the apostles. Yet these controversies remained utterly mysterious to everybody else who was living on the Continent.

When Catholics went to church on Sunday during the Middle Ages, priests recited the words of Holy Scripture in a version of church Latin inherited from the seventh century, which their congregations could not understand. Christians expressed their faith through deeds, not words – kneeling and rising as the ritual proceeded to its climax with the priestly offer of the holy sacrament, representing the body and blood of Christ. By drinking the wine and eating the wafer, believers were affirming their oneness with their Savior. Their wordless but expressive engagement with the priest served as the foundation of their religious self-understanding.

As a historical matter, the church's conduct of its religious rituals varied greatly over the centuries. For our purposes, however, only one point is crucial—the link between the wordless but expressive character of religious ritual and the larger social order in which these rituals were embedded. Although Catholics couldn't understand church-Latin, it did not cause them any problem in conducting everyday life in their tightly knit communities. Within their premodern framework, the crucial question was whether your behavior conformed to entrenched communal expectations. Only by failing to act appropriately in your dealings with your lifelong neighbors could you endanger your standing as a competent human being. When these premodern individuals came to church and bowed before the priest when accepting the Holy Sacrament, their priests were building on the action-centered approach to self-understanding the parishioners exhibited when dealing with their neighbors during the rest of the week.

It was only Gutenberg's breakthrough in the 1450s that enabled Martin Luther to gain massive support for his revolution against the papacy during the following century. This thesis may seem counterintuitive. Despite the printing press, the mass of humanity remained immersed in their premodern communities when Luther took his stand against the papacy in 1517—and yet millions responded enthusiastically to his call for a Protestant Reformation. How could the printing press play such an essential role in mobilizing a massively illiterate population to repudiate their Catholic identities?

My answer requires me to boil down Luther's Ninety-Five Theses—his revolutionary pronunciamento of 1517—into two key arguments. The first involved a critique of traditional forms of meaning-making. In Luther's view, Catholics were making a big mistake in thinking they could save their souls on Judgment Day by bowing down before their priests in the traditional manner. His second claim concerned what they should do instead. Rather than *behaving* in the right way, serious Christians could commit themselves to Jesus only by *reading* the words of the Bible – gaining inspiration from its account of the transformative significance of Jesus's life and death for humanity in general and each believer in particular.

Here is where Gutenberg enters the story. Luther had only a small band of followers when he made his revolutionary call for action in the town of Wittenberg in 1517. By that point, printing presses had been churning out publications on a host of issues for more than 60 years, and European elites were already beginning to educate themselves – and their children – to gain sufficient literacy to comprehend this flood of novel texts. As a consequence, Luther's early followers were able to print and reprint his Ninety-Five Theses in campaigns to mobilize potentially sympathetic elites – and persuade them to lead their uneducated followers to challenge papal authority.

Yet their successes presented Luther and his fellow theologians with an urgent challenge. Before newly established congregations could fulfil their Protestant vision, it was essential to translate the Old and New Testaments into the living languages of sixteenth-century Europe. This was no simple matter. Translation from one language to another invariably requires a host of judgment calls. The Scriptures were written in ancient Greek, Hebrew, and Latin, and there was no serious historical scholarship exploring the special difficulties involved in their interpretation. Worse yet, when comparing different manuscripts, Protestant theologians found that the Catholic Bible included large sections that did not appear in the manuscripts they considered most significant. They agreed that these "apocryphal" texts lacked the authoritative character of divine revelation. Nevertheless, they found it hard to reach a consensus on which portions of the Catholic text should be deemed apocryphal. This issue provoked particularly intense disputes between Luther and John Calvin, whose theological followers identified problematic texts in very different ways.

There was a compelling need, however, to bring these debates to a rapid conclusion. The whole point of the Protestant movement was to call on Christians to repudiate the pope and find their own way to salvation by taking inspiration from their personal encounter with the Holy Scriptures. Doing so was impossible until theologians could provide believers with "authoritative" translations. If they failed to meet the spiritual needs of their followers, the entire movement could readily collapse.

Many previous efforts to reinvigorate the Christian spirit over the centuries had met this fate, with different leaders urging their followers down very different paths to redemption. Gutenberg, however, provided the Protestant leadership with a new way out of their predicament. Rival theologians could simply give up on their search for consensus and order their printing presses to churn out huge numbers of competing versions of the Bible, together with an endless series of tracts explaining why their "authorized version" was superior to those published by rival sects.

The printing press radically transformed the terms on which Lutherans and Calvinists struggled for real-world ascendancy of the Protestant movement. For hundreds of years, parishioners had gone to church on Sunday to hear their priests recite the Holy Truth in seventh-century Latin, which was entirely incomprehensible to them. Suddenly they were confronted by competing Calvinist and Lutheran ministers reading out different versions of the Bible. Because few parishioners had sufficient education to read and reflect upon the Holy Book, they had no choice but to resolve this question based on their response to the charismatic appeals of rival ministers who managed to gain access to their tightly knit communities.

The result was a century of warfare. Despite the dedication and sincerity of Luther and Calvin and their successors, rival Protestant ministers had to rely on rival monarchs to provide the military force required to move through the countryside safely and convince the laity that their particular Bible marked the way to salvation. Meanwhile, Catholic regimes tried to crush both movements and restore the papacy to its rightful place at the center of Western civilization. Not until 1648 and the Treaty of Westphalia was a fragile peace established between warring monarchs upholding different versions of Christianity.[2]

The same bloody scenes took place in the British Isles, with Oliver Cromwell denouncing King Charles I and ultimately beheading him for his papist beliefs. When Cromwell's army entered the battlefield, each soldier carried a printed copy of the Puritan Bible in his pocket. It was only in 1711 – 20 years after the Cromwellian republic was itself overthrown – that the Anglican Church managed to transform its King James Version of the Bible into the kingdom's "authorized" text.[3]

When Gutenberg's printing press appeared on the Continent in the 1450s, nobody suspected that it would, by the 1530s, propel the Christian world into a century of bloody warfare. Yet this is precisely why I have made this seeming detour into the distant past.

The next chapter will argue that the internet revolution threatens the postmodern world with an unanticipated disaster of Gutenberg-like dimensions – but of a very different kind.

Before rushing forward to the present, however, I think the Gutenberg story has more to teach. For starters, it is important to distinguish my thesis from the famous paradigm advanced by Max Weber in *The Protestant Ethic and the Spirit of Capitalism.* He too argued that centuries of religious controversy had paradoxical consequences for serious Protestants. Even as they gained spiritual inspiration from their own version of the Bible, they could not help but recognize that many other committed Protestants were reading very different versions of the Holy Truth, and this realization made them all anxious about the particular path to salvation they had chosen. According to Weber, these pervasive doubts led committed Protestants to search for further evidence that Jesus would intervene on their behalf on Judgment Day, inviting them to look on their economic success in the marketplace as divine affirmation that they were indeed seeking inspiration from the right Bible, generating Weber's famous paradox: Protestant preoccupation with heavenly salvation drove them to emphasize the overriding importance of worldly success.

I find Weber's account of this counterintuitive dynamic entirely convincing – which is why I want to distinguish it from my own. Weber is dealing with the *consequences* of Protestant anxiety emerging from intense sectarian struggle. In contrast, I am trying to explain why Protestants were so anxious in the first place. Here, the causal arrow goes in the opposite direction: Gutenberg's triumph in the *marketplace* was a precondition for Luther's *theological* success in convincing countless Catholics to turn their backs on the pope and seek salvation in the "authorized" Bible designated by their particular sect. If I were writing a book in defense of my thesis, I'd call it *The Printing Press and the Spirit of Protestantism.*

But I'm writing only a chapter. So let me explain why Gutenberg's technological triumph permits a new perspective on my larger story.

The Premodern Predicament

The modernist revolution took place during the nineteenth century, hundreds of years after the Gutenberg revolution. To recall only a few crucial breakthroughs: the separation of home from work; the need to deal respectfully with strangers; the demand for the dignity of labor and the rights of consumers; the rise of democratic citizenship and the secret ballot.

During all this time, the spirit of Gutenberg continued to dominate the communications network. By then, of course, competing theologians shared the system with a host of new protagonists—profit-maximizing capitalists facing off against government bureaucrats and labor union organizers; professional educators confronting perplexed students and anxious parents with demanding textbooks; political parties and charismatic politicians appealing to mobilized voters. Beyond these spherical struggles, printing presses were flooding the public with newspapers and books in response to the enormous range of questions raised by the rise of modernity.

The printed word did not confront big challenges until Alexander Graham Bell's invention of the telephone in the 1880s, which was followed by the rise of the movies, radio, and television in the twentieth century.[4] I will be arguing, however, that this series of media revolutions did not have the impact of Gutenberg's breakthrough in the 1450s. In contrast, I believe that the internet revolution of our own century is indeed transforming modern self-understanding in a fashion comparable to the ways the printing press shattered premodern forms of existence. It is precisely for this reason that the Gutenberg-inspired Protestant revolution serves as my baseline for the assessment of contemporary developments.

These two claims – that the twentieth-century media revolution was not comparable to the Gutenberg revolution but that the twenty-first-century internet revolution is – will prepare the way for my efforts, in the rest of this book, to reflect on the broader implications of this radical transformation of postmodern existence.

A Limited Revolution

When Luther took his stand in Wittenberg, the vast majority of Europeans were peasants who spent their entire lives in the face-to-face communities where they were born. Their outraged neighbors would respond harshly if they persistently refused to conform to deeply entrenched patterns of "normal" behavior. The only place they could not rely on their "commonsense" was in church, where they could not understand what their priests were saying when they recited Holy Scripture. This gave Luther a unique opportunity to evade the repressive response that generally greeted any radical revolutionary launching a self-conscious challenge to the status quo. Although Catholic ritual was a time-honored element in community life, the entire point of Christianity was to invite believers to transcend everyday reality – and realize a higher form of religious identity. Indeed, the very fact that their priests were reciting the Scriptures in unintelligible Latin only emphasized the otherworldly character of their church experience.

This suggests that my description of the "tightly knit community" requires an important modification. In premodern Europe, the church had already carved out religious life as a *separate sphere,* as I have been using the term, giving the rituals practiced by the Catholic priests a special kind of fragility. Although systematic defiance of everyday community practices immediately transformed the transgressor into a deviant, this did not happen with Luther's challenge – the Latin mass already emphasized the compelling need for Christians to transcend their everyday existence in pursuit of their religious identity. Instead, Luther was calling upon villagers to substitute his "authorized" version of the Holy Bible for the Catholic ritual.

To be sure, illiterate peasants were unable to read the text of Protestant Bibles, but at the very least, they could understand what their ministers were saying when they read the holy words aloud during the service. In engaging in this breakthrough form of meaning-making, moreover, parishioners did *not* believe that they were repudiating the entrenched patterns of their daily life. Instead, with the help of their Protestant ministers, they were reinvigorating the divine foundations of their collective existence.

Luther issued his first challenge in 1517, almost 300 years before the dawn of the nineteenth century. During those three centuries, the principal threat to Protestant rural communities was military conquest by a monarch who was a Catholic or who supported a different Protestant sect. Following a successful invasion, members of tightly knit communities would arrive at church to hear Protestant ministers give them a different "authorized version" of Divine Truth or witness the return of Catholic priests to preside over their rituals in ancient Latin. Even when the papacy reemerged on the local scene, it was hard for residents to forget that they had been obliged to forsake their more comprehensible version of revelation through brute force.

It follows, then, that during Gutenberg's first great era of media supremacy, the printing press did not set the stage for a sweeping challenge to the premises of premodern life. Although the Protestants' bookish revolution provoked centuries of violent conflict, it was limited to a single sphere and did not alter basic patterns of lived experience. The techno-revolutions that began with Bell's telephone, by contrast, did have a significant impact. Yet they were not the principal engines of modernization during the twentieth century. It is only the rise of the internet over the last three decades that has generated such a shattering existential challenge.

The End of the Gutenberg Era

Alexander Graham Bell's invention of the telephone in the 1880s dramatically expanded communicative possibilities in two ways. For the first time, it permitted its users to ignore their physical surroundings and hear a human voice speak to them from somewhere else. The printing press had also enabled readers to make communicative contact at a distance, but in a less interactive fashion. They could only guess how an author's stylistic presentations corresponded to his or her face-to-face engagements in "real life." Although a writer's essay might contain impassioned appeals for justice, a phone conversation with him might lead you to conclude that his prosy protestations were bogus – and that he was merely an opportunist trying to draw attention to himself: "He's just an egomaniac!," you tell yourself as you bang down your phone. Of course, your interlocutor may have come away from the conversation with a very different view—and congratulate himself on his persuasive skills.

It takes talent to manage initial phone conversations with strangers, and breakdowns are common. As we have seen, encounters with strangers serve as a central challenge of modern life, and one that we frequently fail to meet. As always, however, I am not trying to provide personal advice on how to succeed. I am arguing that the telephone marked a breakthrough in the very character of human existence. After a century of revolutionary transformation in other social spheres, Bell enabled the increasingly literate populations of the world to transcend their physical surroundings in a new way—not only by casting their eyes on printed pages but by hearing the voices of particular people.

Each form of "distancing," as I will call it, provides a different insight. Even if you believe an author is an egomaniac, you may find his or her essay well-argued. The crucial point is that for the first time in history, Alexander Graham Bell enabled humanity to engage in personal, as well as intellectual, relationships with people they had never met—and experience their reactions in the "here and now."

The telephone also made a decisive breakthrough on a second front—one that permitted conversationalists to enrich their intellectual development in a distinctive fashion. Readers often encounter passages they find ambiguous or confusing. If they could, many would seize the opportunity to talk directly with the author to try to resolve their confusion. But until the telephone, this simply wasn't possible on a long-distance basis. You would have to send a letter and wait for a reply. If you received a response, it might fail to resolve your initial questions in a way you found convincing—and often generate new lines of inquiry as well. As a consequence, you faced the prospect of a time-consuming exchange of words on paper, assuming your interlocutor responded to your questions thoughtfully.

The telephone, however, made it possible for you to make more progress in 30 minutes than you might achieve after months or years of paper exchanges. Over the phone, you and your interlocutor could *immediately* respond to one another's puzzlements and explore different ways of resolving them. This often happens even when the two sides continue to disagree on important matters at the end of their phone call. At the very least, they will have clarified lots of ambiguities in ways that permit them to continue their next phone call in an insightful fashion. Before Alexander Graham Bell arrived on the scene, however, they could have spent six months in a lengthy exchange exploring disagreements they could have resolved in the first few minutes of their first phone call.

Such ground-clearing efforts do not, of course, eliminate continuing misunderstandings. My point is that these telephonic exchanges occur against the background of countless analogous efforts in the face-to-face world—where we are endlessly trying to resolve spherical coordination problems through brief efforts at conversational clarification. After asking, "Are you working overtime tonight?" and hearing my answer, my kids might well respond: "Since you're getting home after dinner, please don't bother us when you arrive because we have lots of homework!"

Just like face-to-face encounters, telephonic engagements with distant voices may lead to rapid clarifications or rapid breakdowns. The crucial point is that during the Gutenberg era, they would never have occurred at all. In short, the telephone made it possible to engage distant voices in the same spontaneous fashion that had been the exclusive domain of face-to-face relationships.

This conclusion permits me to redeem a promise I made at the end of my last chapter's encounter with Heidegger, Sartre, Beauvoir, and Merleau-Ponty. Whatever their standing in twenty-first-century debates, their central concerns were already being vindicated by Bell in the late nineteenth century. Recall that their crucial starting point was Heisenberg's insistence that the dramatic breakdown of the Newtonian paradigm was important not only to physicists but to every thinking person – because their relationships to their own bodies had been radically undermined by the uncertainty principle. So far as these existentialists were concerned, it followed that "I" could hope to fill this sudden scientific vacuum only by understanding the importance of my immediate awareness of my body's relationship to the "here and now."

My twofold analysis of the telephone follows the existentialists' phenomenological path. To translate their mega-concerns into my media analysis, begin with my first – personalist – point: by the simple act of dialing a telephone number, I start talking to a far-off person as if they were sitting next to me in the "*here* and now." My second point moves from the locational to the temporal aspect of telephone talk. Once that person answers the phone, I start talking to my counterpart as if he or she were present in the "here-and-*now*" – engaging in the same spontaneous give-and-take that occurs in a face-to-face conversation.

For the first time in history, human beings had the power to engage in distant relationships on the same terms as the ones they took for granted in real-world encounters. This single machine invited them to give a new answer to a fundamental existential question: *where* am I?

I am *here* in my living room. But at the very same moment, I am also *there* with my distant counterpart – talking to them in the usual manner. I am living in two worlds at once!

It is easy to underestimate the power of this exclamation point. In the twenty-first century, we take it for granted that we can endlessly shift our attention from face-to-face encounters to distant relationships on the internet. But the telephone's invention was celebrated at the time as a great moment of liberation – vastly enriching the cultural resources available to each modern man and woman as they challenged deeply entrenched traditions and searched beyond their immediate surroundings in their ongoing struggle to define their own meaning-in-life. The Bell Telephone Company, moreover, was remarkably successful in responding to worldwide demand for personal liberation, propelling itself into a commanding global position in telecommunications.

Yet from our twenty-first-century perspective, this breakthrough had obvious limitations. When somebody picked up Bell's telephone, they could only hear their partner's voice; they could not see the bodily and facial expressions that modified the meaning of words, as in face-to-face engagements. The telephone offered only a one-dimensional proxy for the everyday encounters of physical existence.

The next great breakthrough occurred in the 1910s with the rise of the motion picture industry. The industry began with one-dimensional "silent movies." A crucial turning point came when audiences could hear, as well as see, performers confront the predicaments of real-world existence. Once again, this breakthrough into *multidimensionality* enabled Hollywood and its worldwide competitors to transform viewers' relationship to virtual reality by presenting it as a more fully realized version of physical reality. From this perspective, the rise of television consolidated this breakthrough.

Rather than going out to the movies, you could come home and watch TV along with your most intimate partners.

Still, the spirit of Alexander Graham Bell called these later achievements into question. When you sat in front of the TV screen, you could witness the distant goings-on only as a spectator. If you didn't like a particular broadcast, the most you could do was change the channel or shut off the TV and complain to your family about wasting time on such a lousy show. But when you talked on the telephone, it was up to you and your counterpart to make good use of the time you spent together. If you ended up shouting at one another, you had only yourselves to blame. The telephone remained the *only* machine that allowed you to take an active role in your engagements with virtual reality. By the end of the twentieth century, virtual reality had assumed a distinctive shape: one-dimensional but active engagement on the telephone, multidimensional but passive engagement with the television/movie screen.

This active/passive stance might have seemed bizarre if it were viewed by a visitor from a far-off planet. But over the preceding century it had become a deeply entrenched pattern of modern existence. Indeed, it helps account for the rapid worldwide response to the internet revolution. Without Bell's telephone and Hollywood's movies, it might have been an overwhelming challenge suddenly to engage with distant friends – and complete strangers – as if they were right beside us in the "here and now." Instead, humanity has staggered into the twenty-first century, managing to engage in its unprecedented struggle to live two lives at the same time without utterly collapsing.

Chapter 10

RECONSTRUCTING EXISTENTIALISM

Does the earth move around the sun?

When Isaac Newton demonstrated why Galileo was right and the Bible was wrong, his mathematical equations required more than a wrenching reexamination of Christian faith. They also shaped the course of Enlightenment thought. Despite their profound disagreements on many subjects, the leading Enlightenment thinkers shared a common premise: there was a scientifically objective way to determine the precise location of every physical object in the universe at any given moment. Including the human body: a Newtonian scientist could calculate, with mathematical precision, exactly where I stood on earth at every single instant. If I refused to believe him, it was a sign that I was irrational, not that the scientist made a mistake.

Immanuel Kant's reflections on the human condition can serve as a paradigm. Newton had explained how "things in themselves" exist in space and time, and Kant didn't try to compete with him. Instead, he began with a basic fact of human existence: when I wake up in the morning, I am immediately aware of the Newtonian world surrounding me. As a consequence, if I hope to understand myself as a rational being, I must search for an explanation of the very possibility of my Newtonian form of self-awareness. This is precisely the ambition of the *Critiques of Pure* and *Practical Reason,* which led Kant to his famous categorical imperative: "Act so that the maxim of your action can be willed into a universal law." On this view, whenever I allow my emotions to propel me to act in an egocentric way, I am betraying my status as a rational being.

Kant failed to persuade many of his successors to accept his Imperative, but leading critics like Hegel and Marx also constructed their understandings of the modern predicament within a Newtonian framework.[1]

Until the dawn of the twentieth century—when Heisenberg's uncertainty principle and Einstein's theory of relativity destroyed the very premises of Newtonian certainty. At that moment, the problem of self-location in space/time not only became a central preoccupation of existentialist philosophy, it also served to provoke novelists like James Joyce and Marcel Proust to portray the way in which Uncertainty required their readers to reorient themselves radically in space and time if they hoped to make sense of their lives. The same was true of the representations of space/time in the cubist paintings of Braque and Picasso or the sculptures of Brancusi and Nevelson, the atonal music of Hindemith and Schoenberg, and the modernist poetry of Eliot and Pound—to name only a few of the great efforts to fill the Newtonian vacuum with revolutionary re-visions of humanity's effort to live a meaningful life in a radically uncertain world.[2]

What is more, these achievements continue to shape the artistic horizons of the twenty-first century. The current generation is moving beyond its predecessors in their efforts to confront postmodern predicaments. Nevertheless, it fully recognizes the decisive breakthroughs of their predecessors as they try to move beyond them.

There is, however, one great exception to this rule. The ongoing debate over the requirements of social justice – and the struggle to achieve it – fails to take seriously the existentialist debates of the past. To be sure, Simone de Beauvoir's work is recognized by leading feminist thinkers. Yet almost nobody reads Heisenberg, Heidegger, Sartre, or Merleau-Ponty any more – or any of the other major participants in this great debate. The decline and fall of existentialist thought began in the 1960s, with the rise of a new generation coming to maturity in a world in which the war against Hitler and the Holocaust was starting to fade into the background of lived experience.

I will be paying special attention to the work of two philosophers who played central roles in this paradigm shift in the ongoing debate over social justice: Jürgen Habermas and John Rawls. Rather than lose myself in the complexities of their elaborate constructions, I will focus on key features of their thought that blinded them to crucial existentialist insights.

Jürgen Habermas

Habermas's organizing framework is basically compatible with the terms developed in this book. He recognizes that modern men and women live multi-spherical lives – engaging in different modes of mutual recognition as they spend time with friends and family, fellow citizens and workers, consumers and entrepreneurs, and many other sphere-mates. To make things more complex, the social skills required to fulfil these disparate role expectations differ dramatically from culture to culture around the world. Nevertheless, the mass of humanity shares a common fate, regardless of where people live.

They are victims of systematic oppression. They confront employers, spouses, or other sphere-mates who use their power to transform them into mere playthings for their own gratification. Yet they were born into social positions that deprive them of the economic and cultural resources required to resist these power-plays. They have no choice but to accept their fate – or spend the rest of their lives in prison.

Habermas was right to insist that the pervasive reality of social domination raises a fundamental question of existential justice. Given the oppressive power structures prevailing in the late twentieth century, billions of people were denied a realistic opportunity to liberate themselves from entrenched injustices and search for new spherical partners with whom they might construct more meaningful lives.

Even when they manage to liberate themselves from entrenched oppression, this will hardly guarantee that their search will prove successful. The struggle for new and fulfilling work opportunities, or loving family relationships, may only lead to heart-wrenching breakdowns. When this happens, however, postmodern people will view themselves in a very different way than if they never had a chance to liberate themselves from pervasive conditions of social domination. They will recognize that they themselves are responsible, in significant part, for the successes and failures in their search for a meaningful existence. This form of self-understanding is a necessary condition for "human dignity," as Habermas came to call it.[3]

I agree. I part company, however, at the next stage of his argument, where he provides a framework within which democratic citizens should conduct a debate over the nature of the real-world resources and fundamental rights required before their fellow human beings have a fair chance to live dignified lives.

Habermas invites us to confront this issue from the vantage point of an "ideal speech situation." He asks each of us to search for common ground by transcending the particular preoccupations of our individual lives and consider a more abstract question: why should we think that human beings have a claim to "dignity" in the first place? On his view, it is only when we come to understand the philosophical foundations of the principle of human dignity that we can thoughtfully determine how much, and what kind, of socio-economic opportunities are necessary for a dignified life.

Habermas's next move makes a good deal of sense – provided his readers accept the decisive importance of his "ideal speech" thought experiment (as I do not). Since its beginnings in Greece and Rome, the Western philosophical tradition has long debated whether and why human beings have superior claims to dignity over other flesh-and-blood creatures that inhabit the earth. If the "ideal speech situation" is the right pathway to real-world legitimacy, it makes perfect sense for all of us to take advantage of the insights of Plato, Aristotle, and their successors in defining our present-day obligations to the billions of our fellow human beings who currently confront overwhelming forms of stigmatization and domination.

What is more, Habermas would be fully justified in offering to help his readers fulfil the "ideal" responsibilities he has imposed upon them. After all, he has devoted his entire life to the study of the Western philosophical tradition's complex debate over the foundations of human dignity. Doesn't it make sense for readers to use his books for guidance as they engage in his thought experiment to define their obligations in the struggle for social justice?

My answer is no—and not only because Habermas and I emphasize very different aspects of the Western tradition. I reject the very idea that citizens should embrace his thought experiment.

To see why, let's assume that I'm wrong and Habermas is right. The hard conclusion is that the only human beings who can take their ideal responsibilities seriously are philosophy professors like Habermas and myself. Almost everybody else will be working at jobs that require them to focus on very different matters—in addition to spending lots of time dealing with the demands of family, friends, and other sphere-mates. To be sure, tens of thousands of people may well take Habermas's challenge seriously and devote the hours and hours necessary to read his books to understand why he thinks an ascent to the "ideal speech situation" is a prerequisite for responsible real-world decision-making. Over the course of a year or two, they may even read a few books by great thinkers of the past whom Habermas has singled out for special attention. But even these people shouldn't suppose they have the time or training to master enough of Hegel or Plato to engage with Habermas on equal terms.

In short, Habermas's appeal to his "ideal speech situation" implicates him in a performative contradiction. Although he considers mutually respectful dialogue supremely important, his extraordinary erudition makes it impossible for even the most thoughtful citizens to deal with his arguments in a serious fashion. In claiming that they have an overriding obligation to enter his "ideal speech situation" to define their civic responsibilities, Habermas is both affirming and denying the crucial role of dignity *at the very same time.*[4] His performative contradiction has even more tragic implications for the billions of stigmatized and oppressed people on this planet. Since they have been deprived of the education required to read any of the great philosophers, they are excluded from the very speech situation that Habermas asserts is necessary for their liberation from bondage.

I have been confronting the problem of existential justice in a different spirit. Part 1 of this book asked readers to consider the implications of the high-tech revolution without seriously engaging with any of the great thinkers of the past. Although I have been arguing with lots of big thinkers in the last two chapters, I have done so only to isolate modes of togetherness and apartness that would otherwise have escaped my attention. At no point have I asked readers to use these philosophical encounters with the existentialist tradition to propel themselves into an "ideal speech situation" in which Ackerman would serve as their guide. If you, as a reader, are unpersuaded by my diagnosis of the postmodern predicament, you should look elsewhere for insight into the dilemmas of the twenty-first century – making a special effort to listen to the most serious victims of oppression. While they lack the formal education required to pick up my book, their tragic life experiences will enrich your understanding of the profound existential implications of postmodernity. And your efforts to reach out to them may also provide new energy for mobilized efforts at radical reform of the oppressive status quo.

Nevertheless, it is important for me to recognize that, whether I like it or not, advocates for "ideal speech" increasingly dominated European debate in the late twentieth century. Not only did Habermas and his followers gain scholarly ascendancy in many universities, their transcendental appeals to "human dignity" increasingly shaped the priorities of real-world campaigns for social justice.

It is a mistake, then, to attribute the decline and fall of existentialism to the rise of "neoliberalism" over the last generation. It was the preceding era of progressive reform, culminating in the fall of the Berlin Wall, which consigned existentialist insights to the periphery of scholarly and political concern.

The next generation's reformers should not repeat this mistake. What is more, there are encouraging signs of a revival of the existentialist tradition—both in the academy and in writings directed to a larger audience.[5] Without a fundamental reassessment, serious reformers will systematically mislead themselves in their struggle to achieve existential justice for the billions left behind by the techno-revolutions of the twenty-first century.

John Rawls

During the same period that Habermas was challenging the existentialist tradition on the Continent, John Rawls was questioning the reigning paradigm for radical reform in the English-speaking world. But he was operating within a different philosophical tradition from the one prevailing in Europe. Since the nineteenth century, utilitarianism had been at the center of the great debate over social justice in the Anglosphere—with Jeremy Bentham and John Stuart Mill taking very different positions on the nature of pain and pleasure and how to measure it.[6] In the twentieth century, these arguments took an increasingly technocratic turn. The rise of the computer encouraged scholars and policymakers to focus increasing time and energy on the statistical aspects of cost-benefit analysis, while ignoring the problematic premises of the entire utilitarian approach.

Here is where John Rawls made his fundamental contribution. Like Habermas, Rawls did not base his critique by focusing on the concrete ways in which technocratic "cost-benefit" analysis trivialized the exploitation of billions of people around the world. He too urged his readers to view the problem of social justice from a transcendent perspective.

Compared to Habermas's model, Rawls's version of the "original position" seems relatively manageable. Rather than reasoning together in an "ideal speech situation," he urges us to put ourselves behind a "veil of ignorance" that makes it impossible to know in advance how we have resolved our real-world problems of self-definition. Once we place ourselves behind the Rawlsian veil, we don't know what our life circumstances will be or what role we will play in society. The only thing we can know is that we are moral agents who are capable of making sense of our lives by adopting one or another "ideal of the good." Our challenge is to join with our fellow citizens, who are also behind the veil of ignorance, and negotiate a social contract defining the principles of social justice that will maximize our chances of fulfilling our ideals – regardless of what they turn out to be.

Rawls tries to persuade us that once we engage in his thought experiment, everybody will reject the utilitarian effort to maximize the welfare of society as a whole. We will focus instead on the fate of our fellow citizens who, once they lift the veil, find themselves among the most impoverished and humiliated members of society. So long as we remain behind the veil of ignorance, all of us have an equal chance of ending up as members of this oppressed class. As a consequence, we will unanimously agree that social justice requires a distribution of resources that will maximize the position of the worst-off – even if these measures significantly diminish the prospects of the better-off.

Rawls calls this the "maximin principle." Before turning to his arguments on its behalf, it is important to see how his contractual approach permits him to escape the performative self-contradiction that undermined Habermas's efforts. Rawls imagines that citizens are *bargaining* with one another in the "original position"—not *reasoning* with one another in an "ideal speech situation." Moreover, his readers already engage in real-world bargaining when operating as consumers in the marketplace. To get them to address the question of social justice from his "original position," he need only persuade them to engage in a familiar activity under different—albeit hypothetical—conditions. He can then move to the second stage of his argument and try to convince them that self-interested bargaining behind the veil of ignorance will lead them to endorse the maximin principle in their social contract.

It's unnecessary for me to consider whether Rawls succeeds in making his case for "maximin"—since I reject the premises of his argument. To be sure, his appeal to self-interested bargaining enables him to engage in a thought experiment that is far more accessible to readers than the "ideal speech situation" offered by Habermas.

But accessibility comes at too high a price. Like Habermas, I believe that we should be struggling to reason with one another, not bargain with one another, when facing the overwhelming reality of social injustice in the twenty-first century. But the wrong way to do this is by engaging in thought experiments. The right way is to spend time and energy in the construction of real-world forms of dialogic engagement that will reinvigorate the democratic struggle against massive subordination and alienation in the "here and now."

An Existentialist Critique

Although the Continental debate between Habermas and leading existentialists profoundly shaped my thinking, it did not occupy an important place in the arguments advanced by *Social Justice in the Liberal State,* the book marking my entry into the debate in 1980. As a newcomer to the discussion, I focused my critique on Rawls's vision of a social contract – which had, with remarkable speed, become a serious challenge to deeply entrenched forms of utilitarian cost-benefit analysis in the English-speaking world.

My existential critique of Rawls in this chapter, however, should not conceal the important ways in which my earlier book joined him in opposing utilitarian orthodoxy. Most obviously, we both emphasized dimensions of human dignity that were trivialized by the utilitarian's exclusive concern with the minimization of pain and the maximization of pleasure. To put it in Rawlsian terms, his *Theory of Justice* imagined contractors defining their principles of justice in terms of an index of "primary social goods" – which measured the extent to which different groups in their real-world society had access to the resources needed to preserve their "self-respect." This idea of self-respect roughly corresponded to my insistence in *Social Justice* that members of oppressed groups cannot legitimately be transformed into mere playthings of the powerful – and that all must be guaranteed sufficient resources to accept personal responsibility in their ongoing struggle to construct a meaningful life for themselves.

Yet there was another, less obvious way in which *Social Justice* was deeply influenced by Rawls's work. In designing the original position, Rawls had created a distinctive problem for himself. It was one thing for his veil of ignorance to make it impossible for contractors to know anything about their future life situations. It was quite another that the veil also concealed the socioeconomic power structures they would confront once the veil was lifted. Suppose, for example, they found they would be living in the low-tech 1850s or the high-tech 2050s. Shouldn't that affect their priorities when negotiating their social contract?

Rawls responded to this question by complicating the original position. At the first stage of their deliberations, participants would make their most fundamental decisions under a very thick veil of ignorance. At this point, they would know only that they were negotiating a social contract for a "well-ordered society" in which their fundamental principles would control the distribution of scarce resources. Then, negotiations would move on to a second stage, conducted under a thinner veil of ignorance. At this point, contractors were permitted to know enough about their particular society to reach agreement on constitutional arrangements that will realize their vision of a "well-ordered society" in the particular country they will actually inhabit. Rawls then develops his multi-stage scenario further, but I have already said enough to suggest its influence on my own work.

Even though I rejected his rejection of existentialism, I engaged in a Rawls-style thought experiment to vindicate my existentialist approach to justice. My own version of the "original position" differed dramatically from Rawls's. It asked readers to throw away their veil of ignorance and suppose that they knew *everything* required to transform their vision of a "well ordered society" into real-world operation.

When viewed from a strictly existentialist perspective, this know-it-all assumption is profoundly problematic. The real-world struggle for justice requires more than a confrontation with entrenched power elites who are grimly determined to defend the status quo. Even when egalitarian reformers gain the upper hand, they face a host of uncertainties in constructing institutional arrangements that will prevent new elites from devising new forms of oppression in the future. If they succeed in devising enduring structural reforms, it will greatly assist the next generation of progressives as they continue the struggle for social justice. But it will be these real-world successes and failures, not solutions to hypothetical thought experiments, that will be of crucial significance to their successors' efforts to reconstruct their societies on more legitimate foundations.

There have been occasions when egalitarian movements have issued grand statements of principle, for example, the *Declaration of the Rights of Man and Citizen,* that have inspired egalitarian movements for generations. Yet, to put it mildly, *Social Justice in the Liberal State* did not pretend to be such a pronunciamento. It was a call to thinkers and doers to face up to the real-world challenges posed by the dramatic social, economic, and technological transformations of the late twentieth century and to formulate reform strategies that respond seriously to the era's distinctive predicaments.

Despite these ambitions, *Social Justice* followed Rawls's example in constructing an "original position" for defining its existentialist approach. Although my thought experiment was based on principles that were diametrically opposed to Rawls's, my book's effort to develop a transcendent vision of a "well ordered society" was deeply problematic. I responded to his version of an "original position" by constructing my own competing "original position"—while insisting on the primacy of the struggle for meaning in the "here and now."

I came to recognize the self-contradiction involved in my own original-positioning only in the course of the scholarly debates that followed the publication of *Social Justice*.[7] Over the next decade, I became convinced that I needed to free myself from Rawls's paradigm entirely, so I tried to construct a self-consciously existential framework for my approach. These essays of the 1990s sketched out some of the themes that, by now, should be familiar to readers of this book—emphasizing ways in which entrenched structures of social domination operate as overwhelming obstacles for billions of people struggling to define their own meaning in life in collaboration with sphere-mates of their own choice.[8]

More recently, however, I've devoted less time to philosophical efforts at reconstruction and more time to concrete proposals that could plausibly respond to the escalating crisis of democracy in America and throughout the world.[9] Yet the looming dangers of technocratic domination have convinced me that our postmodern predicaments require urgent attention. We cannot afford to engage in philosophical thought experiments at a time when megabillionaires and their technocratic servants increasingly define the terms of our very existence.

PART III

FACING THE FUTURE

Chapter 11

CRITIQUE

I suspect that neither Cass Sunstein nor Richard Thaler has paid much attention to Heidegger or Sartre. Nevertheless, their book *Nudge* is by far the most influential existentialist tract of the twenty-first century.

Like its twentieth-century predecessors, *Nudge* takes aim at a form of economic determinism, but its target is very different. As we have seen, Merleau-Ponty rejected Marxism's claim to have "scientifically" demonstrated the inevitability of a proletarian revolution against capitalist oppression. Sunstein and Thaler take their stand against a different form of historical determinism. Neoliberal economists claim to have demonstrated "scientifically" that capitalism inexorably generates "efficient" outcomes, and that state efforts at redistribution will only further impoverish the lower classes.

These anti-Marxist determinists, whose spiritual home is the University of Chicago, try to prove their point through up-to-date scientific methods involving the construction of elaborate mathematical models. But their impressive-looking equations only support their pro-market conclusions if one assumes that all market participants are "rational actors" who consistently pursue the best market options available to them in maximizing their self-interest.[1]

Here is where Sunstein and Thaler respond with their existentialist critique. In *Nudge* they insist that "rational actors" exist only in the mathematical world created by these model builders and that real-world humans lack the time to think through all the choices opened up by the marketplace. Before Chicagoans can call themselves *serious* economists, they require a radically revised kit bag, containing analytic tools designed to deal with distinctive features of real-world decision-making.

Nudge aims to provide these tools, and it is this aspiration that transforms Sunstein and Thaler into existentialists—for two reasons. Most obviously, they focus on the way real-world people respond to real-world problems. Even more significantly, they follow the course marked out by Merleau-Ponty in *Phenomenology of Perception*, exploring the way flesh-and-blood human beings perceive the world around them as they struggle to reach common understandings with their sphere-mates. Moreover, the analysis they offer goes far beyond correcting their Chicago colleagues' mathematical fantasies. *Nudge* presents a sophisticated sociopsychological tool kit that Sunstein and Thaler believe clarifies *all* of the complex problem-solving dilemmas of postmodern existence.

Their efforts have gained extraordinary acclaim. Their book has sold more than 1.5 million copies since it was published in 2008, inspiring a host of reform efforts around the world. It increasingly serves as a policymaking paradigm for aspiring thinkers and doers of the rising generation.

In this chapter I call for serious reconsideration of these enthusiasms. I will emphasize two ways in which *Nudge* blinds itself to key aspects of the modern/postmodern predicament. The first involves the book's failure to appreciate the multi-spherical character of contemporary life. Instead, it proposes a one-size-fits-all style of "nudging" that pays no attention to the particular sphere in which "nonrational" actors are operating.

The second blind spot involves Sunstein and Thaler's deployment of the internet as their tool for reshaping "non-rational" perceptions of real-world opportunities. In constructing their computer algorithms, they systematically ignore the "two-lives problem" posed by postmodern existence. As a consequence, they transform nudging into a mode of manipulation that will dramatically increase the "irrationality" it is intended to correct—upending the lives of enormous numbers of real-world people struggling for a meaningful existence under postmodern conditions.

In advancing my critique, I do not wish to challenge *Nudge*'s larger ambition, which is to channel the computer revolution down pathways that will yield dramatic improvements in the human condition. I will begin, therefore, by considering the ways in which Sunstein and Thaler's approach to real-world problem-solving converges with my own approach to existential justice—and only then explore how a thoughtful confrontation with the postmodern predicament requires a radically different understanding of the directions that serious reform should take in the twenty-first century.

Common Ground

Sunstein and Thaler urge us to reject "perfect rationality" because "most of us are busy, our lives are complicated, and we *can't* spend all our time thinking and analyzing everything."[2]

"Can't" is the crucial word that marks them out as existentialists. They begin with a fundamental fact about everybody's relationship to the "here and now." There simply aren't enough hours in a day to permit people to think through the larger implications of all the decisions they make every day. Human beings simply don't have enough time in their waking lives to operate as perfectly rational actors, even if they wanted to.

Nudge responds to this key point by distinguishing between automatic and reflective responses to real-world problems: "The Automatic System is rapid and is or feels instinctive, and it does not involve what we usually associate with the word *thinking*. . . . The Reflective System is more deliberate and self-conscious."[3]

Note how the authors carefully refuse to equate the Automatic System "with the word *thinking*." Instead, they apply "thinking" only to the "more deliberate and self-conscious" responses of the Reflective System. This is the precise point at which they find common ground with an unlikely philosophical companion: Martin Heidegger. As we have seen, Heidegger also insists on the fundamental difference between an "intuitive and rapid" response to the immediate environment and "deliberate and self-conscious" reflection on the larger implications of your intuitive reactions for the conduct of your life.[4]

Heidegger, however, considers it a big mistake for anybody to reflect about anything. *Being and Time* tries to persuade you that the *only* way to achieve a truly authentic existence is by sustaining an intuitive relationship to the "here and now" at every moment of your life. In his view, once people begin reflecting on the problems they encounter, they are doomed to lose any sense of themselves as genuine human beings.

At no point do Sunstein and Thaler address Heidegger's totalizing rejection of self-reflection. They simply ignore his critique—providing further proof of the extent to which the existentialist tradition has dropped out of sight in contemporary debate. Nevertheless, I am happy to volunteer my services and defend their rejection of Heidegger's totalizing repudiation of reflection.

Recall the wilderness scenarios that played a central role in my Heideggerian critique. I argued that, even when hiking in the wilderness, you can't engage in a single-minded effort to commune with the glories of nature. Otherwise, your all-consuming search for oneness will lead you to stumble on a rock or ignore some other obstacle to your quest for Being Itself. Unless you anticipate these problems in advance, and try to solve them in a thoughtful fashion, even episodic moments of wonder will elude your grasp. To translate this point into *Nudge*-speak, you won't be able to deploy your Automatic System for moments of silent appreciation of nature unless you regularly shift into your Reflective System to deal with real-world problems you encounter in the forest. If this is true of hikes in the wilderness, it is even truer when confronting the everyday predicaments of life in the twenty-first century.

I also endorse the book's next big move. *Nudge* emphasizes the importance of recent breakthroughs by "psychologists and neuroscientists [who] have been converging on a description of the brain's functioning that helps us make sense" of the ways in which all of us deploy our two systems in the ongoing effort to live a meaningful life under postmodern conditions.[5]

I very much agree that these data-driven findings provide genuine insights. This is the point, however, where we part company. Sunstein and Thaler fail to adapt their two-systems approach to the distinctive dilemmas of multi-spherical commitment, blinding themselves to the very different modes of meaning-making that prevail among family and friends, workers and bosses, citizens and consumers, and . . .

I will explore the grim implications of their spherical blindness by considering their discussion of a crucial question that almost all of us face at one time or another: should we get married? Sunstein and Thaler devote an entire chapter to this question.[6] They argue that nudging will greatly improve the thoughtfulness with which lovers confront this decision. I will try to persuade you that they are tragically wrong—and that their proposed nudges would shatter the lives of countless flesh-and-blood people throughout the world.

I will begin my critique, however, by defining some common ground. All three of us agree that modern behavioral science has established that people tend to be myopic when operating automatically, overemphasizing short-term gains even when their immediate decisions have destructive long-term consequences.

This myopia is especially pronounced when people haven't confronted similar problems in the past. In repeat-play scenarios, people often resist short-term temptations after they have experienced, over the long run, the bad consequences of a decision. But they display an overwhelming short-term bias if they have never previously encountered a similar situation.

Sunstein and Thaler take this to mean that two lovers considering a first-time marriage are in desperate need of nudging:

> Unrealistic optimism is at its most extreme in the context of marriage. In recent studies, for example, people have been shown to have an accurate sense of the likelihood that other people will get divorced (about 50 percent). But recall that they have an absurdly optimistic sense of the likelihood that they themselves will get divorced. It's worth repeating the key finding: nearly

> 100 percent of people believe that they are certain or almost certain not to get divorced!

So far as *Nudge* is concerned, prospective newlyweds will continue to rejoice at the prospect of short-term marital bliss – unless they can be induced to shift to their Reflective System, and negotiate a prenuptial agreement that will allow them to confront their long-term breakup risk in a thoughtful fashion.

It's best to let the authors put this point in their own words. Here is how *Nudge* follows up its "key finding" about the lovers' "absurdly optimistic" belief in their future happiness:

> It is in these circumstances, and in part for that reason, that people are immensely reluctant to make prenuptial agreements. *Believing that divorce is unlikely, and fearing that such agreements will spoil the mood, most people will simply take their chances with existing divorce law.*[7]

I have italicized the final line to clarify *Nudge*'s two-pronged diagnosis of the couple's failure to take their contractual opportunity seriously.

The first prong involves cognitive failure: statistical data reveals that almost all couples think their chance of staying married for life is 100 percent – even though the same couples tell pollsters that other prospective newlyweds stand a fifty-fifty chance of divorce. Isn't this utterly irrational?

The second prong is emotional: working out the terms of a prenuptial agreement will spoil the triumphant mood of the moment by forcing the couple to acknowledge that their love might not be everlasting. Shouldn't they recognize that this is their last chance to do the sensible thing and work out the terms of a mutually agreeable settlement in case of a breakup?

So far as Sunstein and Thaler are concerned, the obvious answer to both questions is yes.

I disagree. Their certainty only reveals *Nudge*'s profound spherical blindness.

I hope to persuade you that I am right, but I should enter a caveat: whatever you come to believe, the only opinions that count in the real world are those of a few Silicon Valley mega-billionaires. They now control the World Wide Web, and the fate of nudging is in their hands – even though their dominion is increasingly challenged by rivals in China, Europe, India, and elsewhere.

More precisely: before the Web can function, its technocratic designers – *Nudge* calls them "choice architects" – must construct a complex set of algorithms that permit people to search the network effectively. If Sunstein and Thaler have their way, prospective newlyweds will increasingly confront nudges alerting them to their risk of divorce and encouraging them to negotiate a prenuptial agreement.

In challenging the legitimacy of this strategy, I am not merely calling on the super-elite in control of the internet to repudiate the Sunstein-Thaler project. I am calling upon progressives to mobilize citizens in a serious campaign to end the forms of technocratic mind control that *Nudge* seeks to vindicate.

The Best Case for Nudging

As I did in my discussions of twentieth-century existentialists, I will begin with a thought experiment that enables Sunstein and Thaler to make their best case for nudging. I will argue, however, that their initiative would be utterly counterproductive even under these optimal conditions. Rather than encouraging prospective newlyweds to rethink their decision and cut back on future divorces, their suggested course of action will lead to millions more divorces than would occur in a nudge-free world. I will then turn to the yet more bitter implications of their approach when applied to men and women struggling against entrenched forms of cultural, economic, and racial oppression. But I will defer this worst-case analysis until my best-case critique is concluded.

So let's take the first step – and consider whether nudging will be counterproductive even for prospective newlyweds who are in the best position to take it seriously. For starters, suppose that these couples aren't rushing into marriage after a passionate fling that would make sober consideration of their long-term prospects psychologically impossible. Instead, they have made their decision after a long period of deepening intimacy that has enabled each of them to become extremely familiar with the other's strengths and weaknesses. They are thus in a position to engage in the kind of thoughtful reappraisal that nudging is intended to provoke.

To give Sunstein and Thaler the benefit of the doubt, I will also suppose that the couple's educational backgrounds permit them to understand and appreciate the data-driven analysis that well-designed nudges will bring to their attention. To put the point in operational terms, both partners – call them Alpha and Omega – have college educations that enable them to understand their breakup chances in probabilistic terms.

I should emphasize that this does not transform my scenario into a super-elitist thought experiment. Recall that in the world's rich countries more than 40 percent of adults between the ages of

25 and 40 have college degrees, and that higher education levels are rapidly increasing in many poorer regions as well.[8]

Let's also suppose that Alpha and Omega, like increasing numbers of their peers, are in their late twenties or early thirties when they make this decision, and that they have both embarked on successful professional careers. Each of them has saved $75,000, which they are planning to use for two distinct purposes. They will spend some of their $150,000 on a wonderful wedding celebration; the rest they will put aside, in case they encounter setbacks at work or other spheres during the first few years of their marriage. They plan to use this money as a rainy day fund to help them out during hard times.

At no point, however, has Alpha or Omega given a moment's thought to the grim possibility that, despite their best efforts, their marriage will end in divorce.[9] Instead, they are focused on a more pressing problem: organizing the wedding so that friends and family can join them in celebrating their great moment of love and commitment.

This won't be easy, given the postmodern way in which Alpha and Omega have gotten to know one another. They were raised in different regions of the country and graduated from different universities. Instead of returning to their hometowns, they chose the same Distant City to pursue their high-tech careers—and it was there that they fell in love. When they invite their hometown friends and families to come to Distant City on their wedding day, however, they get some bad news: some can't afford the airfare required to take the trip.

The absence of these old friends would deprive their marriage ceremony of much of its meaning. Both Alpha and Omega confronted many moments of self-doubt and anxiety when they were growing up. Without the support of people like Uncle Harry and Schoolmate Alice, they could have become so demoralized that they might never have gone to university at all! So Alpha and Omega decide to buy airline tickets for Harry, Alice, and other close friends who can't afford them. The overall cost turns out to be substantial, amounting to $50,000, but they agree that it is worth paying. They simply cannot allow the poverty of their beloved hometowners to prevent them from expressing their profound gratitude for their help during their childhood. Although $50,000 is a big price to pay, some moments of face-to-face commitment define the very meaning of life – and this, so far as they are concerned, is one of them.

Having reached this conclusion, Alpha and Omega turn to the internet to buy the necessary tickets, searching for the cheapest fares that would serve their purpose. But to their surprise, they confront nudges that push them in a very different direction. The system's "choice architects" have been monitoring their searches – wedding photographer, florist, and the like – and they conclude that the lovers are planning their own wedding. So Alpha and Omega do not get quick access to airline sites offering tickets between their hometowns and Distant City. Instead, they must first watch a video in which a hip but well-dressed lawyer tells them:

> Hi there, I'm lawyer Doe, and I'm here to tell you some tough facts that you may have overlooked. Did you know that half of all marriages end in divorce? Don't you think you should stop rushing ahead with your wedding plans and take time to consider the implications of this hard truth for your future prospects?

We have finally reached the point at which my critique can proceed in earnest. How will Alpha and Omega respond to Doe's nudge? Will their encounter with Doe lead them to confront their breakup risk in a "rational" fashion – as Sunstein and Thaler predict? Or will it provoke self-destructive forms of irrationality?

To find out, I will be pinpointing a series of real-world problems that could readily provoke a tragic decision by Alpha and Omega to call off their wedding – and invite *Nudge*'s defenders to tell me where I've gone wrong.

Stage One – Framing the Question

DOE: Did you know that half of all marriages end up in divorce?

ALPHA: I'm not impressed by that statistic. Lots of couples get married after a few weeks of passionate romance, and break up with their lover in ways that take them by surprise. But we've been together for years. We've thought this through, and we've decided to spend the rest of our lives together.

Do you have statistics on the breakup rates of couples like us?

DOE: Yes, we do! My firm has been in business since 2002. During the past two decades, we have helped tens of thousands of couples confront their divorce risk in a rational fashion, and our data base contains confidential data on their breakup rates over time. You are right, of course, that many couples get married after a brief acquaintance, but many others reached their decision after knowing each other for years. This permits us to provide a rigorous statistical estimate of breakup rates for couples like you.

OMEGA: Pretty impressive – but I still have my doubts. After all, there are lots of other ways we differ from other serious newlyweds. Most obviously, many couples have lots less money than we have – and this will place a bigger strain on their marriage during tough times. It would be silly for us to make our decision based on such shaky numbers.

DOE: You're perfectly right – which is why I'd like you to fill out a standardized form before we talk seriously about the terms of your prenuptial agreement.

The form asks a series of questions about your cultural, economic, educational, racial, and religious backgrounds. It will allow our analytic team to provide you with the statistically rigorous probability estimates required to confront your future in a rational fashion.

ALPHA: Once we fill out the form, what happens next?

DOE: I am part of a sophisticated network of legal professionals, using the most advanced AI software in the business. As soon as they've analyzed your report, I will connect you with the group of family law experts who specialize in dealing with your distinctive risk scenarios.

This team has lots of experience helping couples like you reach a sensible prenup. They will provide you with brief summaries of the contractual terms that similar couples have often used to reach a mutually acceptable arrangement. After hearing short descriptions of these standard options, you can pick the terms that best serve your purposes. At that point, your family law specialists will explain the key provisions in greater detail – and ask you whether you want to modify them to suit your particular situation. If you do, we'll create a bespoke contract that's specially tailored to your concerns.

OMEGA: Sounds like it could take a long time!

DOE: Maybe not. Some people find it easier to sign one of the standard agreements; others want to explore their options in more detail. It's entirely up to you.

Needless to say, there's an hourly fee for our professional assistance.

ALPHA: I'm sure there is. How much will this cost us?

DOE: I can't say until we've analyzed your completed questionnaires. Once you email them back, we'll provide a preliminary risk analysis for free.

We will only start charging a fee if you decide to engage us to draft a legally binding arrangement.

OMEGA: Can you at least tell us how long it takes to fill out the questionnaire?

DOE: For most people, about an hour, maybe an hour and a half.

OMEGA: Alpha, can we really afford to spend an hour or two on this right now? We haven't even booked airplane tickets for Harry and Alice yet—and there's so much other planning to do! Worse yet, my boss tells me I can't go on our honeymoon until I finish a couple of big reports. This means I'll probably be working overtime for the next few weeks.

So [to the lawyer], Mr. Doe, I suggest we discuss this later. Please send us an email in a year or so—after we've been married for a while and have more time to consider your proposal.

DOE: It's entirely up to you, of course, but our data show that very few couples ever return for an interview after they're married. Instead, they delay and delay and delay—until one day they face a serious crisis without any of the contractual tools for an amicable settlement they might have designed for themselves beforehand.

ALPHA: Well, if that's what Doe's data show, let's work on the questionnaire over dinner tonight and see if his technocrats are more down on this marriage than your cousin Edith. We'll then be in a better position to decide whether to spend time and money dealing with Doe.

OMEGA: OK, we'll give it a try.

DOE (smiling): I very much appreciate the rational way you are organizing your decision-making process. I can tell you're smart, level-headed people who care about their future. See you soon!

Stage Two: Technocratic Predicaments

When Alpha and Omega look over the form at dinner, they encounter some straightforward questions. They have no trouble, for example, reporting that they have $150,000 in savings or that their annual salaries are $X and $Y respectively. Yet their breakup risk depends on lots of other factors. If their work lives are full of frustration, they are more likely to get into shouting matches at home. In contrast, if their job experience fulfils their hopes for self-realization, they will predictably share their sense of accomplishment with their spouse and maybe decide to have kids. It follows that Doe's team must include questions that yield data on the qualitative aspects of their work lives.

In framing these inquiries, however, the technocrats confront a series of dilemmas. The first is temporal: if they expect Alpha and Omega to complete their form within 60 or 90 minutes, they can't afford to explore the issue of job satisfaction at great length – because they must also explore other crucial aspects of the couple's situation that can generate a breakup. So they must settle for a very few questions on each issue. Call this the problem of temporal superficiality.

The problem gets worse when they try to translate each answer into quantitative terms for rigorous statistical analysis. Imagine, for example, that the questionnaire asks prospective newlyweds to rate their work lives on a numerical scale from zero to ten – with 0 indicating deep dissatisfaction and 10 deep fulfilment. Suppose that Alpha proudly gives herself a 9, but Omega gives himself a 4 – since he thinks his boss constantly imposes excessive demands on him and then blames him for underperforming. Nevertheless, since the couple are spending only an hour or so on the entire form, they devote only 60 seconds in providing their numerical answer before moving to the next question. If they had considered the matter for even fifteen minutes, might they have given themselves different scores?

To take this problem into account, Doe's statistical team will attach a margin of error to their answers. Their computer algorithms treat Alpha's 9 as if it might also be an 8 or a 10.

The firm is obliged to increase its error margin further once it confronts a second problem. To assess the chances of an Alpha/Omega breakup, Doe's technocrats must compare the couple's responses to the answers provided by the other prospective newlyweds in its data bank. At this point, they confront their next dilemma: interpersonal comparison.

Suppose, for example, that the technocrats begin by comparing Omega's answers to the ones previously submitted by Gamma—who also rated his job satisfaction as a 4. But Omega's and Gamma's answers to other questions suggest that they gave themselves 4s for different reasons. Gamma believed he was super-qualified for his job and was bitterly disappointed when his boss promoted someone else ahead of him. Omega never considered himself a superstar, and his 4 expressed his belief that his boss was unfairly belittling his work while praising fellow workers for comparable achievements.

It would be a bad mistake for the firm's analysts to treat these 4s the same way. Perhaps Gamma is right about his qualifications and will soon find a new job where he rates his satisfaction as a 10. But Omega, even if he finds a more appreciative boss, will never give his work satisfaction more than a 6. Call this the problem of interpersonal comparison—and it becomes more troublesome once Doe's team moves beyond evaluating the relationship between work life and home life to take a broader view of the problem.

A couple's religious commitments, for example, typically have a statistically significant impact on breakup rates, so it makes sense to ask about this on the questionnaire. It happens that Alpha and Omega are both committed to a religion that, among many other things, is profoundly opposed to divorce. They have doubts about this particular article of faith but are reluctant to discuss these doubts in the few minutes they spend checking boxes in this part of the questionnaire. So they call themselves true believers even though their breakup risk is higher than religious couples who are more deeply committed to the belief that marriage represents a lifetime commitment until "death do us part."

To be sure, the couple's high score on their "religious conviction index" will serve as only one element in the firm's statistical assessment – and it may be offset by low scores on other indicators. Nevertheless, to take their problems of interpersonal comparison into account, Doe's team will have to add an extra margin to the error term generated by the temporal superficiality of their questionnaire. Moreover, this increase in indeterminacy is likely to be large – since it will haunt other key variables dealing with the couple's ethnic, gender, and cultural characteristics.

Yet the analysts must confront a final difficulty before Doe can deliver his breakup estimates to Alpha and Omega. The firm's computers contain only data on past divorce rates, but the prospective newlyweds are concerned with their future prospects: Is it sensible to use backward-looking equations to make these predictions?

Suppose, for example, that couples with the same skill sets as Alpha and Omega did very well on the job market during the last two decades, but that a review of the relevant social science suggests that the future may take a different turn—or two different turns. On one hand, the couple's high-tech skills may become much more valuable in 2050 than they were in 2025. Under this scenario, their job satisfaction index rises to 10 and their incomes soar into the stratosphere, leading the firm to take a very optimistic view of their marriage's chances. On the other hand, Alpha and Omega may find that the technological revolution overwhelms their training and experience—and that employers find it more efficient to replace people with their skill sets with supercomputers and robots. Should this happen, they would be left out in the cold, enduring long periods of unemployment while desperately searching for half-decent jobs. Under this scenario, their job satisfaction sinks to 0 and their income sinks to 1, leading the modelers to predict massive increases in their breakup risk. Or the job market could favor one spouse while making the other's skills obsolete, generating risks somewhere in between the two extremes.

There is, of course, a final possibility—that future trends will be similar to past developments. This scenario makes the computer's backward-looking projections seem relatively unproblematic. When Doe's technocrats turn to the academic literature, however, they find an intense debate, with serious scholars taking optimistic, pessimistic, and moderate views on questions of fateful significance to Alpha and Omega. So they must once again increase their margin of error to take this factor—call it academic indeterminacy—into account.

To sum up: if Doe & Company is to provide prospective newlyweds with serious advice, it can't present them with an impressive-looking series of hard-edged numbers that provide a clear sense of their particular breakup risks—at least if it hopes to maintain its professional integrity. Instead, given the problems raised by temporal superficiality, interpersonal comparison, future uncertainty, and academic indeterminacy, it must accompany its predictions with a very significant margin of error.

This conclusion has large implications for nudging.

Stage Three: The Existential Gamble

ALPHA AND OMEGA: Here are our questionnaires, Mr. Doe. When can we get the results?

DOE: Three days, tops. Our computers process your data in nanoseconds, but we never just rely on algorithms. Experts on our staff check it over, and that takes longer. But it will be quick. After all, you've got to make a quick decision.

ALPHA AND OMEGA: Right you are. See you then.

[Three days later]

ALPHA: So what can you tell us?

DOE: First, some good news. Your prospects look better than the 50 percent breakup rate confronting the average couple. People with your profiles have only a 30 percent chance of getting a divorce—though your odds may vary by 20 percentage points, depending on future socioeconomic developments.

OMEGA: So our risk could be as low as 10 percent or as high as 50 percent. Why such a big range?

DOE: Predicting the future is never an exact science, but in your case our experts have spotted a particular problem. By 2035 or 2040, employers may find it cheaper to have your jobs done by high-tech machines, and you will find yourselves searching for new careers. If this happens, your index of marital satisfaction will take a nose dive. You and your kids will suddenly find yourselves struggling with the humiliations of poverty. Under this scenario, your risk goes to 50 percent.

Don't be too depressed. Many of your answers suggest a deeper-than-usual commitment to one another. When other couples face economic disasters, their breakup rates go even higher.

ALPHA: I don't take joy in the misery of others. Nevertheless, I had somehow supposed that our years of education and professional success would insure against such a catastrophe.

DOE: And you may be right! A lot of academic research suggests that advances in technology will make your job skills more, not less, valuable. Not only will your income soar, but you will take great pride in each other's accomplishments. Your deepening admiration for one another will encourage you to explore many other mutual interests that will further increase your "marital satisfaction index."

OMEGA: So why doesn't our divorce risk sink to zero?

DOE: Perhaps you and Alpha decide to have kids and then can't agree how to share childcare responsibilities. Or maybe you just get bored with each other – and break apart when one of you finds somebody who offers a more meaningful intimate relationship.

But let's not lose time discussing each and every possible scenario. Our challenge is to confront your predicament in a rational fashion. Like it or not, you face a breakup risk ranging from 10 and 50 percent.

I have no doubt that you will try your hardest to avoid your worst-case scenarios. But you might not succeed. I'm offering you the chance to make a prenuptial agreement that will enable you to resolve your crisis on mutually acceptable terms. After all, if you can't agree, the government will resolve your dispute for you – imposing a divorce law that you may profoundly disagree with. Isn't it far better for you to take charge of your own future?

ALPHA: Not so fast. If there's such a wide range of breakdown scenarios, how can we possibly negotiate a sensible agreement before the wedding? It's just a few weeks away.

OMEGA: Not only is there lots more to do on that front. Both of us have promised our bosses that we would complete key job assignments before we take off for our honeymoon!

We simply can't afford the time.

ALPHA: I agree.

ALPHA AND OMEGA: Sorry, Doe, thank you for your offer of assistance. But we really must call it quits for now.

DOE: Just give me five more minutes before you jump to such a despairing conclusion. Let me introduce you to Amity Jones, who heads a family law team that specializes in helping clients with precisely your socioeconomic dilemmas.

AMITY (smiling): Good to meet you. My team has years of experience designing contractual agreements for busy professional couples. To save you time, I'll begin by explaining the key provisions of the Professional Prenup that's most popular with couples from your cultural, educational, gender, political, and religious background. This won't take more than half an hour.

ALPHA: What happens after that?

AMITY: Generally speaking, couples want to discuss the terms by themselves before deciding on their next step. Why don't you look at the agreement and talk it over, and I'll await your return once you've done that.

Many people find that our Professional Prenup provides a very sensible solution to their breakup predicaments – and want to make it into an enforceable contract.

Many others, however, find our initial prenup doesn't meet their needs. If that's you, don't be too worried. Over the decades, we've designed a whole range of alternative prenups tailored to resolve particular issues. Whatever you're concerned about, we almost certainly have an expertly crafted and road-tested clause that will cover it.

Of course, we can't guarantee success. But most clients do find something they're perfectly satisfied with. Shouldn't you also take the future into your own hands?

ALPHA: This all sounds very interesting, but how much will it cost us?

AMITY: The total will be up to you. If you accept our initial proposal without modification, the fee is $7,500. While you may find that a big number, I'd ask you to think about what you're getting for it. It isn't some off-the-shelf prenup offered by most lawyers. We've made an expensive technocratic evaluation of your questionnaire and used it to prepare a custom-made agreement that reflects years of experience working with couples a lot like you. All things considered, we think $7,500 is a fair price for the security and peace of mind this prenup will provide.

If, however, you need individual consultation with a member of our legal team, we charge $500 an hour to help resolve your remaining disagreements. Our past experience suggests that almost no one requires more than six hours of professional assistance to reach an agreement that meets their needs. So your overall fee will most likely amount to $10,000 or less. A small number of couples do require more elaborate negotiations and end up paying $15,000 or more. But that's not the norm.

OMEGA: We only have $150,000 in the bank, and we're already devoting $40,000 to a wedding celebration. If we pay you $15,000, we'll enter our marriage with only $95,000 in our rainy day fund.

ALPHA: Worse yet, you're asking us to deal with one another in a very strange fashion. Your legal team is asking me to suppose that I have come to despise Omega in a hypothetical world in which we are bitterly quarreling over child custody and desperately looking for half-decent jobs. But I *love* Omega and will do everything in my power to sustain our relationship. I haven't the slightest idea of what my bargaining priorities would be if, despite those efforts, the person I love turns into a person I hate. As we approach our wedding day, I could never start wheeling and dealing with Omega in an arm's-length fashion – and treat him as if he were a commercial rival when in fact I love him very much.

AMITY: To be perfectly frank, you are only making it clear how badly you need our assistance. Rather than presenting you with a weird dilemma, I am introducing you to a problem that you will face repeatedly once you're married.

Quite simply, you will be constantly required to confront situations in which you can gain short-term benefits only at the price of long-term costs. If you and Omega face up to this hard fact of human existence, you will be in a position to take sensible steps today that will safeguard you against future misfortune. If you insist on blinding yourself to these long-term implications, you will be acting in an utterly irrational fashion. My invitation to consider your divorce risk is only a special case of a paradigmatic marriage dilemma. It seems strange to you only because you and Omega are just starting out on your experiment in togetherness.

To see my point, you only need to look beyond your wedding day and consider how you will be obliged to bargain with one another when deciding on where to spend your honeymoon. Suppose you've narrowed your choices down to two options. On one hand, you could spend $15,000 celebrating your marriage in a beautiful island resort. On the other hand, you could spend your honeymoon at home in Distant

City and devote precious time to exploring the opportunities it offers for activities that might enrich your lives for years to come. This might lead you to investigate spheres of civic or spiritual or social life that attract you – and let you gain a deeper sense of whether they'll provide mutual self-realization.

Suppose it turns out that Omega wants a magical honeymoon on a romantic island, but you are inclined to stay at home and keep the $15,000 in your rainy day fund. At this point, you will find yourself in the very same position you say is unacceptable when negotiating a prenup. You will smile lovingly at Omega as you try to persuade him to stay at home, and he will do the same as he tries to convince you that a glorious honeymoon is worth spending the money. The bargaining will continue until you settle on one choice or the other.

There is only one difference between that bargaining session and the one I am describing. When negotiating your prenup, you're confronting your worst-case marriage scenario; when negotiating the terms of your honeymoon, you're dealing with your best-case scenario. But so far as I'm concerned, both dilemmas arise because you are thoughtfully confronting the longer-term implications of your current problem – and rightly believe it would be utterly irrational to blind yourself to its implications for the day after tomorrow.

ALPHA: Amity, you are right that both scenarios involve trade-offs between short-run gains and long-term losses. You are also right to point out that, once we are married, it would be irrational to ignore these trade-offs. Our challenge is to confront our honeymoon disagreements candidly and deal with them in a loving fashion. If we let them turn into a shouting match, it will set a terrible precedent for our efforts to face up to the much tougher trade-offs that lie ahead. Our success in resolving our $15,000 question, in short, will confirm the wisdom of our decision to get married.

But you, Amity, are asking us to think about our future divorce when we haven't even made a decisive commitment to one another – and you want me to deal with the problem by maximizing my personal self-interest at Omega's expense. Once seated at the negotiating table, I will be dealing with the man I love as if he were merely an obstacle to my efforts to get the best prenup *for myself*, and vice versa. How can I treat Omega as a hostile rival at the very moment we are committing ourselves to remain together "in sickness and in health" for the rest of our lives?

Even if I could figure out my bargaining priorities in the brave new world you have placed before me, I would be betraying the very marital commitment that I am now determined to make to the man I love.

Don't you see that there is a special problem here?

AMITY: Aha. I think I understand. You are making a point about the "intensity" of your "preferences" – terms I learned from my great teachers, Cass Sunstein and Richard Thaler.

You seem to be saying that your preference for marriage is so intense that you refuse to activate your Reflective System to enable you to confront the prospect of divorce in a rational fashion. This Automatic Response is propelling you away from the bargaining table, even though it means sacrificing your long-run gains in "preference-satisfaction." Is that what you are trying to say?

OMEGA: No, I am challenging the very notion of "preference-satisfaction" that you take for granted in making your case for nudges. It supposes that my commitment to Alpha is merely an "intense" version of the preferences I express for commodities like toothpaste or airline tickets.

Nothing could be further from the truth. In marrying Alpha, I am *committing* myself to her in a way that will define the very meaning of who I am.

ALPHA: I agree. It is you, Amity, who have blinded yourself to this crucial point by treating our rejection of your nudge as if it were an Automatic Response to the horror of divorce. To the contrary, it is based on a rational recognition that we can't sustain the credibility of our mutual commitment if we don't live up to it in our daily existence.

Once we take our vows, for example, we would be *betraying* our marriage if one of us had a secret love affair with somebody else. These acts of betrayal would not necessarily destroy our marriage – even after our partner found out about them. We might be capable of forgiving and forgetting. But our acts of infidelity would be fundamentally incompatible with our commitment to one another.

The same incompatibility would arise if I accepted Amity's offer and sat down at the bargaining table to negotiate a divorce agreement with Omega. Even if I were perfectly polite during the negotiating sessions, I would be trying to get the best breakup deal *for myself.* When I looked across the table, I would see my darling Omega acting in the same way. We would be engaged in an arm's-length relationship that is utterly incompatible with our present commitment to face the future *together*.

AMITY: But in response to our questionnaire, you rated your breakup chances at 0 percent – even though you recognized that the prevailing divorce rate is 50 percent! Doesn't this testify to the profound character of your self-delusion?

OMEGA: Not at all. This was our way of telling you, within the technocratic premises of your questionnaire, that we are determined to remain faithful even in the darkest times – and ultimately count ourselves among the committed couples who will indeed redeem their lifelong pledge to one another.

Since we only spent an hour answering a barrage of questions, the best we could do was to say that, despite your data, we were 100 percent sure that we would remain true to one another.

ALPHA: Even if we're wrong, Amity, you haven't said anything to suggest that you can help us increase our chances. So it's time to say goodbye, and for us to continue our search for cheap airplane tickets!

Omega clicks, and Amity disappears from their screen.

Beyond the Best Case

In framing this conversation, I have tried to give Sunstein and Thaler the benefit of the doubt. Alpha and Omega have the educational background required to understand the statistical and legal arguments that their nudgers are presenting to them. They haven't decided to marry after a brief and passionate love affair, which might make it psychologically impossible to be thoughtful about their breakup prospects. Instead, they have made their decision to wed only after a long period of deepening engagement. Yet they can save themselves from a self-destructive negotiation only by banishing Amity from their computer.

Today, the Alpha-Omega-Amity trialogue is only a thought experiment. Given Sunstein and Thaler's remarkable influence, however, there is a very real chance that these nudges will confront countless couples making wedding day preparations on the internet over the next decade. If this happens, how many couples would Amity persuade to begin adversarial negotiations over a prenup? Once these lovers-turned-adversaries start their negotiations, how many bargaining sessions would blow up into angry confrontations that lead couples to call off their weddings?

I haven't the foggiest notion.

One thing is clear: Sunstein and Thaler would consider it a success if their nudges led couples to call off their marriages before they have even begun. So far as I am concerned, such breakups are tragic failures. They are paradigmatic examples of *Nudge*'s blindness to the multi-spherical character of modern (and postmodern) existence. Sunstein and Thaler fail to recognize the distinctive predicaments that "I" confront in building and sustaining a meaningful relationship with my most intimate companion-in-life and how these challenges differ from those "I" encounter in constructing credible relationships with my co-workers, fellow citizens, co-religionists, and a host of other sphere-mates. Instead, *Nudge* treats all of them as if they were fundamentally similar to my ongoing search, as a consumer, to satisfy my "preferences" in the marketplace.

Their totalizing embrace of commodification represents a fundamental threat to the construction of a just society in the twenty-first century. Sunstein and Thaler's celebration of marriage-nudging is an especially dramatic case of this dangerous dis-ease.

In condemning *Nudge*'s proposed intervention into the sphere of intimate engagement, I don't mean to suggest that prospective newlyweds may never benefit from last-minute efforts to get them to reconsider their decision. I simply deny that technocrats armed with algorithms can serve as competent advisors for couples confronting their existential predicament. These young adults don't require statistical analysis to learn that their marriages may well end up in a divorce. Countless movies and novels portray such breakups, and prospective newlyweds will typically have family members, friends, or fellow workers who have suffered through divorce as well. Moreover, many real-world Alphas and Omegas do indeed experience deep anxiety as their marriage celebration approaches. Rather than turning to legal technocrats, however, they are better off seeking the advice of long-time sphere-mates who know them well enough to be familiar with their personal strengths and vulnerabilities. These people are better positioned to provide genuine assistance in confidential conversations dealing with last-minute hesitations.

To be sure, even the most sympathetic friend or family member may fail to appreciate many aspects of the especially intimate relationship that the prospective newlyweds have developed over time. Still, a good friend or thoughtful family member may offer insights that greatly contribute to Alpha's or Omega's struggle to resolve one of the most fundamental existential questions of their entire lives.

Moreover, if these conversations lead the couple to retreat from their marriage, it is perfectly possible that Alpha and Omega may later regret their decision to heed their advice. Given the twists and turns of multi-spherical life in the twenty-first century, it is simply impossible for anybody to be sure how things will turn out in the long run.

Nevertheless, the positive potential of advice from long-standing personal acquaintances points to a second flaw in the Sunstein-Thaler approach. They do not appear to recognize that internet interventions are *intrinsically* incapable of providing an adequate substitute for many meaning-making forms of face-to-face existence. This point is especially important in the case of marriage, since a loving relationship typically involves the silent modes of togetherness and apartness that, as we saw in part 2 of this book, were central to the work of Heidegger, Sartre, and Beauvoir.

A third flaw in Sunstein and Thaler's approach is their failure to confront the devastating impact of marital nudging on couples further down the socioeconomic hierarchy. The vast majority of couples won't make their wedding plans with the self-confidence provided by Alpha's and Omega's brilliant job prospects or $150,000 bank account. For these couples, even a modest fee for professional services may well be unaffordable. Supposing that they could come up with some money, taking it out of their "rainy day fund" is likely to increase their breakup chances, given the impoverished conditions in which they find themselves.

This last objection is of crucial importance. But it is not decisive – since there are real-world ways of solving it. Rather than requiring prospective marriage partners to pay for their prenuptual negotiations, nudgers could urge local or national governments to subsidize these costs so that citizens can negotiate for free. Or Sunstein and Thaler might persuade some well-intentioned foundation to pay for the initial round of field experiments that might spur governmental nudge-subsidies.

It will be harder for such organizations to respond to another fundamental feature of the current class divide: cultural domination. Despite dramatic increases in education levels, billions and billions of people are culturally unequipped to evaluate technocratic presentations. As a consequence, if marriage-nudgers hope to succeed in reaching these people in a meaningful fashion, they could only do so through mini-dramas in which successes and failures were portrayed in nonstatistical terms.

Yet these portrayals would undermine the fundamental ambition of the Sunstein-Thayer enterprise – which is precisely to encourage people to activate their Reflective System at moments when they most need it. Even if these mini-dramas encouraged prospective newlyweds to overcome their triumphant "mood" of marital success, it would have accomplished this feat by creating a "mood" of anxiety that might well split the newlyweds apart—but without engaging in thoughtful reflection on their real-world chances of enduring happiness.

In short, the Alpha-Omega-Amity trialogue demonstrates *Nudge*'s three fundamental failings—its totalizing embrace of commodification, its blindness to the irreplaceable aspects of face-to-face relationships, and its failure to confront the realities of cultural domination. If Sunstein and Thaler are to redeem their commitment to Enlightenment values in the internet age, it will require a more thoughtful engagement with the existential predicaments confronting us in the twenty-first century.

Chapter 12

RECONSTRUCTION

I will begin with a critique of the buzz word that has come to summarize the worldwide crisis of constitutional democracy: "polarization." This term confuses two very different aspects of our current situation. The first is that political leaders are indeed denouncing each other as "enemies of the people" and refusing to collaborate in an ongoing effort to enact plausible solutions to key problems on the national agenda. Call this elite polarization, and it is on dramatic display in contemporary political practice throughout the world.

Yet it is a mistake to suppose that the larger voting public is equally polarized. Serious pollsters have been exploring this issue for almost a century in the United States. Since George Gallup began operations in the 1930s, pollsters have regularly asked registered voters whether they considered themselves Democrats or Republicans or independents. Throughout the twentieth century, fewer than 20 percent of Americans considered themselves "independents." But over the last two decades, this number has soared to 40 percent – making independents the largest voting bloc in the nation. Moreover, about half of today's Democrats and Republicans describe themselves as "weakly" committed to their party and say they would seriously consider an attractive candidate from the other side. Only 30 percent of registered voters – about half Democrats, half Republicans – are so "strongly" committed that they would put their party loyalty first.

Most Americans view the intransigence of their elected representatives with growing despair. Alienation, not polarization, is the prevailing dis-ease amongst the general public. Given the impasse at the top, citizens are increasingly uncertain whether their political system can sustain a credible version of democracy that can meet the challenges of the twenty-first century.[1]

America is hardly unique in this respect. Democratic disillusionment expresses itself differently in different parts of the world – in ways that depend on each country's constitutional framework, political party system, and cultural traditions. Despite these regional differences, the high-tech revolution contributes everywhere to growing alienation. Demagogues can flood the internet with sloganeering in a way that was impossible during the twentieth century. Even as late as the 1990s, the number of television and radio stations was limited, and democratic governments took strong measures to assure that these stations were not transformed into vehicles for fake news and demagogic propaganda. Most leading newspapers were also committed to the principle that the country's future should be decided by voters at the polls, not violence in the streets – although anti-democratic movements had greater success gaining broad audiences through print media than through radio or television.

Authoritarian movements repeatedly overwhelmed democratic regimes that had been shattered by economic disaster, military defeat, or superpower intervention – or all three. Mostly, however, prevailing structures of mass communication served as a structural source of democratic stability during troubled times.

No longer. The internet enables demagogues to reach vast audiences – and energize them with fake news – on a daily basis. Given their worldwide success, it is easy to lose sight of a longer-term transformation that can serve as an important counterweight. As I have already emphasized, the postmodern world is inhabited by the most educated population in human history. In most of the world, most of the electorate has gained the educational resources needed to move beyond misleading sound bites and engage in an informed debate over the reform priorities that make sense for their sociopolitical context. As always, the question is whether people will take the time and energy required to do so.[2]

Here is where the existentialist approach to reform has a big advantage. Massive numbers of impoverished and stigmatized people have no choice but to engage in a daily struggle for economic survival. Yet they may sometimes find time to talk with their friends, either at home or at work, about politics. These casual conversations provide a special opportunity to mobilize support for existentialist initiatives.

To make my case, suppose that a few friends and relatives have found time to move beyond the sound bites to seriously consider a couple of issues currently at the center of democratic debate. Needless to say, these sphere-mates have many other demands on their time, so their investigations have been relatively superficial and selective. Nevertheless, let's suppose that they have focused on two reforms.

One involves a question that has nothing to do with the problems their impoverished sphere-mates encounter in everyday life.

Suppose, for example, they are trying to follow the raging debate over the way NATO should be reorganized to maintain peace in Europe. Or perhaps it is the debate over the extent to which global warming requires massive cutbacks in air pollution over the next fifty years. Call these "macro-issues," and contrast them with the micro-issues their impoverished sphere-mates directly confront in their everyday lives.

For present purposes, my crucial point has nothing to do with the intrinsic merits of the particular micro-reforms under consideration but with the very different way in which poor people will approach them. Preoccupied with earning a living, they have heard about NATO or climate change only on internet sound bites. As a consequence, they will have a hard time entering into a thoughtful conversation about them. Even if some of their more engaged friends gave them mini-lectures on key issues, it will rapidly become apparent that they can't afford to devote the time and energy required to make a responsible judgment on the macro-reforms championed by leading candidates for elected office.

This won't be true when dinner table conversation turns to micro-reforms near the top of the public agenda. These proposals aim for decisive improvements in the conversationalists' real-world struggle for a meaningful existence in their very own lives – or the lives of people to whom they are deeply committed. As a consequence, it will often seem more democratic to steer the conversation toward these existential issues, since it allows everyone to join in on a relatively equal basis.

Many of these casual give-and-takes won't lead the participants to change their minds, given their relative brevity and superficiality. Nevertheless, they can often encourage participants to pay more attention to candidates who offer serious reforms that promise a significant change in their lives. It will not only create a powerful incentive for rival candidates to engage in thoughtful debate, but it will be especially important in elections in which Democrats or Republicans have backed a demagogue flooding the media with sound bites.

To anticipate a potential misunderstanding, I am not suggesting that real-world activists should ignore macro-questions of existential justice. My thesis is more modest but nonetheless fundamental. Given massive citizen alienation from their system of government, serious reform movements should include at least a few micro-reforms as key priorities in their ongoing effort to gain decisive victories at the polls.

I want to go one step further in my argument for micro-reforms. I will try to persuade you that they will also gain a relatively favorable reception in many privileged households. As this book has repeatedly emphasized, the rich and powerful struggle with many of the same existential predicaments that confront their fellow citizens. At the very least, many of them will be prepared to consider these reforms with a relatively open mind. They will be perfectly aware that if existential reformers gain electoral victories, the rich will be required to pay more taxes. This prospect will predictably lead many to throw lots of money into defeating the reformers at the ballot box.

Yet if micro-reformers manage to win the election, even the rich may come to view the enactment of reforms as a triumph of democracy. After all, they themselves have been struggling with the same existential predicaments that confront their fellow citizens, albeit with the advantage provided by their greater wealth. The fact that their less privileged peers are now struggling on a (somewhat) more equal playing field can significantly contribute to the continuing credibility of democracy in the postmodern world—in which *both* the rich and the poor, the proud and the stigmatized, have reaffirmed their common commitment to one another as fellow citizens. In short, micro-reform can bring us together, not tear us apart.

Given the current triumph of demagogues around the world, I expect a skeptical response to my grimly optimistic thesis. To convince you that my hopes are not wildly utopian, this chapter will develop three initiatives that have gained serious support in real-world politics over the past two decades, beginning with a couple of micro-reforms. I will then advance a more sweeping program for existential justice that could well transform the foundations of everyday life in the postmodern world.

I will only say enough about each proposal to provoke debate over its future prospects – and to encourage readers to come up with more and better ideas. My larger aim is to suggest that you should not sit on the sidelines in despair while demagogues transform themselves into dictators, but that it makes sense to take a grimly optimistic view of the future of postmodern democracy – provided that people like you work hard to construct realistic reforms that make sense to thoughtful voters over the coming decade.

Universal Childcare

One of the great achievements of the Enlightenment was the "discovery of childhood." As infants began to make their way in the world, they were no longer expected to mimic the patterns of existence adopted by the closely knit community in which they were raised. Instead, their elders had an obligation to provide them with the cultural resources they needed to define their own aims – and to break free of their initial cultural environment if it didn't measure up to their evolving self-understandings.

This implied, as the French Declaration of the Rights of Man and of the Citizen proclaimed, "Society ought to favor with all its power the advancement of the public reason and to put education at the door of every citizen."[3] Indeed, if Napoleon had not crushed the Revolution's republican aspirations, Paris of the 1790s—not Boston of the 1830s—would have been the scene of the first great pedagogic breakthrough of the modern era. Instead, France would have to wait until the rise of the Third Republic in the 1870s before it launched its own ambitious project of public education. Over the next century, these early efforts helped inspire a worldwide movement that has culminated in the remarkable breakthroughs of the past half century.[4] Indeed, some Asia-Pacific democracies are now governed by better-educated electorates than almost all of their transatlantic counterparts.[5]

Yet the French are once again leading the world in one respect: early childhood education. Starting in the 1990s, their government has launched an extraordinary nationwide system enabling parents to send their three-year-olds to neighborhood childcare centers, where they are cared for by specially trained clinical psychologists. Each professional supervises a small group of youngsters on an ongoing basis. They encourage the kids to engage with their age-mates in ways that will prepare them to succeed in primary school when they enter at age six.[6]

The nationwide system takes the same approach when dealing with broader issues of cultural subordination. The most compelling problem involves children who have spent their earliest years in Arabic-speaking households. These three-year-olds can go to nearby centers where bilingual specialists do their best to prepare them for their especially challenging transition to elementary schools, where they will be taught in French. The government has also developed a network of centers to assist children with special mental or physical needs.[7]

These extraordinary efforts generated a remarkable public response. Though there was no legal obligation to do so, huge numbers of parents began sending their three-year-olds to these écoles maternelles, as they are called. By 2015, 99 percent of eligible children were entering the system.[8]

Empirical work has demonstrated that these écoles have had a remarkably egalitarian impact. Upper-class youngsters gain a great deal, enabling them to further develop the rich linguistic resources provided by their privileged family backgrounds. But their less privileged counterparts make even more decisive gains – even though they enter preschool at the age of three with far more limited modes of verbal and grammatical self-expression. Nevertheless, this big disadvantage is almost eliminated by the time they leave the écoles and confront teachers speaking the formal style of French that is used in the primary schools. Children from non-French-speaking households also make enormous advances, although they don't entirely erase their initial deficit.[9]

Despite their entry with a relatively equal skill set, different first-graders will have been raised by very different families–and will respond very differently to their teachers and classmates. Yet these differences in classroom response no longer strongly correlate with socioeconomic background and may even give some impoverished youngsters a classroom advantage over some richer fellow students. To put this existential point in grand historical terms: when the children of France enter primary school in the 2020s, they are redeeming, for the first time in history, the proud promise of the Declaration of Rights of 1789, which famously begins by proclaiming that all "men are born and *remain* free and equal [italics added]."

Nevertheless, despite their roughly equal starting point, kids from rich and highly educated families regain their advantage as they move up the academic ladder – since their parents provide them with a host of educational advantages that far outstrip those that poorer parents can provide. Yet it would be a big mistake to underestimate the école's egalitarian breakthrough. Substantial numbers of low-income students use their preschool training as a springboard for extraordinary levels of academic achievement and self-realization.[10]

What's more, the écoles are having a life-changing impact on other impoverished and stigmatized students – even though they are less successful academically. Before the 1990s, many of these students were utterly unprepared for the culture shock they encountered on entering first grade, where teachers spoke a formal French they could barely understand. Millions never managed to overcome their initial bewilderment – and performed so poorly in school that they faced a grim job market.[11]

Thanks to the head start provided by the école, many impoverished students put in a satisfactory performance on their exams that testify to their academic competence. They also succeed in other school activities, ranging from sports to school plays to weekend parties. This multidimensional experience enables them to enter the adult world with a far greater capacity to build a meaningful life with self-confidence.

There is no need to exaggerate. Even with their école training, many impoverished students fail to surmount classroom challenges, and they leave school branded as academic failures – who are forced, as young adults, to engage in desperate efforts to find a decent job, build a rewarding family life, and fulfil the many other demands of postmodern existence. These very real tragedies, however, should not lead us to ignore the decisive breakthrough France achieved at the dawn of the twenty-first century. Instead, they raise the fundamental question emphasized by this chapter: will French citizens of the 2020s follow the path marked out by their predecessors in the 1990s and support another revolutionary reform of preschool education that will further expand the real-world prospects of oppressed youngsters?

President Emmanuel Macron has put this question at the very center of French politics—and has led the voters to answer with a decisive yes. After taking office in 2017, he rapidly moved to redefine the place of the écoles in the life of the country. Until his presidency, parents were not legally required to send their children to preschool. Once he gained office, however, his government enacted a statute that stripped parents of discretion on the matter and made attendance obligatory. This decisive step is especially remarkable given that Macron's victory in 2017 was widely seen as a neoliberal triumph. Yet he immediately moved in the opposite direction. Rather than continuing to nudge parents in the manner of Cass Sunstein and Richard Thaler, the new statute unconditionally required attendance in recognition of the nation's "obligation to future generations."[12]

Even more remarkably, Macron dramatically expanded the école's ambition by opening its doors to children much younger than three. Under the new law, parents could begin to share child-raising responsibilities with specially trained professionals almost immediately after their infants were born. The law left it up to individual parents to decide whether to take this step, but one thing is clear: the citizens most likely to seize this opportunity are impoverished parents who have been abandoned by their spouses. Macron's initiative has freed them from the exhausting demands of round-the-clock childcare – and allowed them to greet their infants with renewed energy when they picked them up at their neighborhood centers. It also enabled some of them to get a part-time job and provide their babies with better food and housing.

In short, Macron's breakthrough is a paradigmatic example of the reformist strategy proposed in this chapter. In running for the presidency, his principal campaign targets were middle- and upper-class voters – and many other elements in his platform directly appealed to their economic and ideological interests. But his childcare initiatives called upon his core constituency to take a very different view of their responsibilities as democratic citizens. Even the richest and most successful voters are intimately familiar with the anxieties of child-rearing – despite having a lot more cash to cushion the conflict between their responsibilities at home and those they confront at work and in other spheres of life. In making his dramatic proposal a centerpiece of his campaign, Macron was calling upon his well-off constituency to rely on these existential understandings to support an unprecedented reform to achieve social justice for their fellow citizens, even though they themselves would never confront the same desperate situation.

It is precisely this appeal to independent-minded voters that is central to the micro-reform strategy I am advancing. Moreover, in Macron's campaign for reelection in 2022, he made his revolutionary educational reforms a key element in his efforts to persuade voters to reject Marine Le Pen's assault on fundamental principles of Enlightenment democracy. And he succeeded: the French people gave him a decisive 59 percent to 41 percent victory at the polls.

It is too early to tell whether Macron's dramatic expansion of childcare will be a real-world success. Countless impoverished parents may confront bureaucratic nightmares when they arrive at their neighborhood centers, or they may find their kids are even more miserable once they have encountered their "therapists." If Macron's government doesn't take effective steps to resolve such problems, his remarkable initiative may backfire.

Nevertheless, I remain grimly optimistic. Despite inevitable start-up problems, Macron may well be in a position to pass on a relatively successful initiative by the time he leaves office. Moreover, any new president will have to think twice before repealing the program. The expulsion of infants from the centers would provoke massive demonstrations that could jeopardize the new incumbent's prospects for reelection.

Macron's reform, in short, is self-reinforcing – precisely because it is based on micro-existential foundations. Not only will the potential backlash give conservative presidents a political incentive to preserve Macron's advance, but it will encourage centrist politicians to include decisive micro-reforms in other spheres when campaigning for office. For this reason, it deserves worldwide attention at a time when constitutional democracy is under such fierce assault. Especially in the United States, where current levels of childcare lag far behind most other economically advanced nations. Before the COVID crisis, preschool facilities were available to just 40 percent of America's three-year-olds, 68 percent of its four-year-olds, and 86 percent of its five-year-olds – with impoverished and non-white youngsters bearing the brunt of the exclusionary burden. Worse yet, employees at day care centers typically lack the specialized training of their French counterparts. Indeed, their median wage was less than $12 an hour.[13]

The COVID pandemic made the situation even worse. Two-thirds of neighborhood centers had to close in 2020 to prevent kids from infecting one another. When the centers began to reopen in 2021, only two-thirds of their childcare personnel returned to work; given their low wages, many had found better-paying jobs elsewhere.[14] This meant that when youngsters returned to preschool, they entered their classrooms to encounter strangers, wearing masks, to take care of them.

During his first two years, President Joe Biden took some tentative steps down Emmanuel Macron's path. Within a month of his entry into the White House, he gained bipartisan support for $2 trillion in COVID emergency funding, including a token $3 billion for preschool. But this issue emerged as a key administration priority only a year later, when Biden looked beyond the COVID crisis. His Build Back Better bill proposed an expenditure of $350 billion over the next five years to create a nationwide system of universal preschool for three- to five-year-olds. But even an appropriation this big will not be nearly enough to give American kids the high-quality help their French counterparts now take for granted. At present, only four states in the Union operate pre-K programs for all children – and they rely heavily on poorly paid caregivers. For every state to live up to French standards, the federal government would have to provide big appropriations over the coming generation to recruit and train the enormous numbers of professionals required to fill the existing vacuum.

Nevertheless, the administration's "budget-busting" proposal provoked strong Republican opposition on Capitol Hill. My micro-thesis gains credibility, however, by the refusal of the most conservative Democrats to embrace this critique. Senator Joe Manchin's views are particularly revealing. He joined the Republicans in rejecting many of the ambitious measures advanced in Build Back Better, but he took a very different position on this particular mega-billion-dollar expenditure – for a simple reason. When he had been governor of West Virginia, between 2005 and 2010, the demand for universal pre-K had already confronted him with a serious political dilemma. His predecessor as governor, Bob Wise, had gained legislative approval of a statute establishing a statewide system of preschool education for three- to five-year-olds – leaving it up to Manchin to transform this legal commitment into a reality. Doing so required him to overcome a host of challenges involved in financing, siting, and staffing centers in each neighborhood.

It would have been easy for Manchin to defer these tough political decisions and preserve his reputation by opening just a few centers to great fanfare. Instead, he did the hard work needed to gain the support of a bipartisan coalition that propelled the initiative into high gear. By the time he left for the Senate in 2010, West Virginia was one of the very few states setting a precedent for President Biden's initiative. Manchin refused to join the Republican opposition to the administration's $350 billion commitment to universal pre-K education and publicly endorsed the measure. But Biden could not convince other swing senators to follow his lead, and his attempted breakthrough became another victim of political polarization on Capitol Hill.

This setback should not lead reformers to give up the fight – especially when viewed against the background of the French revolution in childhood education. Macron's success in persuading voters to recognize their fundamental "obligation to future generations," and Manchin's success in West Virginia, are no less significant than Biden's failure in Congress.

It is far too soon for American thinkers-and-doers to give up efforts to make universal pre-K a key feature of the reform agenda for the coming decade. Instead, candidates of both political parties should make it a central plank in future campaigns for Congress and the presidency. The initiative is based on precisely the kind of commonsense appeal to everyday realities that can convince independent-minded voters to swing to the reformer's side in close elections – and provide a democratic mandate for existential justice.

Deliberation Day

Universal childcare reinvigorates democracy by demonstrating its capacity to respond decisively to an existential dilemma that almost every voter recognizes – even if they vote for candidates who oppose it on fiscal grounds. My second initiative pursues a different micro-strategy to reach the same destination. It responds to the fact that we fail to fulfil our *own* understanding of our responsibilities as democratic citizens, given competing demands on our time in other spheres of life. Only the most dedicated activists, for example, spend as much time mobilizing their fellow citizens as they spend with their families or friends.

Nevertheless, as the 2020 election showed, most Americans take their citizenship seriously. Whether they cast their ballots for Biden or Trump, a precedent-shattering 160 million voters came out to the polls to have their say – 23 million more than in 2016. This dramatic increase was especially remarkable at a time when the COVID epidemic was confronting citizens with massive unemployment and the prospect of death. Nevertheless, citizens found the time to cast a ballot because they rightly saw that the 2020 election was a turning point in American democracy—and that, as citizens, they had a responsibility to join with their fellow citizens in determining the shape of their country's future.[15]

Even in more normal times, 60 to 80 million Americans watch presidential debates in the run-up to Election Day—when they could spend those 90 minutes playing a video game or watching a great movie on another channel. Wouldn't that be a lot more fun than watching a couple of unfunny candidates responding to boring questions?[16]

But Americans aren't turning to the debates in search of fun, though they may sometimes laugh at the candidates' ridiculous answers. The overwhelming majority are watching the debates with a relatively open mind. As professional pollsters have repeatedly shown, only 30 percent of the electorate consider themselves "strong" Democrats or Republicans. In contrast, another 30 percent are only "weakly" committed to their party, and 40 percent tell pollsters that they are "independents" who try to judge each candidate on his or her merits without regard to party affiliation. These 70-percenters recognize that they have been bombarded by sound bites appealing to their anxieties and emotions, and that the debates give them a chance to assess the candidates without an extravagant expenditure of time.

After listening for 90 minutes, many may express disappointment with the candidates' answers and evasions. Nevertheless, when talking afterward with family and friends, they address each other in their role as democratic citizens, not as amateur movie critics. These follow-up conversations are efforts to fulfil their obligation as responsible citizens to cast their ballots in a thoughtful fashion. They aim to determine, however haltingly, which candidate has given them *reasons* for believing that he or she will better serve the public interest.

My second reform proposal builds on these commonplace discussions among citizens. It is based on my work with Professor James Fishkin of Stanford University's Center for Deliberative Democracy. For many years the Center has conducted an ongoing series of "deliberative polls" in which it invites a few hundred voters to engage in one or two days of intensive discussion dealing with central issues on their country's political agenda. Stanford's team of social scientists make special efforts to provide both conservatives and progressives a fair opportunity to argue for their very different solutions to their country's problems. They also take care to assemble groups of deliberators who are statistically representative of the nation as a whole in economic, ethnic, racial, and religious terms. This means that if large numbers of participants change their opinions in response to their sustained discussions, the entire electorate would probably do the same if given a comparable opportunity.[17]

Over the past 30 years, Stanford's Center has supervised deliberative polls in nearly 120 places around the world, from Australia to Bulgaria, China to Denmark, Mongolia to the United States. Fishkin's early field experiments in the 1990s, however, were sufficiently compelling to lead us to publish *Deliberation Day* in 2004. That book proposed a national holiday (known as D-Day) in which citizens would be invited to engage in a day-long discussion of campaign issues before they voted.

According to the proposal, once D-Day was enacted into law, only essential service providers would go to work on the new holiday. Everybody else would have two options: they could enjoy a day off with family and friends, or they could join their neighbors in a common effort to take their citizenship responsibilities seriously.[18]

When Fishkin and I made our initial proposal in 2004, we supposed that D-Dayers would gather for in-person discussions in local community centers. Since then, however, Stanford's Center has moved its field experiments onto the internet, and for reasons that will become clear, this offers a more practical alternative to our original face-to-face version.[19]

Under this postmodern scenario, voters who want to participate click yes to an electronic D-Day invitation, which then links them up with ten to fifteen fellow citizens who will be their conversation partners throughout the proceedings. After briefly introducing themselves to one another, they are admitted into the first event of the day: an hour-long televised debate between the Democrat and the Republican running for president, similar to the debates that have become familiar since John F. Kennedy and Richard Nixon began the modern practice in 1960.

When the give-and-take ends, each small group begins setting the agenda for the rest of the day's deliberations. Members have been asked, while watching the debate, to be on the lookout for key issues that they think deserve more intensive exploration—and to take note of each issue in a few short sentences. After the debate, each group spends the first hour comparing these short issue statements and deciding which ones deserve the highest priority. Their discussion proceeds in a fashion that resembles the way juries traditionally determine the guilt or innocence of a criminal defendant. They don't allow loudmouths to dominate the conversation but instead elect one member to serve as their presiding officer, to assure that each juror has a fair opportunity to participate.

The fifteen D-Dayers in each group have the same objective, but since their agenda-setting conversation lasts only an hour, they can't waste time electing a moderator. Instead, when they assemble via the internet after the candidate debate, they find that the computer program has already randomly assigned each member a four-minute speaking slot. When speaker 1's four minutes expire, the computer screen immediately shifts to speaker 2; and so forth.

Nobody is required to speak when their turn comes up. They may instead go to the end of the line, at which point they can either chime in or assign their minutes to a different speaker. Members are encouraged to use their time to explain why one of the issues raised during the candidates' debate is especially important—and to submit their brief statement to the group. When the 60-minute session comes to an end, members cast a secret ballot on the merits of each issue statement; any statement receiving two or more yeses gets onto the group's priority list, with the highest vote getters earning highest priority. Group members cast another secret ballot to determine who should serve as their spokesperson at later points in the process.

The next stage of deliberation is conducted in a much larger online assembly of 450 participants, all of whom have also spent the previous hour in small groups producing their own short lists—adding up to about 30 lists in all. With a local judge or other impartial official presiding, the next phase of the debate will be conducted by a local Democrat and Republican who has been appointed by their national campaigns to provide answers to each small group's questions. Once again, the presiding officer uses a randomized procedure to determine the order in which individual small groups gain the floor. Once the group's representative raises its highest-priority issue, the local Democratic and Republican representatives each have four minutes to clarify their candidate's position—after which the small group's spokesperson has two minutes to respond. As the deliberative assembly proceeds, groups further down the list may find that their highest-priority question has already been sufficiently explored, in which case, their spokesperson will go down its priority list to expand the debate in a suitable fashion. Since each Q and A lasts for 10 minutes, half of the groups will have a chance to participate during the 90-minute session held before the lunch break.

Deliberators return to their screens at about 2:30, having had a chance to reflect on the morning's conversation. At that point, they have another hour of small group discussion before returning to a concluding 90-minute debate before the larger assembly. This second small group session, however, has a distinctive aim. Members ask themselves whether the debate between the national candidates, followed by the morning's deliberations, has led them to reconsider the views they had previously held before D-Day began.

Strongly committed Democrats and Republicans can be counted on to make the case for their candidates—but they will typically be a minority in their 15-member group. Even if they happen to be in the majority, they will be trying to persuade more independent-minded colleagues. Rather than spending their four minutes on partisan sloganeering, party loyalists will have a compelling incentive to respond thoughtfully to the more complicated views expressed by these swing voters. Moreover, if their small group did not have a chance to interrogate the local debaters during the morning, the majority may vote to push the conversation in new directions when its spokesperson takes the floor in the afternoon.

Citizen assemblies throughout the nation will discuss different issues in very different ways, depending on the interests and ideologies that prevail in different parts of their vast country. Despite these differences, the "polarization" thesis suggests that D-Day will overwhelmingly tend to confirm that citizens will support the candidate they favored when they first clicked onto the internet in the morning to hear the candidates' debate.

Yet overwhelming evidence, collected by Stanford's Center for Deliberative Democracy in 120 "deliberative polls," suggests that the polarizers are wrong. With each poll it organizes, the Center asks invitees to answer a confidential questionnaire designed to reveal their knowledge about, and positions on, the key issues they will confront during their discussion – and then to answer the same questionnaire at the end of their time together. As a consequence, the Center now possesses a formidable data base of before-and-after reports from polls it has conducted throughout the world over the past 30 years.

The Center's statistical analysis generates remarkably consistent findings. Regardless of their different cultures and political predicaments, deliberators greatly enhance their understanding of the issues. They gain a far better appreciation of the ways in which rival interpretations of the facts can credibly support competing positions on the merits. Even more important, their discussions lead many participants to change their substantive views. Conservatives adopt positions they would have considered too liberal, and vice versa.

These big shifts don't cancel each other out. Instead, intensive discussion almost invariably leads the group as a whole to shift its opinion by 10 to 15 percentage points. These big swings, moreover, don't move in the same ideological direction – groups are just as likely, after a day's deliberation, to shift leftwards as rightwards.[20]

The implications of these findings are enormous. Suppose, for example, that Congress and the president gave D-Day a high priority on their reform agenda and enacted it into law in the aftermath of the 2024 election – with the aim of establishing the internet system which would permit Americans to engage in their first deliberative exercise before they cast their ballots in the 2028 election. Suppose, further, that this breakthrough statute creates a bipartisan D-Day Agency to supervise the technocratic construction of the internet network required to enable the nation's 160 million voters to participate in serious discussions. When D-Day finally arrives a few weeks before election day, it turns out that half of these people choose to spend the new holiday with friends and family – but that half decide to talk over the issues with their fellow citizens. If these 80 million deliberators respond like their counterparts in the 120 Stanford studies, it will lead to a swing of 8 to 12 million votes in the presidential election.

Such a tidal wave would almost certainly overwhelm the antimajoritarian features of the Electoral College, putting the candidate whom D-Dayers find most persuasive into the White House for the next four years. No less important, the newly elected Congress will contain lots of representatives and senators who won close contests on the president's coattails. The D-Day swing will not only decide the presidency but give the new administration a majority in both houses.

This doesn't mean that Congress will simply serve as a rubber stamp for the president's campaign platform – because the next nationwide D-Day, held before the off-year election in 2030, will serve as a powerful incentive to scrutinize the administration's grand proposals in a careful and disciplined fashion. Despite their debt to the president, members of both houses will recognize that their opponents will be in a position to launch a powerful counterattack on the next D-Day and that they can't count on an old-fashioned advertising blitz to beat their competitor – even if their incumbency enables them to raise a lot more money for their sound-bite assaults.

In short, my micro-emphasis on the need to encourage Americans to spend more time on citizenship will predictably generate three important macro-consequences. First, it will provide presidents with strong reform opportunities during the first two years of their administrations; second, it will nevertheless create new incentives for public-spirited checks and balances by Congress; third, it will reduce, but not eliminate, the role of big money in politics.

Nevertheless, I need more arguments if I hope to persuade you that D-Day should be taken seriously at the present time. After all, there are plenty of promising reforms that don't stand a chance of adoption, given the present polarized state of politics in Washington, D.C. Rather than inspiring support, why won't my three macro-virtues provoke sustained opposition from the White House and Congress?

Putting aside objections to particular details, the utopian critique depends on one key point. Call it the "incumbency objection." Quite simply, the present incumbents have gained their positions by using the existing levers of political power to win their elections. Yet it is precisely my point that D-Day will make it harder for them to exploit voter ignorance in the old-fashioned ways that they have deployed so successfully in the past. Why, then, would they back a reform that would make it a lot easier for their opponents to win in the future?

My answer comes in two parts. The first involves the significance of Donald Trump's power plays on senators and representatives. Trump's presidency demonstrates the real danger that some future demagogue will strip Congress of all effective control over presidential power – reducing the proudest senators and representatives to mere supplicants as they enter the White House to deal with the de facto dictator. This grim prospect radically revises the cost-benefit analysis of even the most cynical incumbents – leading them to look upon D-Day as a valuable insurance policy against a radical reduction in their real-world power. Moreover, most incumbent senators and representatives aren't total cynics, and they would see D-Day as an opportunity to push for initiatives they genuinely believe to be in the public interest.

Incumbent presidents, in contrast, will take a different view. The current system gives them enormous advantages when running for a second term. Throughout their first four years, the White House gives them the opportunity to dominate the political conversation, win their party primaries without opposition, and overwhelm their opponent with big money in the November election. In contrast, D-Day will give their opponent a dramatic opportunity for a landslide victory. Even if incumbents are deeply committed to democracy, they will be reluctant to make D-Day a high-priority – although even here, D-Day might be a plausible strategy if it seems likely that a Trumpish opponent will emerge as the opposing candidate and that D-Day will serve as the scene of a devastating defeat to demagogic pretentions.

Second-term presidents will view the issue differently, assuming that they don't harbor dictatorial ambitions. Not only will D-Day encourage their successors to appeal to a more thoughtful citizenry, but the incumbent will also take pride in leading American democracy in the right direction—and gain a great deal of praise from succeeding generations if this existential breakthrough proves to be a success.

It is, of course, an optimistic scenario. But at the very least, D-Day would provide a fundamental check on the never-ending propaganda campaigns unleashed by the internet revolution. A single day of deliberation before big elections is hardly a magical solution to the constant misrepresentation flooding our cell phones. But it would encourage serious candidates to move beyond 15-second sound bites and frame their campaigns in ways that make sense to millions of citizens engaged in a reasoned debate over the future of their country.

From a larger historical perspective, D-Day is best viewed as an effort to sustain the Enlightenment commitments of the American founding—despite the radically different conditions in which the country now finds itself.[21] The Bill of Rights, and especially the Sixth Amendment, serves as the decisive precedent. By guaranteeing a trial by jury in criminal cases, the Sixth Amendment repudiated the Crown's past abuses of prosecutorial power. The Founders did not suppose that by guaranteeing a right to trial by jury they were creating an ironclad guarantee against future abuses of power. They knew that criminal prosecutors could beef up a weak case by appealing to the jury's emotions—and that these appeals would sometimes induce the jurors to declare that innocent defendants were guilty "beyond a reasonable doubt." Nevertheless, they relied on the requirement of a jury trial as a crucial check on authoritarian government.

Deliberation Day offers a similarly realistic response to the threat of demagogic dictatorship. Although a single day of citizenship engagement won't eliminate the dangers posed by the endless stream of misinformation on the internet, it will move the electorate in the right direction—and if combined with reforms such as universal childcare, greatly reinforce their confidence in the capacity of democratic government to respond thoughtfully to the challenges of the twenty-first century.

The analogy to the Sixth Amendment suggests another step in building a firm foundation for the new civic holiday. Americans who spend the holiday engaged in D-Day activities should receive a $200 payment in recognition of their contribution to democratic self-government—in the same way that they receive a similar stipend when they are called for jury duty.

But there is an important difference. When citizens are summoned to jury duty, they are not free to refuse but, with certain well-defined exceptions, are legally obligated to leave their jobs to serve their country. In contrast, citizens are free to say no to D-Day and just enjoy their day off. Yet this difference makes the case for D-Day compensation even more compelling. The fact that participation is voluntary shows that those who do participate are serious about reinvigorating democracy in America.

Compensation will also resolve another predictable problem. Once D-Dayers click yes, they may find that the small and large group discussions are boring or stupid—and turn off the internet and return to face-to-face engagement with family and friends. Because participation is voluntary, they have a perfect right to do this, but it will come at the cost of losing their $200 stipend. Some will try to keep the money by misleading their D-Day sphere-mates. They will maintain their link to the other fourteen members of their small group and pretend that they are listening to the discussion though their attention is focused on something else entirely.

Call this the problem of "feigned presence." Computer engineers have developed a straightforward way to deal with it because it arises in many other deliberative contexts on the internet. From time to time, they flash a notice on the screen that gives participants only a short time to click a response button to demonstrate that they are paying attention. If they fail to click, their sphere-mates are put on notice immediately.

D-Day participants should be given a second chance if they fail this test the first time around – since their inattention may have its source in their need to attend to some urgent demand of the "here and now." But they will lose their $200 if they fail a second time, although they are free, of course, to continue their deliberative engagement if they choose.

Some may continue, despite the loss of their bonus; others will not. Regardless of particular decisions, these ground rules will encourage all participants take a more constructive view of their momentary annoyances with the debate. Rather than lose their $200, they may come to recognize that their impatience may stem from the hard truth that they disagree with lots of their fellow citizens – and that the best way to respond is by taking advantage of opportunities to express their very different sense of the public interest. In short: rather than looking upon the potential loss of the stipend as a punishment, they may view it as an incentive to join the debate.

The stipend also responds to the special predicaments confronting people who are working at low pay for lots of hours each week. They will especially appreciate the rare opportunity to relax with their friends and family – and may find it particularly difficult to give it up for D-Day. The $200 grant doesn't solve their dilemma but puts it within a different framework. They can now say to their kids, “Once my engagement with my fellow citizens is done, we can spend the $200 on a special treat. In the meantime, perhaps you would like to sit by my side and tell me what you think of the debate?” Some kids will reject this D-Day invitation; others sit by their parents’ side. Either way, the stipend will increase working-class participation – and it will greatly enhance D-Day’s credibility as a real-world project in which citizens, despite their many differences, come together to shape the future of their country.

The stipend is even more important for men and women who have lost their jobs or whose handicaps have rendered them unemployable. For them, the day off offered by D-Day is meaningless. But the $200 bonus for participating offers a minor, but significant, improvement on the meagre welfare payments they ordinarily receive. Despite its attraction, however, they may well refuse to click into a small group, fearing that their engagement with more successful peers will leave them feeling like failures.

Different people will resolve these anxieties in different ways, but overall the stipend will lead millions to enter the public forum and confront their upper-class Americans with the need to face the question of social justice. Moreover, as Stanford’s social scientists have repeatedly shown in their field experiments, low-income participants typically learn the most from their D-Day engagements, putting them in a far better position to cast a thoughtful ballot in the election.

If 80 million Americans participate, these $200 payments would add up to around $15 billion. This is only a part of the price that Congress must pay if D-Day is to succeed. In its legislation, it must create a D-Day Authority – and appropriate the funds necessary to manage the technology and personnel required for millions to celebrate their first Deliberation Day in the near future. In order to assure relatively glitch-free operation, the authority will need to call upon the Silicon Valley for help, but it can't cede ultimate decision-making authority to private entrepreneurs. Otherwise, they could tell their techies to design the internet network in ways that subtly predispose D-Dayers in the partisan directions that they favor – using all the techniques taught to them by Sunstein and Thaler and their fellow nudgers.

Should this happen, it would discredit the entire enterprise once the technocrats triumphantly announced that their system was ready for real-world operation and Americans began to click into their first nationwide experiment in engaged citizenship. It would quickly become obvious to advocates for the disadvantaged candidate – be it the Democrat or the Republican – that the network had been designed to make it harder for their messages to gain the serious consideration of their conversation partners. By the end of the day, their escalating outrage could well provoke a broad-based backlash and lead to the rapid repeal of the entire initiative.

It is up to the D-Day Authority to create a level playing field in cyberspace. Although private enterprise can provide valuable expertise, the Authority must have a strong professional staff to assure fundamental fairness. Undoubtedly, their real-world efforts will fall far short of perfection, but as staffers supervise system development, they will be in a position to field test alternative designs in a series of Stanford-style deliberative polls. In each field experiment, a representative group of Americans would debate a politically salient issue within a differently designed internet network. As these field experiments accumulate, the Authority will be in a far better position to construct a nationwide system that can gain broad-based credibility.

To be sure, given the ambition of the project, there may well be lots of places around the country in which Democrats or Republicans protest the way in which local judges treat their party spokesperson at particular citizen assemblies, leaving the Authority in a difficult position. Some judges and partisan representatives should be banned from participating in future D-Days—but only after a careful fact-finding effort supervised by bipartisan panels of federal judges. Any other punishment should be strictly prohibited—otherwise it would enable the Authority to transform itself into an engine of repression.

Since extremists will be making these charges in any event, a final reform would serve to put them into perspective. I propose that Deliberation Day replace an already existing holiday—Presidents' Day—that has degenerated into a farce. Rather than celebrating the contributions of Lincoln and Washington to the republic, the third Monday of February has become a time for Americans to dramatize their savvy as bargain-hunting consumers rather than thoughtful citizens.

There is, of course, nothing wrong with bargain hunting, whenever it takes place. But by shifting President's Day from February to October, Congress could honor Washington and Lincoln by providing Americans with an opportunity to take their citizenship responsibilities with high seriousness.

Don't you agree?

A final word: I have been focusing on the United States, since it's best to be concrete, and as an American, I am most deeply familiar with its contemporary political realities. But if you are reading this book somewhere else in the world, I hope that my discussion will encourage you to consider how a version of D-Day might make sense within your own political tradition. The challenge is everywhere the same: how can the most educated citizenry in history redeem the real-world promise of Enlightenment democracy?

The Stakeholder Society

When the Berlin Wall fell in 1989, the United States was already the advanced democracy that allowed the super-rich to appropriate the biggest share of its citizens' overall wealth. In the decades since then, both Democratic and Republican administrations have allowed the rising techno-elite to appropriate an even larger share of the productivity gains generated by the internet revolution—allowing the top 1 percent of Americans to increase their share of the nation's privately held wealth from 30 percent to 40 percent. By the early 2020s, the three richest Americans owned more assets than the entire bottom half of the U.S. population. (Please see the appendix for all the statistics presented in this section.)

Given this extraordinary development, and the ways that the super-rich can legally deploy their wealth in politics, it would hardly be surprising if plutocrats had persuaded realistic reformers to treat scholarly calls for radical redistribution as mere exercises in utopian dreaming that had no chance of statutory enactment. But it hasn't turned out that way. Although she did not win the Democratic presidential nomination in 2020, Elizabeth Warren's advocacy of a wealth tax on the super-rich has greatly reinforced grassroots movements aiming to make the issue a focal point of American politics. This sets the stage for my final proposal: citizenship inheritance.

The basic idea has its roots in the American and French Revolutions. In the 1790s, when both republics were struggling to define their core principles, Thomas Paine urged the creation of "a national fund, out of which there shall be paid to every person, when arrived at the age of twenty-one years, the sum of fifteen pounds sterling," at the time a large amount of money.[22] Only by giving each citizen substantial sums could the new republics allow citizens to define the meaning of their own lives in their own way—and thereby construct a polity that was truly based on the proposition that "all men are created equal." Even more remarkably, Paine demanded that women gain their real-world autonomy on precisely the same terms as men.

Paine's stakeholding proposal has frequently provoked intense debate over the past two centuries, and it regained serious attention when Tony Blair's Labour government enacted a version of Paine's initiative—called the Child Trust Fund—in 2002. While Blair's bill gained broad support among the public, the rise of the Conservative Right in British politics led to its repeal in 2010.[23] Despite this setback, progressive movements elsewhere have succeeded in enacting similar initiatives, most notably in Brazil. When Lula da Silva won the presidency in 2003, he put forward a remarkable reform, the Bolsa Familia, which—like stakeholding—provided impoverished parents with the financial resources needed to keep their children in school and also provide a financial head start when they became young adults. The success of this initiative provided the broad-based popular support that enabled Lula da Silva to overcome the incumbency advantage of President Jair Bolsonaro and regain the presidency in 2022. Lula's commitment to stakeholding, in short, was crucial to his broader effort to reinvigorate the constitutional democracy that Bolsonaro was seeking to destroy.[24]

It is no exaggeration to view Elizabeth Warren's sweeping proposal for wealth redistribution as part of a worldwide movement for existential justice. Of course, this effort may ultimately fail, given the plutocratic forces arrayed against it. I don't possess a crystal ball that lets me predict the future. Nevertheless, it should be clear that it serves as another example of the micro-macro dynamic that serves as the centerpiece of this chapter's reformist agenda—encouraging voters to throw their macro-support behind a micro-initiative that can provide the rising generation with the cultural and economic resources they need before they can confront their postmodern predicaments in a seriously autonomous fashion.

I have been thinking about this particular micro-macro dynamic for a long time. In 1999, I published *The Stakeholder Society*, written with Anne Alstott, which made the case for the Blair/Lula/Warren initiatives of the last two decades, and so it seems appropriate to conclude with some reflections on the key issues that must be confronted if Americans take their intergenerational responsibilities seriously over the coming decades.[25]

One set of questions focuses on the super-rich; another on the young Americans who will be claiming their stakes as they leave school to confront their postmodern dilemmas of self-definition.

First things first. Most obviously, a progressive government must make some controversial decisions about tax rates and tax brackets. How much more should a billionaire pay than a mere multi-millionaire?

There are lots of reasonable answers—some of which I explore in the appendix. For illustration, consider a system that taxes only the top 0.1 percent of American families, those who own more than $50 million. Under my not-so-hypothetical proposal, they would start paying a 3 percent annual tax on assets exceeding this amount in 2032. If they are among the 16,000 households owning more than $175 million, the rate would go up to 5 percent.

This progressive rate structure dramatizes the unprecedented concentration of wealth in America today. Under its provisions, the richest *five* families would pay nearly 5 percent of all the taxes streaming into the Stakeholding Fund. The 500 richest families would pay nearly 30 percent of the requisite tax revenue, and the 3,000 richest would finance half of the fund. All these people would still be in a position to make millions more on their remaining investments – and their personal lives would not change in the slightest. Yet my modeling efforts suggest that the fund would raise enough money to give each young American a stake of $150,000 during their twenties and early thirties – and provide them with real-world freedom to explore life opportunities that only children of the upper middle class presently enjoy.

As the appendix shows, my model generates this remarkable result even if we assume that the super-rich will engage in widespread tax evasion. Yet I think it's a big mistake to suppose this will happen – not because the super-rich are super-moral, but because they will find it in their best interest to obey the law.

To be sure, they will pay big salaries to lawyers and financial advisors to devise clever tax-minimization strategies. But I hope to persuade you that, under the policy I propose, these lawyers and advisors will not find it in their own self-interest to engage in evasive maneuvers. Paradoxically, the fact that so few families own so much of America will induce them to resist their clients' shortsighted efforts to cheat on their returns.

To see why, suppose the Stakeholder law creates a special Wealth Tax Division (WTD) in the Internal Revenue Service to respond to efforts by the super-rich to minimize their tax burden. As long as the IRS keeps its computer systems up to date, the WTD can effectively monitor the tax forms submitted by the super-rich in a rapid-fire fashion that was impossible in the twentieth century. Even as early as 2010, the IRS was auditing more than 32,000 returns submitted by taxpayers reporting net incomes of more than a million dollars.

As a consequence, the WTD will be in a position to create a virtuous cycle in its dealings with the super-rich. If their accountants submit surprisingly low numbers on their clients' tax returns, IRS computers will pick them out for scrutiny and require the accountants to defend their questionable decisions in adversary proceedings. This will require clients not only to pay big fees to their legal and financial representatives for the elaborate preparations required to make their case before the WTD. If their returns are rejected, they will have to pay heavy penalties for failing to file accurate tax reports in the first place.

A very different scenario will prevail amongst super-rich families whose lawyers and accountants refuse to conceal assets. Even if these professionals lose some clients, they will greatly enhance their credibility with staffers in the WTD. When their tax returns generate audits, not only will they be in a position to defend them persuasively, but they will be able to persuade the WTD of their good-faith efforts at compliance. Firms that collaborate with tax evaders, by contrast, will be treated with increasing skepticism by auditors.

As a result, determined tax evaders will find it harder and harder to find reputable firms to defend them. And if they allow lawyers and accountants with shady reputations to represent them, IRS computers will increasingly single them out for scrutiny. Thus the dynamics of a virtuous cycle would reinforce the wealth tax system over a relatively short time: law firms and accounting firms that take their professional responsibilities seriously will drive shady dealers out of the wealth tax business – and the selfish super-rich will have no choice but to obey the law.

But perhaps I am underestimating the power of the super-rich: Why can't they respond by corrupting the staffers in the Wealth Tax Division, paying them millions in order to avoid paying billions?

For starters, the White House and its congressional allies have powerful political incentives to prevent these payoffs. Stakeholding, by hypothesis, served as a key plank in their electoral victory. If the WTD doesn't collect enough taxes to fund $150,000 to eligible Americans, progressive candidates will suffer at the polls in the next election. As a consequence, there is every reason for the White House to make sure that the WTD is staffed by appointees who are deeply committed to its egalitarian aims. There are also (see appendix) several other anti-corruption measures that Congress should seriously consider in drafting its statute.

Apart from corruption, there are a host of accounting issues raised by my claim that a 3 to 5 percent annual wealth tax on the super-rich would generate enough money to fund the program I am advancing – and the appendix will consider these as well. For now, it's better to focus on the fundamental policy issues Congress must confront in designing a credible system.

Begin with a crucial question of transitional justice. Suppose reformers win the 2032 election on a Stakeholding platform, and the newly elected president and Congress set about drafting a statute to serve as the basis for their efforts to mobilize majority support in the midterm elections of 2034. Before confronting a host of other questions, the drafters must define the class of young Americans who will qualify for a grant. If, for example, they propose that stakes would go to every American who had reached the age of 18 on January 1, 2032, how should they deal with people who are already 19 or 20 at that time?

There isn't enough wealth tax revenue in the fund to make it fiscally possible to provide these slightly older Americans with $150,000 stakes. Nevertheless, it would be unjust to cut them off without a penny. When these 19-year-olds were born in 2013, they weren't in a position to choose the time they would come into the world. Yet Congress would be informing them that their birth date had deprived them of the life-defining opportunities that their slightly younger friends will gain as a fundamental principle of social justice. This would generate enormous bitterness among millions of young people – and rightly lead to mass protests at their disparate treatment.

Congress should respond thoughtfully to this problem of transitional justice. There are lots of plausible paths, but I have included a five-year transitional program in my revenue estimates for the wealth tax. As my appendix explains, the 3 to 5 percent wealth tax on the super-rich will raise enough money to provide 19- to 22-year-olds on a sliding scale – with 19-year-olds getting $120,000; 20-year-olds $90,000; and so forth, up to age 22. Although this will understandably cause bitterness among older contemporaries who get nothing, it will nevertheless demonstrate a good-faith inclusionary response, given the finite fiscal resources generated by the wealth tax.

Once the fund delivers its initial round of cash grants, moreover, it will be very tough for the wealthy to repeal the program the next time conservatives come into power in Washington. Such a plutocratic "success" would generate a tremendous backlash as voters asked themselves: why did my neighbor's children receive $150,000 while my youngsters have been left in the cold? Rather than confront the danger of defeat at the next election, even strong conservatives in Congress would resist pressures for repeal—and find other ways of vindicating their free-market commitments.

In short, transitional justice is not just a matter of fundamental fairness in the original design of the program. It will also generate a macro-micro cycle of reinforcement, making it virtually impossible to transition back to the unjust world that a decisive progressive victory would put in the past.

Suppose I've convinced you that wealth taxation isn't merely a pipe dream. The next challenge is to consider the questions raised in the design of Stakeholding itself. Most obviously, $150,000 is far too much money for many 18-year-olds to handle responsibly.[26] Not only do they lack the financial sophistication for the task, but they haven't had sufficient opportunities to explore their career options or define deeply committed relationships to intimate partners. This means that stakeholders should not gain immediate access to their funds when they turn 18. Instead, the money should become available as they move into their twenties, in ways appropriate to their situation in life.

Begin with high school graduates who continue into college, a group that will include more than 50 percent of stakeholders. The fund should pay their tuition and provide a generous grant that will allow them to pursue their educations without financial anxiety. They should get the rest of their stakes only when they leave university and take their next steps into the world.

This will generate a predictable result. Students who enter the adult world after two years at community college will still have stakes of $120,000+—and look forward to the day when they will marry a partner—who may also have $120,000+. In contrast, students who remain in university until they receive doctoral degrees may have spent their entire stake on tuition and living expenses—and marry a graduate school partner with another empty account. The couple would leave university without the $250,000 that their community-college age-mates still possess as they enter the social world as self-defining adults.

These divergent stakeholder balances serve to emphasize one of this book's recurring themes: the predicaments of postmodern existence can't be solved by money alone. The cultural resources provided by higher education are no less important in defining a person's fundamental commitments in life than a financial cushion. Given the wide range of talents and interests, different people will reasonably make different decisions about the right time to stop spending their money on education as students and start spending it exploring opportunities for self-realization as socially competent adults.

Some Ph.D.s will find that their long years of study were crucial in making sense of their lives, but others will find that they were failures as scholars and that their time in the academy had condemned them to decades of despair. The same is true of people who leave school after two years of college – and spend their cash in a failed effort to find self-fulfillment in their search for a loving companion at home, a meaningful job at work, and success in other spheres of personal importance.

The great advantage of Stakeholding is precisely that it isn't a one-size-fits-all initiative but a broad-based effort to help very different people build very different lives for themselves. This fundamental principle of self-determination also requires a different approach when designing a Stakeholding program for high school graduates who move directly into the adult world. Not only are 18-year-olds unprepared to handle $150,000 in a responsible fashion, they have not yet had a chance to broaden their search for self-realization beyond their immediate neighborhoods. Their stakes should be withheld until they have a chance to do so.

Yet many of these 18-year-olds will find themselves in a precarious financial and emotional condition. Until they qualify for their stakes, they should receive the same financial assistance the government extends to older adults in a similar situation; the same is true when they need a broad range of social services. At present, these safety nets are entirely inadequate—and merit serious reform efforts as well.

By requiring them to wait until their twenties, however, the fund is not treating them as second-class citizens. To the contrary, it is respecting their decision to plunge directly into the marketplace, and asking them to recognize that they most likely do not have the life experience and financial savvy to handle their assets responsibly. Nevertheless, when the fund sends them their first account information at the age of 18, they should be guaranteed access to their money (with accumulated interest) when they reach 23. Even then, they should only get $75,000, with the rest becoming available when they are, say, 27. As a consequence, they can use some of their safety-net resources to begin exploring their existential opportunities—in their hometowns or faraway places—in a fashion that will put them in a better position to use their stakes in a way that will give them a serious chance at self-realization.

As a consequence, high school graduates will emerge into adult life with new self-confidence. As they explore their real-world opportunities at 18, they may already have a lover whom, when they both reach 23, they are prepared to marry with the idea that they will face the future together with a $150,000 joint stakeholder account. Or they may defer such a decisive personal commitment and move down a career path which, if they are successful, would benefit from a $75,000 investment in five years' time.

Different high school graduates will choose different paths. Although the overwhelming majority will still struggle against the poverty and prejudice that may have shaped their existence from early childhood, their stakes will enable them to view themselves as autonomous adults who are, to a significant degree, taking charge of their own lives. As they move from 18 to 23 to 27 and beyond, they may rejoice or despair at the way their decisions have turned out. Yet they need no longer view themselves as mere playthings of circumstances beyond their control. They will be able to claim—however problematically—greater personal responsibility for the life path they have taken.

In contrast, a final group will find themselves in a different position. These are the people—about 10 percent of the population—who have dropped out of high school without gaining a diploma and are profoundly disadvantaged in their struggle for a job that will provide the foundation for a fulfilling family life. The Stakeholder Fund should invite them to attend special vocational schools which will permit them to develop the job-related skills appropriate to their capacities—and make their access to their $150,000 dependent on their successful completion of vocational training. When faced with this offer, many will make a serious effort—since, for the first time, their success will be rewarded by $150,000 and the proud forms of self-definition it will make possible. Still, some will never succeed in satisfying their vocational training requirements.

The fund should respond to their predicament by directing their stakeholder account to a special agency that will finance ongoing efforts by social workers to provide effective assistance to these people during the decades of life that lie ahead.

Since 1999 when Anne Alstott and I first advanced this design for Stakeholding, our book has contributed to a worldwide debate that has clarified a host of fundamental questions – including some that I have touched on here. This debate has helped propel a series of legislative enactments of cash-grant programs – not only in Britain and Brazil but in South Africa and many other places as well.[27]

While Elizabeth Warren's campaign for the presidency put a concrete proposal for serious wealth taxation on the American political agenda, her defeat served to emphasize that the United States remains far behind other countries in taking this decisive step forward.

Nevertheless, the real-world successes in other countries suggest that it makes sense for serious American reformers to make Stakeholding a high priority in their electoral campaigns. It would be virtually impossible to repeal the program once it was successfully enacted, given the enormous macro-backlash it would provoke. The overwhelming majority of young Americans will look upon Stakeholding as a great democratic achievement – and will be far more responsive to ongoing efforts to achieve further reforms through the ballot box.

Within a decade or two, it may even be possible for the United States to free itself from plutocratic domination and once again dedicate itself to the proposition that "all men are created equal, that they are endowed by their Creator with certain unalienable Rights, that among these are Life, Liberty and the pursuit of Happiness."

APPENDIX

Funding the Stakeholder Society

In chapter 12, I explained how an ongoing enforcement effort by the Wealth Tax Division can generate a virtuous cycle of tax compliance by motivating the super-rich to file accurate returns. This appendix begins by marking out three additional steps a Stakeholder statute should take to deter tax evasion. If these steps are not taken, the virtuous cycle may collapse—leading to a dramatic drop in revenues that will prevent the government from fulfilling its $150,000 pledge to the rising generation.[1]

Each of my proposals has a basis in existing law. To build a firm foundation for the virtuous cycle, however, it won't be enough for the Stakeholder statute to include one or two of them. Only when all three are combined in a package will they dramatically reduce the risk of significant tax evasion. While my insistence on the entire enforcement package is new, I hope you are persuaded that it is a key element in any serious effort to implement Stakeholding in the real world.

Suppose, next, that the triple package does indeed induce most super-rich families to obey the law. The next question is whether their wealth tax payments will generate the enormous revenue required to fund $150,000 stakes (in 2023 dollars) for all 18-year-olds beginning in 2032, as well as provide smaller transitional stakes to their slightly older contemporaries.

The second part of this appendix explores three basic premises of the mathematical model behind my revenue-raising conclusions. In making these assumptions, I won't elaborate my technocratic framework in all its complexity. This is a task best left to academic journals. My aim is to give you a sense of how I have responded to key problems involved in my effort to generate credible revenue estimates – and to describe my approach in a way that, along with some footnotes, will allow my fellow technocrats to test its plausibility.

ENFORCING THE LAW?

The IRS audited more than 32,000 million-dollar tax returns in 2010. But congressional appropriations for these monitoring activities have dramatically declined over the last decade – thanks especially to budget cuts during Trump's tenure, during which the Tax Cuts and Jobs Act of 2017 created numerous loopholes for the ultra-rich to evade taxes.[2] As a consequence, the Internal Revenue Service's computer system is now terribly obsolete. Not only is it failing to deal responsibly with the flood of tax returns filed by ordinary taxpayers, but the IRS now falls far short of its 2010 performance in dealing with the superrich.[3]

More intensive monitoring will be required if Congress enacts Stakeholding by 2032. As I argued in the last chapter, only the prospect of intensive audits by the Wealth Tax Division can generate the virtuous cycle of voluntary compliance and voter demand for social justice. Without a massive investment in computer modernization for the IRS, many mega-millionaires will underreport their assets, and the amount raised by the Stakeholder Fund will fall short of predictions – disappointing many young Americans who were counting on $150,000 as they confronted the postmodern predicaments of the twenty-first century.

From this perspective, President Biden's recent success in reversing Trump's assault on the IRS is of great significance. Despite Republican resistance to many other initiatives, Congress has granted the agency $60 billion in extra funds to recruit personnel and modernize the computer system over the coming decade.[4] This success testifies to widespread voter frustration in dealing with the IRS. Yet the agency will need much more investment before it can respond rapidly. By the end of this decade, however, the steady stream of investment enacted in 2022 will provide a strong foundation for the Wealth Tax Division to do the intensive monitoring needed to persuade the super-rich to obey the Stakeholder statute, if it is enacted into law.

Even if the government's computers get up to speed, some wealthy families will undoubtedly underreport their wealth. The Internal Revenue Code already contains a strong response to that concern. Section 6663 adds a 75 percent penalty on top of repayment if an initial tax return contains fraudulent misrepresentation.[5] Given the enormous wealth of super-rich taxpayers, a 75 percent penalty may not be enough to deter cheating – since underreporting might save many millions of dollars if it succeeds. To safeguard the system's integrity, the Stakeholder statute should triple the penalty for underpayment of wealth taxes.

Yet some families might take more desperate steps to avoid handing their assets to their fellow Americans. Even under the present system, some multi-millionaires have renounced their citizenship for tax reasons. Once again, existing law provides a remedy, requiring émigrés to pay capital gains on all of their assets at the time they renounce.[6] Building on this precedent, the Stakeholder statute should impose a 40 percent "exit tax" on the "net worth above $50 million of any U.S. citizen who renounces their citizenship in order to escape paying their fair share," to put the point in the words of Senator Warren.[7]

There are strong reasons to believe that this penalty package will suffice to reinforce the virtuous cycle generated by the WTD. Nevertheless, some skeptical readers may believe that significant sums will still escape the WTD auditors. To take this into account, I will present two sets of revenue estimates. The "strict compliance scenario" supposes that the Stakeholding Fund will contain virtually all of the projected revenues. The "moderate compliance scenario" supposes that the fund will experience significant revenue losses.

Under "moderate" assumptions, my model predicts that the IRS will collect enough revenue to provide a stake of $150,000 for every 18-year-old in its first year of operation, so long as the country continues to experience its typical rates of economic growth over the next decade. But even in a sustained recession, Americans can still expect stakes of more than $100,000. It will take more work, however, to elaborate the key premises that provide the framework for these predictions.

REVENUE-RAISING ASSUMPTIONS

My projections assume that all young Americans – including Dreamers – qualify for stakes. I have already argued that fundamental principles of existential justice require Dreamers' inclusion and need not repeat myself here. My calculations also adopt the approach to transitional justice developed in chapter 12. If the statute grants $150,000 to people who become 18 years old when it goes into effect, I will be assuming that 19-year-olds receive four-fifths, 20-year-olds receive three-fifths, 21-year-olds receive two-fifths, and 22-year-olds receive one-fifth of the full amount distributed to 18-year-olds when the program begins in 2032.[8] Given these premises, will the graduated 3 to 5 percent wealth tax raise enough revenue to meet these targets?

My model answers this question by following the guidelines provided by the Congressional Budget Office (CBO), which is charged with assessing the fiscal effects of all major appropriation measures. Since I'm writing this appendix in 2022, my predictions for 2032 incorporate the CBO's current estimates for population growth (0.6 percent per year) and inflation (varying from 1.2 percent to 6.1 percent per year).[9] I follow both the CBO and the Federal Reserve Board in predicting that gross domestic product (GDP) will increase by 2 percent a year.[10] If this growth rate continues over the coming decade, the wealth tax will meet its revenue-raising goals – and members of the rising generation will begin to explore their real-world life-options with unprecedented self-confidence.

Yet the 2 percent estimate of GDP growth may turn out to be wrong. While financial crises have propelled dramatic downturns, the continuing technology boom has generated a strong growth rate over the past generation. This may not be true in the future.

Suppose, for example, GDP grows at just 1 percent a year for the next two decades. Under conditions of "moderate" tax enforcement, that level of growth would yield a stake of only $100,000 for

18-year-olds in 2032 – rising to $130,000 by 2041. In contrast, if GDP increases by 3 percent, stakes would start at $227,000 in 2032 and reach $245,000 by 2041. Under this scenario, it would make sense for Congress to divert a significant share of the wealth tax for other compelling priorities. But even if there is a bust, a stake of $100,000 would be extremely valuable for young Americans confronting a grim economic future.

I simplified my earlier discussion of Stakeholding by focusing exclusively on the standard growth scenario deployed by the CBO and the Fed, which is why I have included this appendix to elaborate the premises for my predictions.

In the same spirit, my treatment of tax evasion requires further elaboration. I have tried to convince you that my proposed enforcement package – involving up-to-date computers and heavy tax penalties – will lead the overwhelming majority of wealthy families to file accurate returns. But I have not used this "strict enforcement" model in my revenue-raising estimates. Instead, I have supposed that despite the government's formidable enforcement weapons, the super-rich manage to evade about 5 percent of their tax obligations. Under this moderate enforcement model, the Stakeholding Fund will suffer an annual shortfall of $52 billion compared to my strict enforcement model.

I should emphasize, moreover, that even my moderate model challenges the conventional wisdom in tax policy circles. Current work emphasizes the way in which the super-rich evade trillions of dollars of taxes by hiding their money in such tax havens as Switzerland and the British Virgin Islands. When Senator Warren consulted leading economists, she was told to expect levels of tax evasion that far exceed the 5 percent built into my moderate enforcement scenario.[11]

These predictions gave opponents of the Warren wealth tax initiative a formidable weapon in their successful campaign to defeat it. The next time around, reformers should not make the same mistake. They should insist that Congress adopt an enforcement package similar to the one I am proposing here. It would prevent the super-rich from sending their trillions to tax havens without fear of detection by the American government. They will only underreport their wealth if they are willing to risk the heavy penalties they will incur should their cheating be detected by the Wealth Tax Division's intensive monitoring of returns. Under this regime, my strict enforcement scenario should serve as the basis for realistic revenue estimates.

Current empirical work has not confronted the possibility of the "virtuous cycle" of voluntary compliance that would prevail under my proposed enforcement regime – for the simple reason that this book represents the first time it has been introduced into serious statistical analysis. To frame the next round of scholarly debate, I have inserted my 5 percent evasion estimate into the revenue-raising model invoked by Senator Warren and other leading progressives in their campaign for the wealth tax. The Warren model was developed by Professors Emmanuel Saez and Gabriel Zucman, who based their predictions of massive evasion on the behavior of the super-rich in the tax haven world that reformers should aim to destroy by adopting my triple-enforcement package.[12]

I hope that my revision of the Saez-Zucman model will shape future research on this subject. The next round of statistical analysis may lead to a revision of the 5 percent evasion rate that serves as the basis for the projected revenue-raising estimates (table 1). Either calculation makes clear the importance of including a triple package of enforcement tools in any serious Stakeholding initiative.

Table 1. Stakeholder Grants

	Stakes		
	1% wealth growth	2% wealth growth	3% wealth growth
2032	$100,000	$150,000	$227,144
2033	$100,000	$150,000	$227,840
2034	$100,000	$150,000	$228,438
2035	$104,559	$150,000	$228,959
2036	$142,402	$150,000	$230,557
2037	$139,772	$150,000	$233,022
2038	$137,295	$150,000	$235,476
2039	$134,995	$150,000	$237,989
2040	$132,854	$153,161	$240,595
2041	$130,831	$179,371	$245,115

So much for the key premises built into the revenue predictions. To make sense of table 1, recall that stakes can't rise above $150,000 until enough money has been raised to provide 19- to 22-year-olds with the smaller cash grants required by principles of transitional justice.

To put all these uncertainties into perspective, I conclude by showing how much of the wealth tax would be paid by the very richest Americans (table 2).

Table 2. Selected Wealth Shares and Tax Contributions

Percentile	Cumulative wealth share	Cumulative share of wealth tax paid
Top 5 households	0.5%	4.3%
Top 500 households	3%	28%
Top 3,000 households	6%	47%
Top 0.01%	9%	73%
Top 0.1%	19%	100%
Top 1%	40%	–
Top 5%	63%	–

Isn't it past time for the country's richest families to recognize that everybody else should also be given a fair opportunity to define the meaning of their lives?

Plutocratic power cannot justify itself. If the super-rich refuse to answer this straightforward question, they have failed the fundamental test of existential justice.

NOTES

INTRODUCTION

1. I am indebted to Ferdinand Tönnies for his crucial insights into the characteristic features of premodern life in closely knit communities – and the revolutionary character of the modernist dilemma of self-definition. WERNER CAHNMAN & FERDINAND TÖNNIES, A NEW EVALUATION (1973). For some recent assessments, Paul S. Adler, *Community and Innovation: From Tönnies to Marx,* 36 ORGANIZATION STUDIES 445–471 (2015); Benedicte Zimmermann, *Ferdinand Tönnies,* 188 ACTES DE LA RECHERCHE EN SCIENCES SOCIALES 44–53 (2011); TÖNNIES HEUTE (eds. Lars Clausen, Volker von Borries, Wolf R. Dombrowsky, Hans-Wener Prahl 1985). Although they do not emphasize Tönnies's contribution, Jean L. Cohen and Andrew Arato's comprehensive account of the rise of civil society – both as an idea and as a reality – is entirely compatible with the approach advanced in this essay. See CIVIL SOCIETY AND POLITICAL THEORY (1992) – though we differ, of course, in many particular assessments. For a complementary perspective, emphasizing the real-world limits on the power of premodern empires to impose centralized control over activities beyond the imperial capital, see LAUREN BENTON, LAW AND COLONIAL CULTURES: LEGAL REGIMES IN WORLD HISTORY: 1400–1900 (2002).

2. Statista Research Department, *Largest Cities in Western Europe in 1980* at https://www.statista.com/statistics/1022001/thirty-largest-cities-western-europe-1800/.

3. For an insightful account of these decisive transformations, JEROME BLUM, THE END OF THE OLD ORDER IN RURAL EUROPE (1986).

CHAPTER 2. THE STRANGER

1. Paul M. Hohenberg & Lynn Hollen Lees, The Making of Urban Europe, 1000–1950 (1985). For specific population estimates, see Statista, "Largest Cities in Western Europe in 1800," http://www.statista.com/statistics/1022001/thirty-largest-cities-western-europe-1800. In contrast, by 1850, Paris's population had already increased to 1.3 million.

2. John M. Merriman, Police Stories: Building the French State, 1815–1851 (2006); Eugène-François Vidocq, Mémoires de Vidocq: Chef de la Ofice de Sûreté Jusqu'en 1827 (1998).

3. Angela J. Davis Ed., Policing the Black Man: Arrest, Prosecution and Punishment (2017); Tom Tyler & Tracey Meares. *Revisiting Broken Windows: The Role of the Community and the Police in Promoting Community Engagement,* 76 N.Y.U. L. Rev. 637–656 (2021).

CHAPTER 3. CITIZEN V. CONSUMER

1. Geoffrey Crossick & Serge Jaumain Eds., Cathedrals of Consumption: The European Department Store (1999).

2. Ryan Catterwell, *Autonomy and Institutionalism in the Law of Contract,* 42 Oxford J. Leg. Stud. 1067 (2022), John D. T. Wood, *Consumer Protection: A Case of Successful Regulation,* Regulatory Theory: Foundations and Application (ed. Peter Drahos) 633–653 (2017).

3. See Civil Rights Act of 1964, 42 U.S.C. 2000(a). For further elaboration of the crucial role of the civil rights movement in transforming the "anti-humiliation principle" into a fundamental national commitment, Bruce Ackerman, We The People: The Civil Rights Revolution 133–152 (2014). For a broader survey of the worldwide recognition of similar principles, Aharon Barak, Proportionality: Constitutional Rights and Their Limitations (2012); Alec Stone Sweet & Judd Matthews, *Proportionality Balancing and Global Constitutionalism,* 47 Columbia J. Transnatl Law 68–149 (2008).

CHAPTER 4. DEMOCRACY V. PLUTOCRACY

1. I attempt a systematic analysis of these remarkable achievements in Bruce Ackerman, Revolutionary Constitutions (2019).

2. Mary Beard, SPQR: A History of Ancient Rome (2016); Edward Gibbon, A History of The Decline and Fall of the

Roman Empire (1776). The face-to-face republics of Renaissance Italy also failed to sustain themselves in their confrontations with military strongmen – and these failures profoundly reshaped the democratic ideals of the French Revolution and subsequent Enlightenment efforts at constitutional construction. J. G. A. Pocock, The Machiavellian Moment: Florentine Political Thought and the Atlantic Republican Tradition (1975).

3. James Madison, *Federalist 1* (1788).

4. Bruce Ackerman, We the People: Foundations 165–322 (1991).

5. Robert Hughes, Fatal Shore: The Epic of Australia's Founding (1988); William Coleman ed., Only in Australia: The History, Politics and Economics of Australian Exceptionalism (2016); David Clark, *The Australian Ballot in New Zealand: A Study in Legal Transplantation,* 14 Flinders Law Journal 69 (2012).

6. Jon Lawrence, Electing Our Masters: The Hustings in British Politics from Hogarth to Blair 45–48 (2009); Ben Smyth, *A Foundation for Secret, Verifiable Elections,* Cryptology ePrint Archive, Report 2018/225. https://eprint.iacr.org/2018/225.pdf.

7. Article 31, French Constitution of the Year III (1795): "All elections are to be held by secret ballot."

8. Julia Maskivker, The Duty to Vote (2019).

9. *A Half-Century of Learning: Historical Statistics on Educational Attainment in the United States, 1940 to 2000,* Report Number PHC-T-41, Table 4. Percent of the Population 25 Years and Over with a Bachelor's Degree or Higher by Sex, Race, and Hispanic Origin, for the United States: 1940 to 2000, U.S. Census Bureau (April 06, 2006) https://www.census.gov/data/tables/2000/dec/phc-t-41.html; *Educational Attainment in the United States: 2010,* Table 1. Educational Attainment of the Population 18 Years and Over, by Age, Sex, Race, and Hispanic Origin: 2010, U.S. Census Bureau, https://www.census.gov/data/tables/2010/demo/educational-attainment/cps-detailed-tables.html; *Educational Attainment in the United States: 2020,* Table 1. Educational Attainment of the Population 18 Years and Over, by Age, Sex, Race, and Hispanic Origin: 2020, U.S. Census Bureau (April 21, 2021) https://www.census.gov/data/tables/2020/demo/educational-attainment/cps-detailed-tables.html; Table 10. Educational Attainment of People 25 Years and Over, by Nativity and Period of Entry, 1 Age, Sex, Race, and Hispanic Origin: March 2000, U.S. Census Bureau (December 19, 2000) https://www2.census.gov/programs-surveys/demo/tables/educational-attainment/2000/p20–536/tab10.pdf. *Educational Attainment in the United States: 2020,* Table 1. Educational Attainment of the Population 18 Years and Over, by Age, Sex, Race, and Hispanic Origin: 2020

(Table 1.1 All races), U.S. CENSUS BUREAU, https://www.census.gov/data/tables/2020/demo/educational-attainment/cps-detailed-tables.html.

10. The Organization for Economic Cooperation and Development has organized the most comprehensive data-analysis of the worldwide breakthrough in educational attainment over the past half-century at: https://www.oecd-ilibrary.org/education/data/oecd-education-statistics_edu-data-en.

11. For an incisive analysis of the contemporary situation, RICHARD L. HASEN, PLUTOCRATS UNITED: CAMPAIGN MONEY, THE SUPREME COURT AND THE DISTORTION OF AMERICAN ELECTIONS (2016). For my own contributions to this debate, BRUCE ACKERMAN & IAN AYRES, VOTING WITH DOLLARS (2002); Bruce Ackerman and Ian Ayres, *The Secret Refund Booth,* 73 U. CHICAGO LAW REVIEW 1107 (2006); Bruce Ackerman and Ian Ayres, *Democracy Dollars' Can Give Every Voter a Real Voice in American Politics,* WASHINGTON POST (November 5, 2015) at https://www.washingtonpost.com/opinions/democracy-dollars-can-give-every-voter-a-real-voice-in-american-politics/2015/11/05/48100ae8-8345-11e5-a7ca-6ab6ec20f839_story.html.

12. Sentenza nel procedimento a carico di Berlusconi Silvio (Tribunale di Napoli: 8 luglio 2015) at https://acrobat.adobe.com/link/track?uri=urn%3Aaaid%3Ascds%3AUS%3A837d8199-7717-34d9-ae0f-d6149e28bfcb&viewer%21megaVerb=group-discover.

13. BRENNAN CENTER FOR JUSTICE: CAMPAIGN FINANCE REFORM: https://www.brennancenter.org/search/?q=campaign%20finance&langcode=en&; SAVE DEMOCRACY IN AMERICA: https://savedemocracyinamerica.org/media-and-events/; for the domination of big-money interests at the present time: https://www.opensecrets.org/news/2020/10/cost-of-2020-election-14billion-update/

14. JACOB HACKER & PAUL PIERSON, LET THEM EAT TWEETS (2020).

15. *Supra* n. 9.

16. *See* 1–3 BRUCE ACKERMAN, WE THE PEOPLE (1991, 1998, 2014).

CHAPTER 5. MEANINGFUL WORK

1. MAGALI SARFATTI LARSON, THE RISE OF PROFESSIONALISM: A SOCIOLOGICAL ANALYSIS (1977) provides a particularly insightful perspective to which I am greatly indebted.

2. For the challenge of modernity to traditional forms of professionalism in the Islamic world, see MOHAMMED HADDAD, MUSLIM REFORMISM–A CRITICAL HISTORY (2020); for analogous developments in China, TAISU ZHANG, THE LAWS AND ECONOMICS OF CONFUCIANISM (2019).

3. Chapter 9, pp. 166-72.

4. ARNOLD PACY & FRANCESCA BRAY, TECHNOLOGY IN WORLD CIVILIZATION: A THOUSAND YEAR HISTORY 155–75 (2021). As their title indicates, Pacey and Bray place the rise of professional engineering in a much larger context. A more focused account is provided by JULIAN GLOVER, MAN OF IRON: THOMAS TELFORD AND THE BUILDING OF BRITAIN (2017). Telford's pioneering role is suggested by his election as founding president of the Institution of Civil Engineers in 1820 – which, two centuries later, serves as a leading association for 92,000 professionals in the British Isles and beyond. https://www.google.com/search?gs_ssp=eJzj4tTP1TcwrCowy1BgNGB0YPCSy8wrLsksKS3JzM9TyE9TSM4sy8xRSM1Lz8xLTS0qBgBRtQ-Y&q=institution+of+civil+engineers&rlz=1C1GCEU_enUS819US819&oq=INSTITUTION+OF+CIVIL+&aqs=chrome.

5. DANIEL T. ROGERS, ATLANTIC CROSSINGS: SOCIAL POLITICS IN A PROGRESSIVE AGE (2000).

6. For a remarkable effort to put these particular Progressive initiatives in a broader historical and political context, JOSEPH FISHKIN & WILLIAM FORBATH, THE ANTI-OLIGARCHY CONSTITUTION: RECONSTRUCTING THE ECONOMIC FOUNDATIONS OF AMERICAN DEMOCRACY (2022).

7. Dartmouth College began experimenting with graduate education in 1900, but its Tuck School initially attracted very few students and was eclipsed by Harvard's decisive entry into the field. DUFF MCDONALD, THE GOLDEN PASSPORT CHAPS. 1–8 (2017).

8. HOWARD THOMAS, PETER LORANGE & JAGDISH SHETH, THE BUSINESS SCHOOL IN THE TWENTY-FIRST CENTURY (2013) provides an impartial assessment of the challenges involved in adapting business school education to the computer age. DUFF MCDONALD, *supra* n. 7, provides a longer and richer account of the 125-year evolution of the educational project – with a far grimmer diagnosis of future developments than offered by Thomas, Lorange, and Sheth. My own real-world engagements with business schools are far too superficial to support an independent judgment on the key issues involved. My aim instead is to encourage business school leaders to participate in the larger debate over the postmodern predicament that my own book seeks to provoke.

9. Watson, Lehmann & Braddock, *The Essential Role of Medical Ethics Education in Achieving Professionalism: The Romanell Report,* 90 ACADEMIC MEDICINE 744 (2015).

10. MICHAEL SANDEL, THE TYRANNY OF MERIT (2020).

CHAPTER 6. BECOMING A PERSON

1. Under appropriate conditions, it is possible for an infant to master three or even four "native languages" – that's why my counterexample invokes the possibility of six different tongues, with very different grammars.

2. Jean Piaget's great works mark the decisive breakthrough on this front. See, e.g., THE EQUILIBRATION OF COGNITIVE STRUCTURES (1985); SCIENCE OF EDUCATION AND THE PSYCHOLOGY OF THE CHILD (1970). For an incisive and comprehensive assessment of contemporary research, which provides a compelling framework for my approach, see MICHAEL TOMASELLO, BECOMING HUMAN: A THEORY OF ONTOGENY (2019).

3. JEAN PIAGET, INTELLECTUAL EVOLUTION FROM ADOLESCENCE TO ADULTHOOD (1977).

4. CARL KAESTLE, PILLARS OF THE REPUBLIC: COMMON SCHOOLS AND AMERICAN SOCIETY 64 (1983).

5. LAWRENCE CREMIN, AMERICAN EDUCATION 64–65 (1980).

6. *Id.*

7. WILLIAM H. JEYNES, AMERICAN EDUCATIONAL HISTORY: SCHOOL, SOCIETY, AND THE COMMON GOOD 150 (2007); KAESTLE, *supra* n. 4, at 64, 75 (1983).

8. KAESTLE, *supra* n. 4, at 71–93; Joseph Perksy, *American Political Economy, and the Common School Movement,* 37 J. HIST. OF ECON. THOUGHT 247, 265 (2015).

9. RUSH WELTER, POPULAR EDUCATION AND DEMOCRATIC THOUGHT IN AMERICA 84 (1962).

10. JEYNES, *supra* n. 7.

11. CREMIN, *supra* n. 5, at 64-65. HORACE BUSHNELL, VIEWS OF CHRISTIAN NATURE, AND OF SUBJECTS ADJACENT THERETO (1848).

12. JEYNES, *supra* n. 7, at 105; JOHN L. RURY, EDUCATION AND SOCIAL CHANGE 80 (3d ed. 2009).

13. KAESTLE *supra* n. 4, at 114.

14. *Id.* at 125

15. Derek Black, *Freedom, Democracy and the Right to Education,* NW. U. L. REV. 116:1 (2022).

16. PHILIPPE ARIES, THE DISCOVERY OF CHILDHOOD (1960).

17. In his later writings, Rousseau came to appreciate the profound risks, as well as rewards, of an education seeking to liberate the next generation from parental domination. Abbie LeBlanc, *Seeing Like Sophie: Developing Judgment in Rousseau's Émile,* 84 REV. OF POLITICS 183–93 (2022).

18. YVES DÉLOYE, ÉCOLE ET CITOYENNETÉ: L'INDIVIDUALISME RÉPUBLICAIN DE JULES FERRY A VICHY, 13–15, 87 (1994), JEAN-JACQUES ROUSSEAU, EMILE OU DE L'EDUCATION 38–43 (1966).

19. As early as 1833, the French monarchy, in collaboration with the papacy, enacted the Loi Guizot, which created free schools on the local level – enabling the clergy to teach the young to repudiate the Enlightenment ideals of the Revolution and embrace the True Religion. It was only after a generation of mobilized debate that the Third Republic self-consciously affirmed the fundamental link between public education and the imperatives of democratic citizenship. See PATRICK WEIL, DE LA LAÏCITÉ EN FRANCE (2021). YVES DÉLOYE, ÉCOLE ET CITOYENNETÉ: L'INDIVIDUALISME RÉPUBLICAIN DE JULES FERRY A VICHY, 13–17, 216 (1994). JACQUES GADILLE, LA PENSÉE ET L'ACTION POLITIQUE DES ÉVÊQUES FRANÇAIS AU DÉBUT DE LA TROISIÉ ME RÉPUBLIQUE, 1870–1883, 31–37, 85 (1966).

20. BRUCE ACKERMAN, REVOLUTIONARY CONSTITUTIONS (2019).

21. Clare Ryan, *Children as Bargaining Chips,* U.C.L.A L. REV. 410 (2021).

CHAPTER 7. POSTMODERN LIFE CYCLES

1. Vasilis Kontis, James Bennett, Colin Mathers, Guangquan Li, Kyle Foreman & Majid Essati, *Future Life Expectancy in 35 Industrialised Countries: Projections with a Bayesian Model Ensemble,* 389, 1323–35 LANCET (February 21, 2017) at http://dx.doi.orglio.1016/50140-6736(16)32381-9.

2. This question is gaining increasing salience in public discussion. OLIVER BURKEMAN, FOUR THOUSAND WEEKS: TIME MANAGEMENT FOR MORTALS (2021) provides a notable contribution. My own approach differs fundamentally from Burkeman's – but it is far more important to emphasize our common appreciation of the existential problem and to call on others to join the conversation.

3. DEREK PARFIT, REASONS AND PERSONS (1984).

4. Bruce Ackerman, *With a Single Climate Initiative, Biden Could Generate $4 Trillion for Green Investment,* YALE MACMILLAN CENTER NEWS (December 18, 2020) at https://macmillan.yale.edu/news/single-climate-initiative-biden-could-generate-4-trillion-green-investment.

CHAPTER 8. UNCERTAINTY

1. J. L. HEILBRON, GALILEO 218 (2010).

2. ISAAC NEWTON, PHILOSPHIAE NATURALIS PRINCIPA MATHEMATICA (1687); ISAAC NEWTON, THE PRINCIPIA: MATHEMATICAL PRINCIPLES OF NATURAL PHILOSOPHY (trans. Bernard Cohen & Anne Whitman 1999).

3. Historical antecedents to these path-breakers in each artistic sphere go back for centuries. But there had never been a time when poets and painters, novelists and sculptors, joined together to confront the challenge that Heisenberg and Einstein posed to the very meaning of human existence. Arthur Miller provides a compelling biographical account of this relationship in EINSTEIN, PICASSO: SPACE, TIME, AND THE BEAUTY THAT CAUSES HAVOC (2001).

4. This book is only dealing with my reactions to *Being and Time*, which served as the culmination of Heidegger's work before his embrace of Hitler and his passionate commitment to Nazism. I also do not deal with Heidegger's desperate efforts to restore his philosophical respectability after the war. Although Heidegger explicitly acknowledges his debt to Husserl in the first edition of *Being and Time*, they differ in the basic frameworks that define their philosophical efforts. Husserl emphasizes the crucial role of Descartes in framing the skeptical alternative to phenomenology. Heidegger instead roots his position in an interpretation of ancient Greek thought. But as should be apparent, this book is neither a history of philosophy nor a biography of particular philosophers. It is an effort to confront some of the thinkers who have deeply influenced my own existential understanding. You should read Husserl and Heidegger, not Ackerman, to figure out what you really think of their efforts to make sense of the world.

5. Given the particularly obscure character of English-language translations of Heidegger's German prose, PETER GORDON, CONTINENTAL DIVIDE: HEIDEGGER, CASSIRER, DAVOS (2010) is the place to go for a remarkably illuminating introduction to the central concerns of *Being and Time*.

6. There has been a great deal of scholarly controversy surrounding Sartre's underground dealings with different elements of the French Resistance after his release from a Nazi detention camp. STÉPHANE ISRAËL, LES ÉTUDES ET LA GUERRE: LES NORMALIENS DANS LA TOURMENTE (1939–1945) (2005). But for present purposes, it is unnecessary for me to enter this debate – since the key point is that he was not willing to wait until Hitler's defeat before authorizing the Resistance to publish his book.

7. At a much later time in her life, Parks was granted a special award by Congress in recognition of her "great contributions to the Nation." See 31 USC

5111 (May 4, 1999). Yet even this high honor did not immunize her from the humiliations of everyday life.

8. When Andrej Sakharov was later awarded a Nobel in 1975, his Soviet overlords didn't allow him to go to Copenhagen to accept it—so Elena Bonner was invited to give a speech in his place. https://www.nobelprize.org/prizes/peace/1975/sakharov/lecture/.

9. For an account of the historical situation in 1964, see ACKERMAN, *supra* n. 3, at chap. 3.

10. Sartre first permitted journalists to learn of his decision, and the Academy received a letter from him only after the newspapers had made it public. Alison Flood, *Jean-Paul Sartre Rejected the Nobel Prize in a Letter to Jury That Arrived Too Late,* THE GUARDIAN (January 5, 2015) at https://www.theguardian.com/books/2015/jan/05/sartre-nobel-prize-literature-letter-swedish-academy.

11. SIMONE DE BEAUVOIR, THE SECOND SEX 359–74 (trans. Constance Borde & Sheila Malovaney-Chevallier 2010).

12. *Id.* at 479–500.

13. ACKERMAN, *supra* n. 4, at chap. 4.

14. My discussion of *The Second Sex* includes elements of de Beauvoir's larger program that she developed more elaborately in later writings. Deirdre Bair provides a comprehensive account in SIMONE DE BEAUVOIR: A BIOGRAPHY (1991).

15. DE BEAUVOIR, *supra* n. 11, at 844–45.

16. MAURICE MERLEAU-PONTY, THE WORLD OF PERCEPTION 86–89 (trans. Oliver Davis 2004; orig. pub. in French, 1948, as CAUSERIES).

17. *Id.* at 84.

18. *Id.* at 72–73; 88.

19. *Id.* at 66.

20. *Id.* at 44.

21. *Id.* at 45–46.

22. *Id.* at 88.

23. *Id.* at 88–89.

CHAPTER 9. WHERE AM I?

1. Although Johannes Gutenberg invented the printing press in Europe in the 1430s, Korean bookmakers were printing with moveable metal type a century before that. Woodblock printing in China was invented sometime in the ninth century – though, for reasons I will suggest, Gutenberg's invention had a far more transformative impact on the course of history.

2. Davide Cantoni, *Adopting a New Religion: The Case of Protestantism in the 16th Century,* 122 THE ECONOMIC JOURNAL 501–531 (2012).

3. This reassertion of royal authority provoked the radical Protestants in the New World to return to their printing presses to denounce the King James Version as apocryphal and insist on the sanctity of their own – rival – versions of the biblical text.

4. Samuel Morse's invention of the telegraph in the 1840s was a technological breakthrough of importance. Yet it served to reinforce, rather than undermine, the hegemony of the written word by permitting its more rapid dissemination than had been possible previously.

CHAPTER 10. RECONSTRUCTING EXISTENTIALISM

1. Newtonian certainties were not entirely immune from philosophical challenge in the nineteenth century. The contributions of Ralph Waldo Emerson and Charles Sanders Pierce remain of enduring significance, and the same is true of Søren Kierkegaard and Friedrich Nietzsche. Nevertheless, these thinkers served as remarkable exceptions to the Newtonian self-confidence exhibited in the more general debate – until Heisenberg and Einstein shattered its very foundations. In contrast, twentieth-century existentialists self-consciously confronted this radical transformation in the reigning scientific paradigm. As a consequence, I will be emphasizing the way in which their insights provide a crucial perspective upon our postmodern predicaments. For present purposes, it would require too great a detour to consider the complex ways in which their exceptional predecessors also contribute enduring insights.

2. SAMUEL JAY KEYSER, THE MENTAL LIFE OF MODERNISM: WHY POETRY, PAINTING, AND MUSIC CHANGED AT THE TURN OF THE TWENTIETH CENTURY (2020).

3. My own thinking has been particularly influenced by two of Habermas's major works. THEORY OF COMMUNICATIVE ACTION (1981); BETWEEN FACTS AND NORMS (1992).

4. Over the last decade, Habermas has engaged in a remarkable paradigm shift – repudiating his lifelong commitment to the Enlightenment and embracing Christianity in his response to the current legitimacy crisis afflicting the West. 1-2 AUCH EINE GESCHICHTE DER PHILOSOPHIE (2019). I will defer my critique of his turnaround to another time.

5. Wolfram Eilenberger, Time of the Magicians (2018) provides a compelling historical account of the great philosophical debate, culminating in the confrontation between Cassirer and Heidegger at Davos in 1929, over the rise of Einstein and the fall of Newton at the dawn of the twentieth century – and then explores the tragic ways in which the Great Depression and the rise of Hitler transformed the existentialist debate over the next generation. For an insightful philosophical effort to reinvigorate foundational existentialist concerns, see David Couzens Hoy, The Time of Our Lives: A Critical History of Temporality (2009). For a recent book reaching out to a larger audience, see Oliver Burkeman, Four Thousand Weeks: Time and How to Use It (2021). My own views depart from those presented by each of these writers in significant ways. Taken together, however, they suggest an increasing recognition of the relevance of existentialist themes in meeting the distinctive challenges of contemporary life.

6. Compare J. H. Burns & H. L. A. Hart Eds., The Collected Works of Jeremy Bentham 283 (1996) with Harriet Taylor Mill & John Stuart Mill, The Subjection of Women (1869).

7. Brian Barry, *Introduction to The Symposium,* 93 Ethics 328–390 (1983); Bruce Ackerman, *What Is Neutral About Neutrality?*, 93 Ethics 372–390 (1983).

8. Bruce Ackerman, *Why Dialogue,* 86 Journal of Philosophy 5–22 (1989); Bruce Ackerman, *Rooted Cosmopolitanism,* 104 Ethics 516–35 (1994).

9. Bruce Ackerman, Revolutionary Constitutions: Charismatic Leadership and the Rule of Law (2019); Bruce Ackerman, The Decline and Fall of the American Republic (2010); Bruce Ackerman, Before the Next Attack (2006); Bruce Ackerman, The Failure of the Founding Fathers (2005).

CHAPTER 11. CRITIQUE

1. Although Milton Friedman was the leading figure driving the Chicago School's systematic opposition to activist government, *see* Capitalism and Freedom (1962), George Stigler played a decisive role in emphasizing the central role of "rational actor" models in the technocratic analysis of free market activity. Stigler, *The Theory of Economic Regulation,* 2 Bell J. Econ. & Manage Sci. 3–21 (1971). For an overview, see Edmund Kitch, *Chicago School of Economics,* The New Palgrave Dictionary of Law and Economics 227 (ed. Peter Newman 1998).

2. Richard H. Thaler & Cass R. Sunstein, Nudge: Improving Decisions about Health, Wealth, and Happiness 226 (2008). Hereafter cited as *Nudge.*

3. *Nudge* at 21. Daniel Kahneman, Thinking Fast and Slow (2011) further develops *Nudge*'s organizing insight.

4. *Nudge* at 19–20.

5. *Nudge* at 19.

6. In the original edition of their book, Sunstein and Thaler devote an entire chapter to the marriage issue, *Nudge* at 217–228 (2008). In 2022, the authors published a "Final Edition," which once again endorsed the compelling need for nudging prospective newlyweds. *Nudge,* at 33–34 (2021). For present purposes, however, it seems more sensible to quote from the original edition's more extended discussion of the marriage question, since the Final Edition continues to endorse it.

7. *Nudge* at 226.

8. *Supra* n. 9, at chap. 4.

9. For present purposes, I won't be addressing the problems of the super-super-rich. Even if a billionaire couple doesn't consider the breakup problem on their own, their parents might predictably pay high-powered lawyers to negotiate a prenuptial agreement on their behalf. They won't require a nudge to assure that a divorce, if it occurs, will take advantage of all available tax breaks and enable both sides to leave the marriage with a significant share of the assets.

CHAPTER 12. RECONSTRUCTION

1. Jacob Hacker & Paul Pierson, Let Them Eat Tweets (2020); Yochai Benkler, Robert Faris & Hal Roberts, Network Propaganda (2018); Megan M. Ruxton & Kyle L. Saunders, *Declining Trust and Efficacy and Its Role in Political Participation,* Why Don't Americans Vote? (eds. Bridgett A. King & Kathleen Hale 2016); Derek Bok, The Trouble with Government (2001) anticipates many of the features of the current crisis and remains of enduring relevance.

2. World Population Review, Most Educated Countries (2022) at https://worldpopulationreview.com/country-rankings/most-educated-countries.

3. Declaration of the Rights of Man and Citizen, art. XXII (1793). See Declaration of the Rights of Man and of Citizens, in Thomas Paine, The Rights of Man 94–101 (1951).

4. Yves Déloye, École et Citoyenneté: L'individualisme Républicain de Jules Ferry a Vichy 16 (1994); Jacques Gadille, La Pensée et L'action Politique des Évêques Français au Début de la Troisième République 1870–1883 (1966).

5. World Population Review, *supra* n. 2.

6. For an illuminating overview, Samira Malik, *France's Nursery and Primary School System: Maternelle & École Primaire,* French Entrée (2021), https://www.frenchentree.com/living-in-france/education/french-primary-school-system/.

7. Marguerite Delatour, L'École Maternelle: Guide Pratique Pour Tous 255–268 (2020).

8. Ève Leleu-Galland, *L'école Maternelle: Une École Pour Apprendre à Grandir,* 23 Enfances & Psy 23–32 (2015).

9. Samira Malik, *supra* n. 6; Ève Leleu-Galland, *supra* n. 8; Christelle Dumas & Arnaud Lefranc, *Early Schooling and Later Outcomes: Evidence from Pre-school Extension in France,* Cergy-Pontoise (2010), https://2012.economicsofeducation.com/user/pdfsesiones/088.pdf.; Sylvia Edwards Davis, *Nursery Schools in France (maternelle),* French Entrée (2009), https://www.frenchentree.com/living-in-france/education/nursery-schools-in-france-maternelle/.

10. Samira Malik, *supra* n. 6; Ève Leleu-Galland, *supra* n. 8; Christelle Dumas & Arnaud Lefranc, *supra* n. 9.

11. Ève Leleu-Galland, *supra* n. 8; Christelle Dumas & Arnaud Lefranc, *supra* n. 9.

12. Press Release, *Discours du Président de la République aux Assises de l'école maternelle,* L'Elysée (2018), https://www.elysee.fr/emmanuel-macron/2018/03/27/discours-du-president-de-la-republique-aux-assises-de-lecole-maternelle.

13. Department of Education, A Matter of Equity: Preschool in America (2015) at https://www2.ed.gov/documents/early-learning/matter-equity-preschool-america.pdf.

14. Childcare workers who have returned to their old centers are also leaving their positions at unprecedently high rates when offered better-paying jobs in other economic sectors. Emilie Le Beau Lucchesi, *Finding Child Care Is Getting Even Harder,* The Atlantic (2021) at https://www.theatlantic.com/family/archive/2021/08/delta-child-care-shortage-unvaccinated-kids/619919.

15. https://en.wikipedia.org/wiki/Voter_turnout_in_United_States_presidential_elections#History_of_voter_turnout.

16. https://www.statista.com/chart/23075/estimated-tv-viewership-of-presidential-debates/.

17. The Center typically tests its results by recruiting a second representative sample—which does not deliberate but answers the same questions. By comparing the two sets of responses, the Center can consider whether the demographic and party identification variables it has used in selecting its group of deliberators captures the full range of policy attitudes that are relevant to the issue under discussion. The two samples rarely diverge from one another, but if they do, the Center takes these disparities into account when estimating how the entire voting population would respond to a similar form of deliberative engagement. For further discussion of the internet format and its deployment in a series of cases, see https://cdd.stanford.edu/online-deliberation-platform/.

18. BRUCE ACKERMAN & JAMES FISHKIN, DELIBERATION DAY (2004).

19. My text focuses on a few crucial design issues involved in the construction of real-world exercises in deliberative democracy. For consideration of additional key issues in the light of the Center's recent experience, see JAMES FISHKIN, DEMOCRACY WHEN THE PEOPLE ARE SPEAKING (2018).

20. For a more elaborate investigation of the Center's findings, go to: https://cdd.stanford.edu/.

21. For my own effort to put this problem in a larger perspective, see ACKERMAN, WE THE PEOPLE: FOUNDATIONS (1992).

22. THOMAS PAINE, AGRARIAN JUSTICE (1797), https://www.ssa.gov/history/paine4.html (entire original text reproduced, but there was no pagination in the original version).

23. Nick Green, *Trace Your Child Trust Fund This Autumn,* UNBIASED (2022), https://www.unbiased.co.uk/news/financial-adviser/trace-child-trust-fund.

24. For Brazilian developments, see DAVID TRUBEK ED., LAW AND THE NEW DEVELOPMENTAL STATE: THE BRAZILIAN EXPERIENCE IN LATIN AMERICAN CONTEXT (2013); TIMOTHY POWER & PETER KINGSTONE, DEMOCRATIC BRAZIL DIVIDED (2017); *Bolsonaro Rushes to Scrap Remnants of Bolsa Familia,* The Brazilian Report at: https://brazilian.report/liveblog/2022/05/11/bolsonaro-vestiges-bolsa-familia/.

25. BRUCE ACKERMAN & ANNE ALSTOTT, THE STAKEHOLDER SOCIETY (1999). Once Tony Blair became convinced of the merits of a similar proposal, the British breakthrough provoked a worldwide debate. Ackerman & Alstott, *Tony Blair's Big Idea,* NEW YORK TIMES (2001) at https://www.nytimes.com/2001/05/06/opinion/tony-blair-s-big-idea.html?scp=2&sq=%22Tony+Blair%92s+Big+Idea&st=nyt; JOAO CARDOSO ROSAS ED., IDEIAS E POLITICASA PARA O NOSSO TEMPO (2004); ACKERMAN, ALSTOTT, & VAN PARIJS EDS., REDESIGNING DISTRIBUTION (2005), DOWDING, DE WISPELAERE & WHITE EDS., THE ETHICS OF STAKEHOLDING (2005); OFFE, GROZINGER, & MASCHKE, DIE TEILHABEGESELLSCHAFT – MODELL EINES NEUEN WOHLFAHRTSSTAATES (2006). With the rise of the internet, the ongoing discussion has confronted the decisive ways in which the technorevolution has made it far more realistic to design and implement such measures in an effective fashion. See generally, Basic Income Earth Network at: https://basicincome.org/.

26. Financial competence does increase with age, although a majority of adults do not presently possess the basic financial proficiency required for thoughtful investment decisions. Stakeholding, however, will greatly increase individual incentives to increase financial competence and encourage Congress to fund this effort on an ongoing basis – providing yet another example of the micro-macro dynamics deployed in my reform proposals. For assessments of the present situation, see Annamaria Lusardi & Olivia S. Mitchell, *The Economic Importance of Financial Literacy: Theory and Evidence,* 52 J. ECON. LIT. 5 (2014); Roland Happ & Manuel Förster, *The Relationship between Migration Background and Knowledge and Understanding of Personal Finance of Young Adults in Germany,* 30 INT'L REV. ECON. ED. 1 (2019); Christin Siegfried & Eveline Wuttke, *What Influences the Financial Literacy of Young Adults? A Combined Analysis of Socio-Demographic Characteristics and Delay of Gratification,* 12 FRONT PSYCHOL. 663254 (2021).

27. See ACKERMAN, ALSTOTT & VAN PARIJS, *supra* n. 25. Brazil enacted a cash transfer program in 2004 with the stated purpose of establishing a right to basic income "regardless of socioeconomic condition." Lena Lavinas, *Brazil: The Lost Road to Citizen's Income,* Citizen's Income and Welfare Regimes in Latin America: From Cash Transfers to Rights 29–30 (2012). That right was never fully recognized, and Brazil instead implemented a means-tested welfare program, *Bolsa Família. id.* at 30; Gary Duffy, *Family Friendly: Brazil's Scheme to Tackle Poverty,* BBC News (2010), https://www.bbc.com/news/10122754.

APPENDIX

1. Zachary Shelley, a recent Yale Law graduate, provided outstanding research assistance.

2. IRS Budget & Workforce, https://www.irs.gov/statistics/irs-budget-and-workforce; Consolidated Appropriations Act, 2018, Pub. L. No. 115–141, 132 Stat. 348; Tax Cuts and Jobs Act of 2017, Pub. L. No. 115–97, 131 Stat. 2054.

3. *Millionaires and Corporate Giants Escaped IRS Audits in FY 2018,* TRAC IRS (2019), https://trac.syr.edu/tracirs/latest/549/.

4. The Democratic Congress included an $80 billion appropriation to the IRS as part of its Inflation Reduction Act of 2022, but once the Republicans gained control of the House of Representatives in the mid-term elections, they initially demanded a complete repeal of the measure in their campaign to resolve the nation's debt default crisis in June of 2023. When Biden rejected this demand, the Republicans settled for a $20 billion reduction as part of the last-minute compromise that enabled the country to avoid default. Catie Edmundson, *House Passes Debt Limit Bill in Bipartisan Vote to Avert Default,* NEW YORK TIMES (2023) at https://www.nytimes.com/2023/05/31/us/politics/debt-ceiling-house-vote.html.

The ultimate fate of IRS modernization, however, will depend on the next few elections. If hard-line conservatives win control of the government in 2024 or 2028, there is every reason to believe that they will repeal Biden's breakthrough initiative and destroy the capacity of the IRS to enforce a wealth tax in a credible fashion. It is only if the next two electoral cycles move in the progressive direction that Stakeholding will seem realistic by 2032.

5. "If any part of any underpayment of tax required to be shown on a return is due to fraud, there shall be added to the tax an amount equal to 75 percent of the portion of the underpayment which is attributable to fraud." 26 U.S.C. § 6663.

6. 26 U.S.C. § 877 (2022). Paul R. Organ, *Citizenship and Taxes: Evaluating the Effects of the U.S. Tax System on Individuals' Citizenship Decisions* 6–8 (Working Paper, 2021), https://www.irs.gov/pub/irs-utl/21rpcitizenshipandtaxes.pdf.

7. https://www.warren.senate.gov/newsroom/press-releases/warren-jayapal-boyle-introduce-ultra-millionaire-tax-on-fortunes-over-50-million#:~:text=their%20fair%20share.-,The%20Ultra%2DMillionaire%20Tax%20would%20bring%20in%20at%20least%20%243,the%20University%20of%20California%2DBerkeley.

8. The Bureau only provides data on the number of individuals who have reached 18 by July 1 of each year – and my model uses this number as the basis for calculating the number of 18-year-olds born throughout the entire year. Census Bureau, Census Population Estimates for 2014–2060 (2014), https://wonder.cdc.gov/population-projections-2014–2060.html; Census Bureau, Methodology, Assumptions, and Inputs for the 2014 National Projections (2014), https://www2.census.gov/programs-surveys/popproj/technical-documentation/methodology/methodstatement14.pdf.

9. https://www.minneapolisfed.org/about-us/monetary-policy/inflation-calculator/consumer-price-index-1913-.

https://www.cbo.gov/publication/57950#:~:text=In%20CBO's%20projections%2C%20assuming%20that,by%203.1%20percent%20this%20year.

10. https://www.federalreserve.gov/monetarypolicy/files/fomcprojtabl20211215.pdf. The Fed's data is not adjusted for inflation. I rely on the CBO's guidelines to take this factor into account.

11. Letter from Emmanuel Saez & Gabriel Zucman to Senator Elizabeth Warren (Feb. 24, 2021), https://www.warren.senate.gov/imo/media/doc/

Wealth%20Tax%20Revenue%20Estimates%20by%20Saez%20and%20Zucman%20-%20Feb%2024%202021.pdf; WEALTH TAX SIMULATOR, http://wealthtaxsimulator.org/ (last visited Nov. 17, 2021). The data, as well as code from Saez & Zucman's Wealth Tax Simulator, are available here: https://github.com/BITSS-OPA/opa-wealthtax.

12. Letter from Emmanuel Saez & Gabriel Zucman to Senator Elizabeth Warren (Feb. 24, 2021), https://www.warren.senate.gov/imo/media/doc/Wealth%20Tax%20Revenue%20Estimates%20by%20Saez%20and%20Zucman%20-%20Feb%2024%202021.pdf.

Saez and Zucman rely on the following tax haven studies to provide Senator Warren with an estimate of a tax evasion rate of 16 percent: David Seim, *Behavioral Responses to an Annual Wealth Tax: Evidence from Sweden,* 9 AM. ECON. J.: ECON. POL. 395 (2017) (0.5 percent elasticity of wealth tax evasion); Kristian Jakobsen, Katrine Jakobsen, Henrik Kleven & Gabriel Zucman, *Wealth Accumulation and Wealth Taxation: Theory and Evidence from Denmark,* NBER WORKING PAPER NO. 24371 (2018) (0.5 percent elasticity of wealth tax evasion). Juliana Londono-Velez & Javier Avila, *Can Wealth Taxation Work in Developing Countries? Quasi-Experimental Evidence from Colombia,*" UC BERKELEY WORKING PAPER (2018) (2–3 percent elasticity of wealth tax evasion in a setting with weak enforcement); Marius Brülhart, Jonathan Gruber, Matthias Krapf & Kurt Schmidheiny, *Taxing Wealth: Evidence from Switzerland,* NBER WORKING PAPER NO. 22376 (2016) (23–24 percent elasticity of wealth tax evasion estimated based on limited variations in wealth tax).

Their 16 percent estimate, moreover, may well be an underestimate, given the ease with which the super-rich can hide their wealth from all public sources available to empiricists. Rather than exploring existing data more intensively, however, it is far more important for future work to move beyond "tax haven" premises and develop models that use my triple-enforcement framework as the basis for their tax evasion predictions.

INDEX

Tables are indicated by "t" following the page numbers.

INDEX

INDEX

INDEX

INDEX

INDEX